Praise for

Train Your Mind, CHANGE YOUR BRAIN

"A thrilling account of recent breakthroughs in neurology that have profound implications for Buddhist practitioners and anyone interested in human potential and how the mind works."
—*Shambhala Sun*

"Reading this book is like opening doors in the mind. Sharon Begley brings the reader right to the intersection of scientific and meditative understanding, a place of exciting potential for personal and global transformation. And she does it so skillfully as to seem effortless."
—Sharon Salzberg, author of
Faith: Trusting Your Own Deepest Experience

"Neuroplasticity has enormous implications not only for our physical health but for our mental health."
—*Slate*

"It is very seldom that a science in its infancy is so skillfully unpacked that it reads like a detective novel. The fact that this science includes the collaborative efforts of neuroscientists, psychologists, contemplatives, and philosophers, and the full engagement of the genius of the Dalai Lama is not only fascinating but uplifting and inspiring. This book lets you know that how you pay attention to your experience can change your entire way of being."
—Jon Kabat-Zinn, author of *Coming to Our Senses*

"Does a good job of detailing the history behind the discovery [that the human brain is not fixed at adulthood] and how it is changing our approach to learning, neurological diseases, and emotional understanding." —*BusinessWeek*

"This is a truly illuminating and eminently readable book on the revolutionary new insights in mind sciences. I recommend it highly to anyone interested in understanding human potential."
—JACK KORNFIELD, author of *A Path with Heart*

"A clearly written account of recent discoveries about brain plasticity."
—*New Scientist*

"I have meditated for forty years and have long felt that the potential of mind training to improve our emotional, physical, and spiritual well-being has barely been tapped. Thanks to Sharon Begley's fascinating book, though, that is about to change. As human beings, we really do have inner powers that can make a world of difference, particularly if our goal is not merely to advance our own agendas but to cultivate compassion for the benefit of all living beings."
—JOHN ROBBINS, author of *Healthy at 100* and *Diet for a New America*

Train Your Mind,

CHANGE YOUR BRAIN

Train Your Mind,

CHANGE YOUR BRAIN

How a New Science Reveals Our Extraordinary

Potential to Transform Ourselves

Sharon Begley

BALLANTINE BOOKS NEW YORK

2008 Ballantine Books Trade Paperback Edition

Copyright © 2007 by Mind and Life Institute

Published in the United States by Ballantine Books,
an imprint of The Random House Publishing Group,
a division of Random House, Inc., New York.

BALLANTINE and colophon are registered
trademarks of Random House, Inc.

Originally published in hardcover in the United States by
Ballantine Books, an imprint of The Random House Publishing Group,
a division of Random House, Inc., in 2007.

Library of Congress Cataloging-in-Publication Data

Begley, Sharon.
    Train your mind, change your brain : how a new science reveals our
extraordinary potential to transform ourselves / Sharon Begley.
        p.   cm.
    ISBN 978-0-345-47989-1
    1. Neuroplasticity.   2. Brain.   3. Mind and body.   4. Philosophy of mind.
5. Buddhism and science.   I. Title.
QP 363.5.B44 2007
12.8—dc26   2006042952

Printed in the United States of America

www.ballantinebooks.com

9   8   7   6   5   4

Book designed by Cassandra J. Pappas

To Ned, Sarah, and Daniel,

for seeing me through

THE DALAI LAMA

FOREWORD

The Dalai Lama

It is now nearly twenty years since the first Mind and Life Conference took place in Dharamsala. Some of those who fostered and encouraged those initial dialogues between Buddhism and modern science, such as the late Robert Livingston and Francisco Varela, are no longer with us. Nevertheless, I'm sure they would share the pride and enthusiasm the eminent scientists, contemplatives, and other contributors who have subsequently been involved, have expressed about what our conversations have achieved so far.

Although modern science and the Buddhist contemplative tradition arose out of quite different historical, cultural, and intellectual circumstances, I have found that they have a great deal in common. By some accounts, both traditions are motivated by an urge to relieve the hardships of life. Both are suspicious of notions of absolutes, whether these imply the existence of a transcendent creator or an unchanging entity such as a soul, preferring to account for the emergence of life in the world in terms of the natural laws of cause and effect. Both traditions take an empirical approach to knowledge. It is a fundamental Buddhist principle that the human mind has tremendous potential for transformation. Science, on the other hand, has, until recently, held to the convention not only that the brain is the seat and source of the mind, but also that the brain and its structures are formed during infancy and change little thereafter.

Buddhist practitioners familiar with the workings of the mind have long been aware that it can be transformed through training. What is exciting and new is that scientists have now shown that such mental training can also change the *brain*. Related to this is evidence that the brain adapts or expands in response to repeated patterns of activity, so that in a real sense the brain we develop reflects the life we lead. This has far-reaching implications for the effects of habitual behavior in our lives, especially the positive potential of discipline and spiritual practice. Evidence that powerful sections of the brain, such as the visual cortex, can adapt their function in response to circumstances reveals an astonishing malleability unforeseen by earlier, more mechanistic interpretations of the brain's workings.

Findings that show how a mother's expressions of love and physical contact with her child can affect the triggering of different genetic responses tell us a great deal about the importance we need to give to bringing up our children if we wish to create a healthy society. On the other hand, it is also tremendously encouraging to know that some therapeutic techniques may successfully be employed to help those people, who, due to childhood neglect, find it difficult to generate warm, compassionate feelings toward others. Reports of cases where normal function has been restored through therapy indicate exciting and innovative discoveries. Finally, there has been a positive answer to the question I have been asking for many years; investigators have shown that how people think really can change their brains.

In addition to my interest in science, readers may also know that I'm a keen gardener. But gardening is often a hit-and-miss activity. You can put a lot of time into preparing the soil, carefully sowing the seeds, watching over them, and watering the seedlings. And yet, other conditions beyond your control—particularly in places such as Dharamsala, where I live, with its occasionally excessive heat, humidity, and rainfall—can prevent these efforts from ever coming to fruition. Therefore, as other gardeners will attest, there is a special joy to be had from seeing the plants you have nurtured emerge and blossom. I feel a somewhat similar emotion toward the findings related to neuroplasticity (revealed and discussed at our conference and recounted in this book): that we have reached a watershed, an intersection where Buddhism and modern science become mutually enriching, with huge practical potential for human well-being.

A great Tibetan teacher once remarked that one of the mind's most marvelous qualities is that it can be transformed. The research presented here confirms that such deliberate mental training can bring about observable changes in the human brain. The repercussions of this will not be confined merely to our knowledge of the mind: They have the potential to be of practical importance in our understanding of education, mental health, and the significance of ethics in our lives.

The Mind and Life Institute has grown into a substantial network of scientists, scholars, and interested individuals focused on the creation of a contemplative, compassionate, and rigorous experimental and experiential science of the mind. This we hope will be able to guide and inform medicine, neuroscience, psychology, education, and human development. I personally feel that its activities are extremely worthwhile and am very grateful—not only to the many busy individuals who have taken the time and trouble to share and explain their research but also to those who organize and coordinate our occasional meetings and conferences. In addition, part of the Institute's mission is to support the preparation of accessible publications of the proceedings of our conferences, so that what takes place as semiprivate conversation can be presented to a wider interested public. I am grateful, therefore, on this occasion to Sharon Begley for her artful work presenting this material accurately and attractively. I am optimistic that the exciting discoveries related here have great potential to contribute positively to the betterment of humanity and the way we may develop our future.

September 5, 2006

Daniel Goleman

When Tenzin Gyatso, the fourteenth Dalai Lama, met for a week with a handful of neuroscientists at his home in Dharamsala, India, in October 2004, the topic was neuroplasticity, the brain's capacity to change. That this capacity was even a subject of serious scientific discussion would have been unthinkable just a decade or two earlier; the received dogma in neuroscience for a century had held that the brain takes its shape for life during our childhood years and does not change its structure thereafter.

But that assumption has joined countless others in the trash heap of scientific "givens" that the march of research has forced us to discard. Neuroscience now has a vibrant branch exploring the many ways the brain continues to reshape itself throughout life. This volume stands as an excellent introduction to this hopeful new science.

What's particularly intriguing about the discussion recounted here are the partners involved. Many world leaders in the study of neuroplasticity traveled thousands of miles to India to consider the implications of their findings with the Dalai Lama, a surrogate for the tradition of Buddhist practice that he leads. The reason: the meditative practices of such contemplative paths seem to offer neuroscientists an "experiment of nature," a naturally occurring demonstration of the upper regions of neuroplasticity.

For millennia, meditation adepts have been exploring the potentials of brain plasticity, systematizing their findings and passing them on as instructions for future generations, down to our day.

One of the questions raised by the Dalai Lama was particularly provocative: can the mind change the brain? He had raised this point many times with scientists over the years, usually receiving a dismissive answer. After all, one of the cardinal assumptions of neuroscience is that our mental processes stem from brain activity: the brain creates and shapes the mind, not the other way around. But the data reported here now suggest there may be a two-way street of causality, with systematic mental activity resulting in changes in the very structure of the brain.

How far this can be carried, no one knows. But the fact that neuroscientists are even acknowledging the possibility is a second revolution in thinking for the field: it's not just that the brain changes its structure throughout life but that we can become active, conscious participants in that process. This poses yet another challenge to the received gospel in neuroscience: the assumption that mental systems such as perception and attention are subject to fixed constraints. Buddhism tells us these can be overcome, through the right training.

How far such neural systems might be pushed was shown by Richard Davidson, the University of Wisconsin neuroscientist who convened this round of dialogue. With the cooperation of the Dalai Lama, a series of lamas highly adept in meditation (with fifteen hundred to fifty-five thousand lifetime hours of practice logged) have undergone tests in his laboratory. Davidson shared some key findings with the scientists gathered at this meeting, showing that, during a meditation on compassion, these practitioners activated neural areas for positive feeling and preparedness to act to a degree never seen before. Old assumptions about the constraints on our mental apparatus must be examined anew.

This volume represents the tenth in a continuing series of books, each capturing for a wider audience one of the dialogues arranged by the Mind and Life Institute (see www.MindandLife.org for more information). Founded by the late Francisco Varela, a Chilean cognitive neuroscientist working in Paris, and Adam Engle, a businessman, the institute works closely with the Dalai Lama in planning its programs. Originally the institute's focus was on orchestrating scientific dialogues such as the one recounted in this book. While those continue, additional activities include a yearly seminar for graduate and postdoctoral students on research the dialogues have spawned, notably in cognitive neuroscience. The institute also administers research grants to young scientists who want to work in these fields. Called Mind and Life–Francisco J. Varela Research Awards, they honor the institute's visionary founder.

Each book in the Mind and Life series has its own shape and character, reflecting both the nature of the conversation and the strengths of the author. Sharon Begley, one of the world's leading science journalists, brought her unique aptitude for probing a field of research to the task, using the dialogue itself as a graceful springboard into a thorough and lively exploration of the science leading up to what was said in Dharamsala. The result goes beyond what went on in that room: she has surveyed the state of the field of neuroplasticity, one of our day's most exciting scientific revolutions.

ACKNOWLEDGMENTS

The scientists and Buddhist scholars who made this book possible probably never imagined what they were getting into when they agreed to tell me about their work. For their patience with my unending questions, and for infectious enthusiasm that I hope I have conveyed at least in part, my thanks in particular to Richard Davidson, Fred Gage, Phillip Shaver, Helen Neville, Michael Meaney, Alvaro Pascual-Leone, and Mark Hallett. Thupten Jinpa, Alan Wallace, and Matthieu Ricard never faltered in their efforts to help me understand the consilience between Buddhism's philosophy of mind and the discoveries of modern neuroscience. I am grateful to Adam Engle and Daniel Goleman for believing that I would capture for readers the excitement of the collaborations they, through the Mind and Life Institute, are forging between brain scientists and Buddhists. Without Nancy Meyer's assistance getting me to Dharamsala and nursing me back to health while there, I would never have been able to cover the historic 2004 meeting between scientists and the Dalai Lama. And this book would not exist without the support of my agent, Linda Loewenthal, and editor, Caroline Sutton; as soon as they heard what this book would be about, they got it.

CONTENTS

Train Your Mind,

CHANGE YOUR BRAIN

Chapter 1

Can We Change?

Challenging the Dogma of the Hardwired Brain

The northern Indian district of Dharamsala is composed of two towns, lower Dharamsala and upper. The mist-veiled peaks of the Dhauladhar ("white ridge") range hug the towns like the bolster on a giant's bed, while the Kangra Valley, described by a British colonial official as "a picture of rural loveliness and repose," stretches into the distance. Upper Dharamsala is also known as McLeod Ganj. Founded as a hill station in the nineteenth century during the days of British colonial rule, the bustling hamlet (named after Britain's lieutenant governor of Punjab at the time, David McLeod) is built on a ridge, where hiking the steep dirt path from one guesthouse to another requires the sure-footedness of a goat and astute enough planning that you don't make the ankle-turning trek after dark and risk tumbling into a ravine.

Cows amble through intersections where street peddlers squat behind cloths piled with vegetables and grains, and taxis play a game of chicken with oncoming traffic, seeing who will lose his manhood first by edging his car out of the single lane of the town's only real thoroughfare. The road curves past beggars and holy men who wear little but a loincloth and look as if they have not eaten since last week, yet whose many woes are neatly listed on a computer printout that they hopefully thrust at any passerby who slows even half a pace. Barefoot children dart out of nowhere at the sight of a Westerner and plead, "Please, madam, hungry baby, hungry baby," pointing vaguely toward the open-air stalls that line the road.

From the flagstoned terrace of Chonor House, one of the guesthouses, all of Dharamsala spreads out before you. As soon as the sun is up, the maroon-robed monks are scurrying to prayers and the holy men crouched in back alleys are chanting *om mani padme hum* ("hail to jewel in the lotus"). Prayer scarves fluttering from boughs carry the Tibetan words *May all sentient beings be happy and free from suffering.* The prayers are supposed to be carried by the wind, and when you see them, you think, Wherever the wind blows, may those they touch find freedom from their pain.

Although lower Dharamsala is inhabited mostly by Indians, residents of McLeod Ganj are almost all Tibetan (with a sprinkling of Western expatriates and spiritual tourists), refugees who followed Tenzin Gyatso, the fourteenth Dalai Lama, into exile. Many of those remaining in Tibet, unable to flee themselves, have their toddlers and even infants smuggled across the border to Dharamsala, where they are cared for and educated at the Tibetan Children's Village ten minutes above the town. For the parents, the price of ensuring that their children are educated in Tibetan culture and history, thus keeping their nation's traditions and identity from being erased by the Chinese occupation, is never seeing their sons and daughters again.

McLeod Ganj has been the Dalai Lama's home in exile and the headquarters of the Tibetan government in exile since 1959, when he escaped ahead of Chinese Communist troops, which had invaded Tibet eight years earlier. His compound, just off the main intersection where buses turn around and taxis wait for fares, is protected around the clock by Indian troops toting machine guns. The entrance is a tiny hut whose physical presence is as humble as the guards are thorough. From its anteroom, large enough for only a small sofa, dog-eared publications in a wooden rack, and a small coffee table, you pass through a door into the security room, where you place everything you want to bring in (bags, notebooks, cameras, tape recorders) on the X-ray belt before entering a closet-size booth, curtained at both ends, for the requisite pat-down by Tibetan guards.

Once cleared, you amble up an inclined asphalt path that winds past more Indian security guards draped with submachine guns and lounging in the shade. The sprawling grounds are forested with pines and rhododendrons; ceramic pots spilling purple bougainvillea and saffron marigolds surround the widely spaced buildings. The first structure to your right is a one-story building that houses the Dalai Lama's audience chamber, also guarded by an Indian soldier with an automatic weapon. Just beyond is the Tibetan library and archives, and farther up the hill, the Dalai Lama's two-story private compound, where he sleeps, meditates, and takes most of his meals. The large structure to the left is the old palace where the Dalai Lama lived before his current residence was built. Mostly used for ordinations, for the next five days its large main room will be the setting for an extraordinary meeting. Brought together by the Mind and Life Institute in October 2004, leading scholars from both the Buddhist and the Western scientific traditions will grapple with a question that has consumed philosophers and scientists for centuries: does the brain have the ability to change, and what is the power of the mind to change it?

Hardwired Dogma

Just a few years before, neuroscientists would not even have been part of this conversation, for textbooks, science courses, and cutting-edge research papers all hewed to the same line, as they had for almost as long as there had been a science of the brain.

No less a personage than William James, the father of experimental psychology in the United States, first introduced the word *plasticity* to the science of the brain, positing in 1890 that "organic matter, especially nervous tissue, seems endowed with a very extraordinary degree of plasticity." By that, he meant "a structure weak enough to yield to an influence." But James was "only" a psychologist, not a neurologist (there was no such thing as a neuroscientist a century ago), and his speculation went nowhere. Much more influential was the view expressed succinctly in 1913 by Santiago Ramón y Cajal, the great Spanish neuroanatomist who had won the Nobel Prize in Physiology or Medicine seven years earlier. Near the conclusion of his treatise on the nervous system, he declared, "In the adult centers the nerve paths are something fixed, ended and immutable." His gloomy assessment that the circuits of the living brain are unchanging, its structures and organization almost as static and stationary as a deathly white cadaver brain floating in a vat of formaldehyde, remained the prevailing dogma in neuroscience for almost a century. The textbook wisdom held that the adult brain is hardwired, fixed in form and function, so that by the time we reach adulthood, we are pretty much stuck with what we have.

Conventional wisdom in neuroscience held that the adult mammalian brain is fixed in two respects: no new neurons are born in it, and the functions of the structures that make it up are immutable, so that if genes and development dictate that *this* cluster of neurons will process signals from the eye, and *this* cluster will move the fingers of the right hand, then by god they'll do that and nothing else come hell or high water. There was good reason why all those extravagantly illustrated brain books show the function, size, and location of the brain's structures in permanent ink. As late as 1999, neurologists writing in the prestigious journal *Science* admitted, "We are still taught that the fully mature brain lacks the intrinsic mechanisms needed to replenish neurons and reestablish neuronal networks after acute injury or in response to the insidious loss of neurons seen in neurodegenerative diseases."

That is not to say that scientists failed to recognize that the brain must undergo some changes throughout life. After all, since the brain is the organ of behavior and the repository of learning and memory, when we acquire new knowledge or master a new skill or file away the remembrance of things past, the brain changes in some real, physical way to make that happen. Indeed, researchers have known for decades that learning and memory find their physiological expression in the formation of new synapses (points of connection between neurons) and the strengthening of existing ones; in 2000, the wise men of Stockholm even awarded a Nobel Prize in Physiology or Medicine for the discovery of the molecular underpinnings of memory.

But the changes underlying learning and memory are of the retail variety—strengthening a few synapses here and there or sprouting a few extra dendrites so neurons can talk to more of their neighbors, like a household getting an extra phone line. Wholesale changes, such as expanding a region that is in charge of a particular mental function or altering the wiring that connects one region to another, were deemed impossible.

Also impossible was for the basic layout of the brain to deviate one iota from the authoritative diagrams in anatomy textbooks: the visual cortex in the back was hardwired to handle the sense of sight, the somatosensory cortex curving along the top of the brain was hardwired to process tactile sensations, the motor cortex was hardwired to devote a precise amount of neural real estate to each muscle, and the auditory cortex was hardwired to field transmissions from the ears. Enshrined from clinical practice to scholarly monographs, this principle held that in contrast to the ability of the developing brain to change in significant ways, the adult brain is fixed, immutable. It has lost the capacity called neuroplasticity, the ability to change its structures and functions in a fundamental way.

To some extent, the dogma was understandable. For one thing, the human brain is made up of so many neurons and so many connections— an estimated 100 billion neurons making a total of some 100 trillion connections—that changing it even slightly looked like a risky undertaking, on a par with opening up the hard drive of a supercomputer and tinkering with a circuit or two on the motherboard. Surely that was not the sort of thing nature would permit and, in fact, something she might take steps to prevent. But there was a subtler issue. The brain contains the physical embodiment of personality and knowledge, character and emotions, memories and beliefs. Even allowing for the acquisition of knowledge and memories over a lifetime, and for the maturation of personality and character, it did not seem reasonable that the brain could or would change in any significant way. Neuroscientist Fred Gage, one of the researchers invited by the Dalai Lama to discuss the implications of neuroplasticity with him and other Buddhist scholars at the 2004 meeting, put the objections to the idea of a changing brain this way: "If the brain was changeable, then we would change. And if the brain made wrong changes, then we would change incorrectly. It was easier to believe there were no changes. That way, the individual would remain pretty much fixed."

The doctrine of the unchanging human brain has had profound ramifications, none of them very optimistic. It led neurologists to assume that rehabilitation for adults who had suffered brain damage from a stroke was almost certainly a waste of time. It suggested that trying to alter the pathological brain wiring that underlies psychiatric diseases, such as obsessive-compulsive disorder (OCD) and depression, was a fool's errand. And it implied that other brain-based fixities, such as the happiness "set point" to which a person returns after the deepest tragedy or the greatest joy, are as unalterable as Earth's orbit.

But the dogma is wrong. In the last years of the twentieth century, a few iconoclastic neuroscientists challenged the paradigm that the adult brain cannot change and made discovery after discovery that, to the contrary, it retains stunning powers of neuroplasticity. The brain can indeed be rewired. It can expand the area that is wired to move the fingers, forging new connections that underpin the dexterity of an accomplished violinist. It can activate long-dormant wires and run new cables like an electrician bringing an old house up to code, so that regions that once saw can instead feel or hear. It can quiet circuits that once crackled with the aberrant activity that characterizes depression and cut pathological connections that keep the brain in the oh-god-something-is-wrong state that marks obsessive-compulsive disorder. The adult brain, in short, retains much of the plasticity of the developing brain, including the power to repair damaged regions, to grow new neurons, to rezone regions that performed one task and have them assume a new task, to change the circuitry that weaves neurons into the networks that allow us to remember, feel, suffer, think, imagine, and dream. Yes, the brain of a child is remarkably malleable. But contrary to Ramón y Cajal and most neuroscientists since, the brain can change its physical structure and its wiring long into adulthood.

The revolution in our understanding of the brain's capacity to change well into adulthood does not end with the fact that the brain can and does change. Equally revolutionary is the discovery of how the brain changes. The actions we take can literally expand or contract different regions of the brain, pour more juice into quiet circuits and damp down activity in buzzing ones. The brain devotes more cortical real estate to functions that its owner uses more frequently and shrinks the space devoted to activities rarely performed. That's why the brains of violinists devote more space to the region that controls the digits of the fingering hand. In response to the actions and experiences of its owner, a brain forges stronger connections in circuits that underlie one behavior or thought and weakens the connections in others. Most of this happens because of what we do and what we experience of the outside world. In this sense, the very structure of our brain—the relative size of different regions, the strength of connections between one area and another—reflects the lives we have led. Like sand on a beach, the brain bears the footprints of the decisions we have made, the skills we have learned, the actions we have taken. But there are also hints that mind-sculpting can occur with no input from the outside world. That is, the brain can change as a result of the thoughts we have thought.

A few findings suggest that brain changes can be generated by pure mental activity: merely thinking about playing the piano leads to a measurable, physical change in the brain's motor cortex, and thinking about thoughts in certain ways can restore mental health. By willfully treating invasive urges and compulsions as errant neurochemistry—rather than as truthful messages that something is amiss—patients with OCD have altered the activity of the brain region that generates the OCD thoughts, for instance. By thinking differently about the thoughts that threaten to send them back into the abyss of despair, patients with depression have dialed up activity in one region of the brain and quieted it in another, reducing their risk of relapse. Something as seemingly insubstantial as a thought has the ability to act back on the very stuff of the brain, altering neuronal connections in a way that can lead to recovery from mental illness and perhaps to a greater capacity for empathy and compassion.

It is this aspect of neuroplasticity—research showing that the answer to the question of whether we can change is an emphatic yes—that brought five scientists to Dharamsala this autumn week. Since 1987, the Dalai Lama had opened his home once a year to weeklong "dialogues" with a hand-picked group of scientists, to discuss dreams or emotions, consciousness or genetics or quantum physics. The format is simple. Each morning, one of the five invited scientists sits in an armchair beside the Dalai Lama at the front of the room used for ordinations and describes his or her work to him and the assembled guests—in 2004, a couple of dozen monks and monastery students, as well as scientists who had participated in previous dialogues. It is nothing like the formal papers scientists are accustomed to presenting at research conferences, where they barrel through their findings to a rapt (they hope) audience. Instead, the Dalai Lama interrupts whenever he needs a clarification, whether for a point of translation (the scientists speak in English, which the Dalai Lama understands well, but a casually thrown-off scientific term such as *hippocampus* or *BRDU* will prompt a hurried tête-à-tête with one of his interpreters) or because one of the scientific findings reminds him of a point of Buddhist philosophy. The morning is punctuated by a tea break, during which the Dalai Lama either stays in the room for informal conversation with the scientists or takes a breather, and everyone else decamps to a huge adjacent room for tea and cookies. In the afternoon, the Dalai Lama and the Buddhist scholars he has invited respond to what the scientist has presented that morning, explaining what Buddhism teaches about the topic or suggesting further experiments to which Buddhist contemplatives might lend their minds and brains.

This time, the scientists were those working at the frontiers of neuroplasticity. Fred Gage, of the Salk Institute in La Jolla, California, works with laboratory animals; he has made seminal discoveries in how the environment can change their brains, in ways applicable to people. He also led a study on human subjects, demolishing the dogma that the adult brain does not generate new neurons. Michael Meaney, from Montreal's McGill University, has toppled the idea of genetic determinism. Also working with lab animals, he showed that the way a mother rat treats her babies determines which genes in the baby's brain are turned on and which are turned off, with the result that the genes with which it is born become merely an opening gambit on nature's part: the animal's traits—fearful or shy, neurotic or well adjusted—are shaped by maternal behavior, something that also has relevance for people. Helen Neville, of the University of Oregon, has done as much as any scientist to show that brain diagrams depicting what region does what should be printed in erasable ink. In work with people who are blind or deaf, she discovered that even something as seemingly fundamental, as hardwired, as the functions of the visual cortex and the auditory cortex can be completely overturned by the life someone leads. Phillip Shaver, of the University of California–Davis, is one of the leaders in the field of psychology called attachment theory. He discovered that people's sense of emotional security, based on their childhood experiences, has a powerful effect not only on their adult relationships but also on seemingly unrelated behaviors and attitudes such as their feelings about people who come from different ethnic groups and their willingness to help a stranger. For these four scientists, it was their first trip to Dharamsala and their first meeting with the Dalai Lama.

Richard Davidson was the veteran of these dialogues. More than that, however, his research on the science of emotions had grown to include

studies of Buddhist contemplatives, men who devote their days to meditation. The Dalai Lama had helped arrange for Buddhist monks and yogis to
trek all the way to Davidson's lab at the University of Wisconsin–Madison
so he could study their brains. His work was beginning to show the power
of the mind to change the brain. He would orchestrate the meeting, intro-
ducing each of the scientists for their morning presentation and leading the
discussion each afternoon.

"Of all the concepts in modern neuroscience, it is neuroplasticity that
has the greatest potential for meaningful interaction with Buddhism,"
Davidson said.

Buddhism and Science

Although science and religion are often portrayed as chronic opponents
and even enemies, that misses the mark for science and Buddhism. There is
no historic antagonism between the two, as there has been between science
and the Catholic Church (which put Copernicus's work on the Index of
forbidden books) and, lately, science and fundamentalist Christianity
(which, in the United States, has used the wedge issue of creationism to
argue that science is "just" another way of knowing). Instead, Buddhism
and science share the goal of seeking the truth, with a lowercase *t*. For science, truth is always tentative, always subject to refutation by the next experiment; for Buddhism—at least, as the Dalai Lama sees it—even core
teachings can and must be overturned if science proves them wrong. Perhaps most important, Buddhist training emphasizes the value of investigating reality and finding the truth of the outside world as well as the contents
of one's mind. "Four themes are common to Buddhism at its best: ratio-
nality, empiricism, skepticism, and pragmatism," says Alan Wallace, who
spent years as a Buddhist monk in Dharamsala and elsewhere before turning in his robes to become a Buddhist scholar and who is a longtime participant in the dialogues between scientists and the Dalai Lama. "His Holiness
embodies these. He often says with delight that if there is empirical evidence that contradicts something in Buddhism, 'Into the garbage!' He is
quite adamant that Buddhism has to yield to rational argument and empiricism."

Consonances between Buddhism and science were recognized as early as 1889, when Henry Steele Olcott argued in *Buddhist Catechism* that Buddhism is "in reconciliation with science," that there is "an agreement between Buddhism and science as to the root idea." Olcott based this on the fact that Buddhism, like science, teaches "that all beings are alike subject to universal law." By this reasoning, says José Ignacio Cabezón, a former Buddhist monk and now a scholar of religion and science at the University of California—Santa Barbara, "Buddhism and science are in agreement because they subscribe to the view that there are natural laws that govern the development of both persons and the world." In 1893, at the World Parliament of Religions in Chicago, part of the World's Columbian Exposition, Buddhist leader Anagarika Dharmapala of Sri Lanka spoke passionately of how Buddhism, not Christianity, could bridge the chasm that for centuries had divided science and religion. He based his hope on Buddhism's status as a nontheistic tradition, one with no creator god and with "no need for explanations that went beyond that of science, there being no need for miracles or faith," Cabezón explains. As Alan Wallace puts it, "Buddhism is not a religion; it is a philosophy. It is not some eastern version of Christianity or Judaism. Buddhism does not culminate in faith, as the Abrahamic traditions do. It culminates in insight."

Some scholars have gone so far as to proclaim Buddhism the "Religion of Science." As the Sri Lankan scholar K. N. Jayatilleke argued in his essay "Buddhism and the Scientific Revolution" in the late 1950s, Buddhism "accords with the findings of science" and "emphasizes the importance of a scientific outlook" in that "its specific dogmas are said to be capable of verification." Like science, Buddhism is "committed to critically (and not dogmatically) establishing the existence of universal laws," José Cabezón says.

Which is not to deny that some silliness swirls around efforts to find consonances between science and Buddhism. Through the decades, there have been claims that Buddhism *is* science, that the Buddha was the founder of psychology, that Buddhism discovered the size of elementary particles and of the universe, that modern physics merely confirms what Buddhist sages knew centuries ago. But while such assertions are over the top, a growing number of neuroscientists are at least open to the notion that Buddhism has something substantive to say about the mind. If so, then

Buddhism and science both stand to benefit from their interaction. "Science stands to gain by being pushed to consider mind or consciousness nonmechanistically, or by having to confront extraordinary inner mental states that are not normally within the purview of its investigations," says José Cabezón. "Buddhists stand to profit by gaining access to new facts concerning the material world (body and cosmos)—facts that have lain outside of traditional Buddhist speculation due to technological limitations."

The discoveries of neuroplasticity, in particular, resonate with Buddhist teachings and have the potential to benefit from interactions with Buddhism. The reason gets to the very core of Buddhist belief. "Buddhism defines a person as a constantly changing dynamic stream," says Matthieu Ricard, a French-born Buddhist monk. A veteran of the scientific dialogues with the Dalai Lama, he is anchoring the "Buddhist side" of the 2004 meeting.

Even scholars who were not involved in the meeting—but who have followed the dialogues closely—point out the consonances between Buddhist teaching and the idea, and potential, of neuroplasticity. "There are many strong parallels between the neuroscientific findings and the Buddhist narrative," says Francisca Cho, a Buddhist scholar at George Washington University. "Buddhism's is a story of how we are in pain and suffering and how we have the power to change that. The scientific findings about neuroplasticity parallel the Buddhist narrative of enlightenment because they show that, although we have deeply ingrained ways of thinking and although the brain comes with some hardwiring, we also have the possibility of changing. The idea that we are constantly changing means there is no intrinsic nature to the self or the mind, which is what Buddhism teaches. Instead, both self and mind are extremely plastic. Our activities inform who we are; as we act, so we shall become. We are products of the past, but because of our inherently empty nature, we always have the opportunity to reshape ourselves."

The discovery that mere thought can alter the very stuff of the brain is another natural point of connection between the science of neuroplasticity and Buddhism. Buddhism has taught for twenty-five hundred years that the mind is an independent force that can be harnessed by will and attention to bring about physical change. "The discovery that thinking something produces effects just as doing something does is a fascinating consonance with Buddhism," says Francisca Cho. "Buddhism challenges the traditional belief in an external, objective reality. Instead, it teaches that our reality is created by our own projections; it is thinking that creates the external world beyond us. The neuroscience findings harmonize with this Buddhist teaching."

Buddhist narratives have another consonance with the discoveries of neuroplasticity. They teach that by detaching ourselves from our thoughts, by observing our thinking dispassionately and with clarity, we have the ability to think thoughts that allow us to overcome afflictions such as being chronically angry. "You can undergo an emotional reeducation," Cho says. "By meditative exertion and other mental exercises, you can actively change your feelings, your attitudes, your mind-set."

Indeed, Buddhism believes that the mind has a formidable power of self-transformation. When thoughts come to the untrained mind, they can run wild, triggering destructive emotions such as craving and hatred. But mental training, a core of Buddhist practice, allows us "to identify and to control emotions and mental events as they arise," says Matthieu Ricard. Meditation, the most highly developed form of mental training, "is about coming to a new perception of reality and of the nature of mind, about nurturing new qualities until they become integral parts of our being. If we place all our hopes and fears in the outside world, we have quite a challenge, because our control of the outside world is weak, temporary, and even illusory. It is more within the scope of our faculties to change the way we translate the outside world into inner experience. We have a great deal of freedom in how we transform that experience, and that is the basis for mental training and transformation."

And why does the Dalai Lama hope to contribute to scientific understanding, whether by engaging in these dialogues with researchers or by encouraging Buddhist monks to lend their brains to science? "His Holiness believes that today's dominant worldview is the scientific one, and he wants to keep Buddhism growing and developing by engaging with science," says Thupten Jinpa, a Tibetan Buddhist scholar who earned a Ph.D. in religious studies from Cambridge University in 1989. The Dalai Lama's primary English translator and a collaborator on several of his books, Jinpa directs the Institute of Tibetan Classics, in Montreal, editing and translating Tibetan texts. "His Holiness," he says, "hopes to inspire a younger generation of Buddhist scholars to engage with science. But also, he is personally curious."

Of Timepieces and Telescopes

That curiosity dates from his youth. The boy who would become the fourteenth Dalai Lama was born on July 6, 1935, the fifth of nine children in a family of subsistence farmers who used cattle to plow their barley fields on the high Tibetan plateau in the northeastern province of Amdo and to pound grains out of tough husks. At the age of two, Tenzin Gyatso was recognized, after a nationwide search, as the reincarnation of the thirteenth Dalai Lama, Thubten Gyatso, who had died in 1933. He was formally installed as the head of state of Tibet on February 22, 1940. Science was unknown in his world, and when he looked back on his youth seventy years later, the only technology he recalled was the rifles carried by local nomads.

Between lessons in reading, writing, rote memorization of Buddhist rituals and scriptures, and Buddhist philosophy, the young Dalai Lama amused himself by embarking on sporadic treasure hunts in the one thousand rooms of Potala Palace in the capital of Lhasa. The palace held what he termed "assorted oddities" belonging to his predecessors, especially the thirteenth Dalai Lama. In a poignant foreshadowing of the current Dalai Lama's own desperate escape from Tibet after the Chinese invasion, the thirteenth Dalai Lama had fled Tibet in 1900, when word came that the armies of the last Chinese emperor were poised to invade. He spent a brief time in India, long enough to awaken to how the world beyond Tibet was charging ahead into the new century. Upon his return to Tibet, he established several political and social reforms, including mail service and secular education, as well as technological ones: a telegraph system and Tibet's first electric lights, powered by a small generating plant. He also brought back to the palace a fascination with mechanical objects, including those given to him by a British political officer posted to nearby Sikkim, Sir Charles Bell.

So when the fourteenth Dalai Lama explored the palace's chambers, he came upon an old brass telescope, a mechanical clock, two film projectors, a simple pocket watch, and three automobiles—all of which had been carried across the mountains in pieces from India, on the backs of donkeys, mules, and porters, since there were no roads fit for cars across the Himalayas or, indeed, anywhere in Tibet beyond Lhasa. The clock especially intrigued him. It perched atop a sphere that made a complete rotation every twenty-four hours and was covered with mysterious patterns. One day, paging through his geography books, the Dalai Lama realized that the drawings on the sphere were a map of the world, and the globe's rotation showed the sun's apparent movement from east to west across the sky. Other tokens of technology came the Dalai Lama's way as gifts. In 1942, a group of Americans presented him with a gold pocket watch. British visitors gave him a train set and a pedal car.

"There was a time, I remember very clearly, when I would rather fiddle with these objects than study philosophy or memorize a text," the Dalai Lama wrote in his 2005 book *The Universe in a Single Atom.* "They hinted at a whole universe of experience and knowledge to which I had no access and whose existence was endlessly tantalizing."

Indeed, he derived his greatest enjoyment of these gifts not from using them in the usual way but by taking them apart. He disassembled his wristwatch and managed to get all the pieces back together in working order. He took apart his toy cars and boats, rooting around for the mechanisms that made them work. As a teenager, he scrutinized an old movie projector that was powered by a hand crank, wondering how a spinning wire coil could generate electricity. There was no one in the palace he could ask, so he took it apart, too, and gazed at the pieces hour after hour, finally figuring out that a wire coil rotating around a magnet indeed generates an electric current. Thus began a lifelong love of dismantling and reassembling gadgets, something at which he grew adept enough to become the go-to man for friends in Lhasa who owned clocks or watches. (He never managed to repair his cuckoo clock after his cat attacked the poor bird, however.) Emboldened by what he took as evidence of a mechanical knack, the young Dalai Lama set his mind on fathoming the workings of his predecessor's automobiles, though he confined himself to learning to drive rather than turning the cars into a pile of parts. He did not lack for ingenuity, however. When he had a minor accident and broke the left headlight, he was terrified of what the palace attendant in charge of the fleet would say and quickly managed to procure a replacement. But while the original was of frosted glass, the replacement was clear. So he coated it with melted sugar.

His exalted status had a few disadvantages, notably the Tibetan custom that the Dalai Lama must remain sequestered in Potala Palace. Yearning for a glimpse of the outside world, he seized on the thirteenth Dalai Lama's telescope. In the daytime, he turned it on the hustle and bustle of the town spread out below the palace. At night, though, he turned it to the stars, asking his attendants the names of the constellations. On a night with a full moon, he peered at the lunar surface, where Tibetan folklore says a rabbit resides (akin to the Americans' and Europeans' "man in the moon"). Seeing shadows, he excitedly called over his two tutors to see for themselves. Look, he exclaimed; the shadows on the moon belie the fourth-century Buddhist cosmology that holds that the moon is a heavenly body like the Sun and other stars, radiating with light from an internal source. The moon is clearly "just a barren rock, pocked with craters," he saw, and the shadows that fall across its uneven surface proof that the moon, like Earth, is illuminated by the reflected light of the Sun. His own empirical observation had disproved an ancient Buddhist teaching. The discovery left a lasting impression. Observation, he realized, can challenge traditional Buddhist teachings.

"Looking back over my seventy years of life, I see that my personal encounter with science began in an almost entirely prescientific world where the technological seemed miraculous," he wrote. "I suppose my fascination for science still rests in an innocent amazement at the wonders of what it can achieve."

To the Dalai Lama, whose lessons included nary a whiff of math, physics, chemistry, or biology—and who had no clue, as a child, that these subjects even existed—the gadgets and rudimentary technologies that fascinated him *were* science. But slowly, once he was formally enthroned as the temporal leader of Tibet on November 17, 1950, and began visiting China and India, he came to understand that science is not merely the foundation for gadgets but a coherent way of questioning and understanding the world. It was this facet of science, he says today, that intrigued him and in which he saw profound similarities to Buddhism.

Just as science observes the minutiae of the world and the beings and objects within it, constructing theories and making predictions, refining or jettisoning a theory when experiments contradict it, so the Buddhism he learned in his contemplative practice and philosophical lessons is imbued with the same spirit of open-minded inquiry. "Strictly speaking," the Dalai Lama has written, "in Buddhism scriptural authority cannot outweigh an understanding based on reason and experience."

That tradition began with the Buddha himself, who admonished his acolytes twenty-five hundred years ago not to accept the authority of his own words, as set down in the scriptures, nor the rightness of his teachings simply out of respect for him. *Test* the truth of what I say, he told them, through the application of your reason and your observations of people and the world around you. "Therefore, when it comes to validating the truth of a claim, Buddhism accords the greatest authority to experience, with reason second and scripture last," the Dalai Lama has said. If science discovers that a belief of Buddhism is wrong, that it violates an indisputable truth of science, he has said repeatedly, then Buddhism must abandon that view or scriptural teaching even if it has prevailed for millennia. "Buddhism must accept the facts," he says. For instance, Buddhist physics, which holds that form, taste, smell, and tactility are basic constituents of matter, has to be modified, he says.

On March 17, 1959, the Dalai Lama fled Tibet after an uprising against the occupying Chinese failed. Some eighty thousand Tibetans eventually followed him into exile, many settling in or near Dharamsala, where he made his home and established the Tibetan government in exile. During his first three decades in exile, almost everything the Dalai Lama knew about science came from news seeping into Dharamsala—through the BBC, *Newsweek,* and the occasional astronomy textbook. But by the late 1980s, his curiosity was turning into something more pressing. Science's "inevitable dominance in the modern world fundamentally changed my attitude to it from curiosity to a kind of urgent engagement," he wrote. "The need to engage with this powerful force in our world has become a kind of spiritual injunction as well. The central question . . . is how we can make the wonderful developments of science into something that offers altruistic and compassionate service for the needs of humanity and the other sentient beings with whom we share this earth."

In 1983, the Dalai Lama traveled to Austria for a conference on consciousness. There he met Francisco Varela, a thirty-seven-year-old Chilean-born neuroscientist who had begun practicing Buddhism in 1974. The Dalai Lama had never met an eminent neuroscientist who was also knowledgeable about Buddhism, and the young researcher and the older Buddhist hit it off immediately. Even with his busy schedule, the Dalai Lama told Varela, he wished he could have such conversations more often.

The Mind and Life Institute

The year after Varela met the Dalai Lama, he heard about a plan that Adam Engle, an entrepreneur in California, was working on. In 1983, Engle was serving on the board of the Universal Education Organization, which had been founded by Lama Thubten Yeshe. At one board meeting, someone mentioned that His Holiness was supposedly keenly interested in science. What an odd pairing, Engle thought: the spiritual head of Tibetan Buddhism, leader of the Tibetan government in exile—and science? I wonder if it's true. As the meeting ended, he decided that if it were, he wanted to "put some energy" into making the Dalai Lama's interest in science something more than a passing fancy.

Engle, who had become a practicing Buddhist eight years before, began asking acquaintances in California's Buddhist community about the Dalai Lama's rumored interest in science. To a person, they all assured Engle that His Holiness loved science. The idea began gestating in Engle's mind. A year later, he attended a public teaching by the Dalai Lama in Los Angeles with a friend and colleague, Michael Sautman. As he waited for the doors to open, Sautman introduced him to the Dalai Lama's youngest brother, Tendzin Choegyal (Ngari Rinpoche), who was part of His Holiness's entourage. As Engle shook his hand, he recalled more than twenty years later, "part of me said, 'Don't bother him with this now,' while another part said, 'It's now or never.' " The second voice won. Keeping Rinpoche's hand in a desperation grip, Engle scraped up the courage to blurt out that he had heard that His Holiness was interested in science and that he would like to "organize something." Rinpoche offered to meet after the teaching in the lounge of the Century Plaza Hotel.

At six o'clock that evening, Rinpoche swept into the lounge, and Engle plunged right in. He had heard through the Buddhist grapevine, he said, that His Holiness was interested in science. If that were so, he'd love to try to set up something, perhaps a meeting where the Dalai Lama could hear from and talk with scientists. But please be sure to explain to him that this was not to be yet another event to which the Dalai Lama lent his name and perhaps a few minutes of his time for a keynote address. I'll do this, Engle explained, only if His Holiness wants to be a full participant. Rinpoche agreed to talk to his brother.

Two days later, at another of the Dalai Lama's teachings, Rinpoche told Engle that the Dalai Lama was truly interested in participating in something substantive about science. Engle began brainstorming just what, exactly, he might put together. He assumed the subject would be something in physics; Fritjof Capra's book *The Tao of Physics* had just introduced millions of readers to the notion of a consonance between the wisdom of the East and the discoveries of quantum physics. In early 1985, Engle and Sautman visited Capra in Berkeley, but the writer was lukewarm to the idea of convening a meeting between the Dalai Lama and physicists to explore some of the ideas in his book. There seemed to be an unending stream of New Agey meetings, Capra groused, and he was getting tired of them: people get up and make speeches, and nothing happens next. Engle left, no closer to knowing what he was supposed to be organizing.

Soon after, Francisco Varela, the neuroscientist who had met the Dalai Lama in Austria, phoned Engle from Paris. He had heard that Engle was trying to put together a meeting between the Dalai Lama and a group of scientists. He told Engle about his own chance meeting with the Dalai Lama, who invited Varela to continue the dialogue. But Varela wasn't sure how to do that. Hearing of Engle's own inchoate plans, he knew one thing. *"Adam,"* he said, *"you don't want to do this on physics; cognitive science makes much more sense."*

Varela knew there would be hurdles. Soon after he began practicing Buddhism, he had embraced meditation as a tool of cognitive research. He believed that cognitive science, a fusion of psychology and neuroscience that attempts to parse the workings of the mind and brain, could benefit from introspective accounts of mental activity—but not haphazard accounts from untrained observers. Just as casual observations of, say, how the leg moves are unlikely to yield any reliable insights into muscle metabolism, so casual observations of what one's mind is doing would rightly be suspect. But a trained observer, Varela thought, was a different story: such a person could turn meditation into a tool of cognitive research. By giving practitioners greater access to the contents and processes of their minds, he thought, meditation could augment the traditional study of the mind and brain, providing a reliable first-person account of mental activity.

His proposal was not exactly embraced by the neuroscience world, many of whose scientists regarded introspection as hardly better than entrails when it came to understanding the workings of the mind. When Varela met with Engle, he therefore warned him about the importance of inviting scientists who would be open-minded about what the first-person accounts of contemplatives, and centuries of Buddhist scholarship on the mind, could contribute to scientific understanding. Nothing would be accomplished if the scientists came gunning for Buddhism.

In March 1986, after more than a year of corresponding with the Dalai Lama's office, Engle flew to New Delhi and, after an overnight train and a three-hour car ride that took him past more traffic of the bovine than the vehicular variety, arrived in Dharamsala. He walked to the gate of the Dalai Lama's compound, just up the hill from the town's central intersection, and asked to see the Dalai Lama's secretary, Tenzin Geyche Tethong. The guard called the office, and soon a young assistant trotted down the curving asphalt walkway. Engle showed him his sheaf of correspondence with the Dalai Lama's office, in which letters had passed back and forth about setting up some sort of meeting with scientists, hoping that would distinguish him from every other acolyte who showed up wanting some contact with His Holiness. The poor kid was so confused about who exactly Engle was and what he wanted that he gave up and led him up to see Tenzin Geyche.

In the stucco building where the Dalai Lama keeps his private office, Engle introduced himself to Tenzin Geyche and described his months of correspondence with the office. It was the first Tenzin Geyche, who had just recently taken the post of secretary, had heard about any proposed meeting with the Dalai Lama and scientists. Engle asked for an audience with the Dalai Lama. I'll get back to you, Tenzin Geyche said; where are you staying? I haven't found the place yet, Engle answered, but I'll be at Kashmir Cottage. Walking back down the path and past the security booth at the bottom of the hill, Engle wandered the winding streets of Dharamsala until he came upon Kashmir Cottage, which was owned and run by Tendzin Choegyal and had been the home of the Dalai Lama's mother until her death.

Tendzin Choegyal remembered Engle from the Century Plaza lounge in Los Angeles eighteen months before. Would you talk to Tenzin Geyche about the Dalai Lama's interest in having this meeting with scientists? Engle asked. Two days later, Engle had his audience with the Dalai Lama. He explained what he and Francisco Varela had in mind, and after listening intently, the Dalai Lama said that this was something he very much wanted to do. But Engle had a question: "What's in it for you?" He was personally interested in science and wanted to keep learning about it, the Dalai Lama said. He also wanted to introduce science into the monastic curriculum. He was deeply aware that, in the modern world and especially in the West, science is the dominant mode of discovering reality; the monastery students needed to know about it, for understanding science was crucial to the continued vitality of Buddhism.

Things moved quickly. Varela met with the Dalai Lama in Paris that June, confirming his interest in the proposed meeting, and Engle got a formal okay on it from the Dalai Lama's secretary. He returned to Dharamsala to work out dates. How much time do you want? Tenzin Geyche asked. A week in October, Engle replied. Tenzin Geyche laughed. That's impossible, he said; we're here for only two weeks next October, and the only thing His Holiness has ever done for a full week is teach Buddhism. Engle, dejected, returned to Kashmir Cottage. But two days later, a letter arrived from the private office. He got the exact dates he'd proposed—and the full week of the Dalai Lama's time.

In October 1987, the Dalai Lama hosted the first conference of what Engle and Varela had named the Mind and Life Institute, in Dharamsala. Five scientists and one philosopher engaged him in seven days of informal give-and-take on cognitive science and Buddhism. The format became the model for every subsequent dialogue between the Dalai Lama and scientists: each scientist presenting his or her work to the Dalai Lama, followed by exchanges between the scientists and the Dalai Lama and other invited Buddhist scholars.

Just a few years before the Mind and Life meetings began, the Dalai Lama recalled, he had had a conversation with an American woman married to a

Tibetan. She cautioned him that science has a long history of "killing" religion and thus might threaten the survival of Buddhism. He should not befriend these people, she warned. He thought otherwise. Recalling that first Mind and Life meeting years later, he says, he "leapt at this idea." He saw the dialogues with leading scientists as an opportunity to learn about the latest scientific thinking, of course, but also as part of his mission to open Tibetan society and culture to the modern world. He therefore ordered that science be part of the curriculum in the children's schools and even in the monastic colleges, whose focus is classical Buddhist thought and whose students are all monks-in-training. "If as spiritual practitioners we ignore the discoveries of science, our practice is also impoverished," he later wrote.

The Dalai Lama has become much more than the leader of the Tibetan people, the spiritual leader of Tibetan Buddhism, and the head of the Tibetan government in exile. He is also an international icon; symbol of forgiveness, enlightenment, peace, and wisdom; able to attract throngs to the "teachings" he offers in locales from New York's Central Park to the holiest sites of Buddhism in India. To a small but growing group of scientists, he is also a bridge between the world of spirituality and the world of science, someone whose expertise in mental training might offer Western science a perspective that has been lacking in its investigations of mind and brain.

That brought him an invitation to address the annual meeting of the Society for Neuroscience in 2005—and more controversy than he counted on. Some five hundred members signed a petition protesting his appearance, arguing that religion has no place at a scientific conference. (Many of the leaders of the protest were Chinese-born scientists, which fueled rumors that the protest was more political than scientific.) Even the Dalai Lama recognized the seeming incongruity of his association with neuroscience. "So what is a Buddhist monk doing taking such a deep interest in neuroscience?" he asked rhetorically. He offered an answer in his most recent book. "Spirituality and science are different but complementary investigative approaches with the same greater goal, of seeking the truth," he wrote. Specifically, he told the neuroscientists, although Eastern contemplative practices and Western science arose for different reasons and with different goals, they share an overriding purpose. Both Buddhists and scientists investigate reality: "By gaining deeper insight into the human psyche, we might find ways of transforming our thoughts, emotions and their underlying properties so that a more wholesome and fulfilling way can be found."

It is little wonder that neuroplasticity, the topic of the 2004 meeting organized by the Mind and Life Institute, resonated with the Dalai Lama. He is intrigued that the Buddhist understanding of the possibility of mental transformation has parallels in the plasticity of the brain. "The Buddhist terms in which this concept is couched are radically different from those used by cognitive science, but what is significant is that both perceive consciousness as highly amenable to change," he has written. "The concept of neuroplasticity suggests that the brain is highly malleable and is subject to continual change as a result of experience, so that new connections between neurons may be formed or even brand-new neurons generated." And as he wrote in his 1998 bestseller *The Art of Happiness,* "The wiring in our brains is not static, not irrevocably fixed. Our brains are also adaptable."

Not static. Not fixed. Subject to continual change. Adaptable. Yes, the brain can change, and that means that we can change. It is not easy. As we will see, neuroplasticity is impossible without attention and mental effort. At the risk of invoking an old joke, in order to change, you have to *want* to change (whether or not you are a lightbulb). But if the will is there, the potential seems immense. Depression and other mental illnesses can be treated by enlisting the mind to change the brain, not by flooding it with problematic drugs. A brain afflicted with dyslexia can change into one that reads fluently, merely by repeatedly changing the sensory input it receives. A brain with no special ability in sports or music or dance might be induced to undergo a radical rezoning, devoting more of its cortical real estate to the circuitry that supports these skills.

The Dalai Lama has thrown his personal and official resources into supporting research into neuroplasticity because it resonates so well with Buddhism's wish that all sentient beings be free from suffering. It is not so far-fetched a goal: a brain whose existing circuitry leads to suspicion and xenophobia might, through disciplined effort and commitment to self-improvement, be rewired to respond with compassion and altruism. Because the science is so new, the limits of neuroplasticity are largely unmapped. But there is no question that the emerging science of neuroplasticity has the potential to bring radical changes, to both individuals and the world, raising the possibility that we could train ourselves to be kinder, more compassionate, less defensive, less self-centered, less aggressive, less warlike. This world of possibilities opened up by the discoveries of neuroplasticity is why scientists and Buddhist scholars met that autumn in Dharamsala.

Just a word about the organization of this story. The five researchers who met with the Dalai Lama have made seminal contributions to the revolutionary science of neuroplasticity. Their stories are told in chapters 3, 4, 7, 8, and 9. But it's impossible to grasp the extent of the brain's power of neuroplasticity without knowing about other discoveries; those are described in chapters 2, 5, and 6.

I began by quoting Ramón y Cajal's view that "the nerve pathways are something fixed, ended, and immutable." Most scientists who quote Ramón y Cajal stop there. But in fact, Ramón y Cajal continued, "It is for the science of the future to change, if possible, this harsh decree." As we will now see, it did.

Chapter 2

The Enchanted Loom

The Discovery of Neuroplasticity

W hen it came to neuroplasticity and the question of whether the adult brain can undergo dramatic change, scientists got it right before they got it wrong.

The second half of the nineteenth century had seen a whirlwind of activity in brain mapping that, for sheer cartographic hubris, rivaled the fifteenth-century expeditions to map the Earth. Scientists were determined to show that specific regions of the convoluted cortex performed different functions.

The Mapmakers

The first big step in this direction came in 1861, when French anatomist Pierre-Paul Broca announced his discovery of the brain region responsible for speech. During the autopsy of a patient who could speak but a single syllable, *tan* (and who was therefore known around the hospital where he was treated as Monsieur Tan), Broca discovered a lesion toward the back of the frontal lobes. He inferred correctly that the damaged region is responsible for articulated speech, and ever since, it has been known as Broca's area.

The announcement had the effect of a starter's pistol at a race. Anatomists rushed to pin particular functions on specific neural real estate. In 1876, Carl Wernicke, born in what is now Poland and educated in Germany, discovered that a region behind and below Broca's area plays a role in language, too, not so much in forming spoken words as Broca's area does but in understanding speech and in stringing together words in a way that makes sense; people with damage to this region can speak just fine, but what comes out is on the order of jabberwocky. Not one for halfway measures, German neurologist Korbinian Brodmann analyzed the brains of cadavers and determined that the cortex has fifty-two distinct regions, based on their appearance. For his efforts, the regions are still designated as BA (for Brodmann's area) 1, BA2, BA3 . . . up to BA52. BA1, 2, and 3, for instance, form the somatosensory cortex, where the brain receives signals from various points on the surface of the body and interprets them as the sense of touch.

These brain maps raised an obvious question for the scientists of the day. Were the boundaries and functions of the specialized regions set in the neuronal equivalent of stone? If so, then a region that received the signal "Your right big toe has just touched something" would always and forever receive signals about the right big toe and nothing but the right big toe, and such a region in the brain of one person would have an exactly corresponding region in every other person's. Or did the regions move around from person to person or even within the same person, so that my right big toe region is different from yours and what is the right big toe region one month might be the right middle toe another month?

By the early twentieth century, these questions had come to a head. Neuroanatomists began investigating what were called "movement maps" of the brain. This kind of brain map is essentially a drawing of the motor cortex, which runs in a strip roughly from ear to ear across the top of the brain, in which each point is labeled with the part of the body it controls. Rather than receive signals that the right big toe has been touched, as the somatosensory cortex does, the motor cortex transmits signals telling it to move. To make a movement map, scientists touch tiny electrodes to one spot after another on the motor cortex of a laboratory animal (something that causes the creature no pain, since the brain, somewhat paradoxically, can't feel). Then they see which part of the body moves. If the spot they touch causes the left pinkie to jerk, then they know that that spot controls the left pinkie . . . on and on through lips and cheeks, feet and fingers, and everything in between.

There was a peculiar thing about these movement maps, however. They varied from one animal to another. Electrical stimulation of a particular spot in the motor cortex of one monkey moved the creature's index finger. But stimulation of the same spot in another monkey moved the entire hand. There was no such thing as *the* movement map. Each monkey's was pretty nearly unique.

Why? One obvious possibility was that the neuroanatomists were sloppy. After all, the distance from the spot in the motor cortex that moves the right foot to the spot that moves the right ankle is minuscule. In 1912, two British neuroscientists, T. Graham Brown and Charles Sherrington, therefore decided to see whether movement maps varied from monkey to monkey because the anatomists were imprecise or because the movement maps really did reflect something unique about the individual. In landmark but long-forgotten experiments, they took tiny electrodes and zapped lab animals' motor cortexes. After each zap, the scientists carefully noted which muscles twitched. Then they zapped another region, on and on until they had constructed a movement map of the animal's entire motor cortex. And then they moved on to the next animal.

It was true: movement maps were as individual as fingerprints. Stimulating one animal's motor cortex *here* produced a twitch of a cheek muscle; stimulating another animal in the precisely corresponding spot caused its lip to twitch. In speculating how this variability arises, Sherrington suggested that a movement map reflects an animal's history of movement, like footprints.

It's not that every single movement over the course of an animal's life leaves a physical trace in the motor cortex. But repeated, habitual movements do. Say there is a monkey that gets into the habit of holding fruit with its thumb and pinkie. In that case, those two fingers repeatedly and regularly flex at the same time so the monkey can grasp its snack. As a result, Sherrington suggested, the clusters of neurons in the motor cortex that move those two fingers would lie close together. A monkey in the same troop that has different table manners, holding fruit with its thumb and forefinger, would have a different movement map, with neurons moving the thumb lying close to those moving the forefinger. Movement maps reflect not only which fingers or other parts of the body tend to move in unison but also how often an animal uses that part of the body. Not to get ahead of ourselves, but musicians who regularly use certain fingers would be expected to have larger clusters of neurons in the motor cortex devoted to moving those fingers than do nonmusicians; dancers who repeatedly practice particular foot extensions should have larger clusters of neurons responsible for moving the foot muscles than people who do little more than place one foot ploddingly in front of the other. Sherrington's and Brown's experiments provided the earliest empirical evidence for a notion that had been kicking around psychology a century ago, that habits both produce and are reflections of changes in the brain.

The studies also launched the first flowering of research into neuroplasticity. In 1915, a neurologist named S. Ivory Franz compared movement maps in the motor cortexes of macaques. He, too, found that the map in one monkey differed from that in another and speculated that the differences probably reflect the unique motor habits and skills of the monkeys. In 1917, Sherrington himself famously described the brain as "an enchanted loom, where millions of flashing shuttles weave a dissolving pattern, always a meaningful pattern, though never an abiding one."

There was one logical flaw in all this, however. None of the studies uncovering the idiosyncratic movement maps of experimental animals had actually ruled out a competing explanation: that the differences between the movement map of one animal and that of another were inborn rather than a reflection of the animals' different life experiences.

In 1923, Karl Lashley, a former colleague of Franz's, began a series of experiments intended to rule out that possibility once and for all. He realized that it was not very illuminating to compare one animal to another, as Sherrington and Franz had, since any differences in the animals' movement maps could be attributed to innate brain differences as plausibly as to different experiences. Instead, he laboriously determined the movement maps of the same adult rhesus monkey four times over the course of a month. If differences in movement maps are present at birth, then the map of a monkey's motor cortex should be the same today as it was last week and the week before. But if the differences reflect an animal's habits of movement, then—if a monkey picks up a new habit during the course of a month—the map of the monkey's motor cortex should change.

It did. Each time Lashley worked out a movement map, he found that it was slightly different from the previous one and even more different from maps derived longer ago. From this, he inferred what he termed a "plasticity of neural function" that allows the movement map in the motor cortex to remodel itself continuously to reflect its owner's recent patterns of movement. Foreshadowing the fundamental discoveries of neuroplasticity a century later, Lashley concluded that muscles that move more have larger clusters of neurons in the motor cortex devoted to them than muscles that move less. That makes sense, and it will come up time and again in research on neuroplasticity: the more habitually you make a particular movement, the more of the brain's real estate is zoned for that movement.

By the middle of the twentieth century, then, neuroscientists had accumulated a compelling body of evidence that the brain is dynamic, remodeling itself continually in response to experience. In 1949, Canadian psychologist Donald Hebb made a proposal that would eventually explain how. Hebb was not trying to explain the kind of neuroplasticity that allows regions of the brain to change in response to an animal's experiences. He wanted to explain learning and memory. Both, he proposed, are based on the strengthening of synapses. Somehow, either the neuron that fires first in the chain (the presynaptic neuron) or the neuron that fires next (the postsynaptic neuron), or both, change in such a way that the firing of the first is more likely to cause the firing of the second.

It took years for synaptic plasticity to catch on. Partly because Hebb was "just" a psychologist and not a neuroscientist, brain researchers were slow to take him seriously. Eventually, however, they tested his hypothesis, and the data were irrefutable: when neurons fire simultaneously, their synaptic connections become stronger, raising the chance that the firing of one will trigger the firing of the other. This property of neurons is summed up by the maxim "Cells that fire together wire together." Much as traveling the same dirt road over and over leaves ruts that make it easier to stay in the track on subsequent trips, so stimulating the same chain of neurons over and over—as when a child memorizes what comes after "Do, a deer"—increases the chances that the circuit will fire all the way through to completion. And the child sings the entire song.

Scientists have worked out in detail the neurochemistry that underlies Hebbian plasticity, but it's enough to know that it is a complicated cascade that begins with the release of a neurotransmitter from a presynaptic neuron and ends with an increase in synaptic strength. The two neurons that meet at the synapse become locked in a sort of physiological embrace. This is the physical basis for the formation of functional circuits during brain development, for learning and memory, and—as neuroscientists are beginning to understand—for the changes brought about by the kind of mental training at the center of Buddhist contemplative practices. It was clear even in the 1950s that this sort of plasticity must be a response to experience.

So there were Sherrington and Franz, Lashley, and Hebb, all giants in the history of neuroscience, all arguing—well, more than that: they were producing solid evidence—that the brain is the child of experience, undergoing physical changes in response to the life its owner leads. It didn't matter. For the greater part of the twentieth century, neuroscience dogma held that, with the exception of synaptic strengthening, the adult brain is fixed, hardwired, unable to change—a done deal. Of all the scientists who championed this view, none had a greater influence than the great Spanish neuroanatomist Ramón y Cajal, mentioned in the previous chapter, who in 1913 argued that the pathways of the adult brain are "fixed, ended, immutable." Oh sure, the adult brain can learn new facts and skills—any fool can see that—but only up to a limit. According to the dogma that had taken hold by the 1950s, the brain establishes virtually all of its connections in fundamental systems such as the visual cortex, auditory cortex, and somatosensory cortex in the first years of life. A region responsible for one function cannot assume a different one; don't bother, then, trying to train neurons to take the place of those wiped out by a stroke. If the brain sustains injury through stroke or trauma to, say, a region responsible for moving the left arm, then no other region can pinch-hit. The function of the injured region is lost forever.

So convinced were neuroscientists that the adult brain is essentially fixed that they largely ignored the handful of (admittedly obscure) studies suggesting that the brain is actually malleable and shaped by experience. The "truth" is spread out in glossy color in any lavishly illustrated brain book. There, diagrams confidently map and label the structures of the brain. Here is the region that controls language. There is the one that moves the left thumb. Over there, the one that processes feelings on the tongue. Every bit of neural real estate is assigned a fixed function. A parcel zoned for, say, processing sensations from the right palm is no more able to process sensations from the left cheek than the *B* on your keyboard is able to start producing *W*s. The discovery of links between structure and function gave rise to the view that different parts of the brain are hardwired for certain functions. Different regions of the brain, held the dogma, figure out early what they're going to be and stick to it for life. The work of Sherrington, Franz, and Lashley was largely forgotten.

Hardwired Not

But not by everyone. Among the doubters was Michael Merzenich. A rudimentary experiment he had performed as a postdoctoral fellow at the University of Wisconsin–Madison got him thinking that the brain of a monkey might reorganize as a result of experience. So in 1971, by then at the University of California–San Francisco, he determined to see just how extensive that reorganization could be. He reconnected with Jon Kaas, who had also been a postdoc at Madison. Now at Vanderbilt University in Nashville, Kaas was doing experiments with little New World primates called owl monkeys. When Merzenich told him his plan for seeing whether monkey brains can reorganize as a result of experience, Kaas said his owl monkeys would be perfect: this species has a flat, easy-to-map somatosensory cortex, free of the fissures and bumps that make working with the somatosensory cortices of other species like trying to draw a hopscotch board on cobblestones. Just as one can construct a movement map of the motor cortex, so can one construct a feeling map of the somatosensory cortex. In the first case, you stimulate a point in the motor cortex and see what part of the body moves. In the second, you gently touch one point on the skin and determine which point on the somatosensory cortex registers it. In owl monkeys, the hand gets a big chunk of space in the somatosensory cortex. It would therefore be relatively easy to see how that might change as a result of changing what the monkeys felt.

Kaas and Merzenich took a fairly crude approach, cutting the medial nerve in a monkey's hand. That left the monkey unable to feel anything in the thumb side of the palm and the underside of the neighboring fingers. In anatomical terms, no signal from this part of the monkey's hand reached the somatosensory cortex. Several months after the surgery, time enough for the monkeys' brains to realize they had not received any messages from the hand for quite a while, it was time to look at the animals' somatosensory cortices. How had the absence of a signal from the monkey's hand to its brain affected it? "The standard view was that when you deprive the brain of this sensory input, there should be like a black hole in the cortex where it used to receive that input," says Mriganka Sur, who was a graduate student of Kaas's at the time.

To find out how lack of sensory input had affected the monkeys' brains, the scientists recorded electrical activity in hundreds of locations in the somatosensory cortices. This mapping takes hours and hours, so they would start in the morning and not leave until two days later, at which point they had either completed the map or were too punch-drunk to work. No one wanted to miss a single recording. "There was a feeling that you didn't know what would be seen next, and if you weren't right there, you wouldn't believe it," Kaas said.

Their incredulity was understandable. The region of the somatosensory cortex that had originally received signals from the severed nerve in the hand, and that should now have been as silent as that nerve itself, responded to stimulation of other parts of the hand. Instead of receiving signals from the thumb side of the palm and fingers (which were not arriving, since the nerve had been cut), this region processed signals from the pinkie side of the palm and the back of the fingers. "These results," the scientists wrote in 1983, "are completely contrary to a view of sensory systems as consisting of a series of hardwired machines."

Discoveries that challenge the prevailing dogma are rarely embraced by dogmatists, and this one was no exception. "We were working in an atmosphere where the brain was seen as having plasticity early in life, as had been shown with young kittens," says Sur. "But in older cats, the brain could not change, which seemed to close off the possibility of plasticity in the adult brain. It was a very difficult time." The conventional wisdom that the adult brain is fixed and immutable was so strong that the study was dismissed as a quirk or an experimental error. The paper was almost not published at all, so hostile were the reviewers whom journal editors asked to judge it. As it was, Kaas's and Merzenich's first three papers reporting changes in the brain of an adult monkey as a result of a change in sensory input eventually appeared in relatively obscure journals. "People were very antagonistic," Merzenich recalled years later. Studies that were to win a Nobel Prize for the scientists who conducted them, Torsten Wiesel and David Hubel, "had shown just the opposite: that after a critical period early in life, the brain does not change as a result of changes in sensory input."

Undaunted, Merzenich and Kaas pushed ahead in their search for evidence of plasticity in the adult brain. The experiment in which they found that a spot on the brain that once processed the sense of touch from one part of the hand can rezone itself to process the sense of touch from a different part of the hand was admittedly pretty crude: the rezoning had occurred in response to a fairly radical event, the severing of a major nerve. What about ordinary life—can that rezone the brain? Merzenich had a strong hunch that it could. "We propose that the differences in the details of cortical map structure are the consequence of individual differences in lifelong use of the hands," he and his colleagues wrote. Looking back fifteen years later, Merzenich remembered thinking that "the cortex is not static but dynamic. What, we asked, was driving this dynamism? It could only have been behavior."

But the brain reorganization that he and Kaas had discovered wasn't all that impressive to most neuroscientists. That was because it either had come in response to fairly extreme changes, such as a monkey's nerves being cut, or was not that extensive. Skeptics could, and did, argue that while rare and extreme events might trigger brain reorganization, that fell short of proving that the adult brain changes in response to normal, everyday experiences. Merzenich took this criticism to heart. What he needed to do next, he realized, was investigate whether the brain can remodel itself in response to anything like normal behavior.

William Jenkins, working with Merzenich, got the job of seeing whether teaching old monkeys new tricks changed their somatosensory cortex. He needed a task that monkeys could learn without too much trouble, one that would give them a sensory experience unlike any they had had before—and that might therefore change their brain just as severing a nerve had. Since monkey fingers are as sensitive as people's, Jenkins decided to see if changing what monkeys felt with their fingers, day in and day out, would change the part of the brain that processes information from fingers.

Jenkins positioned a four-inch disk incised with wedge-shaped grooves outside a cage where an owl monkey waited expectantly. He trained the monkey to reach through the bars and gently touch the disk, letting a couple of fingers lightly skim the top and stay in contact with the disk as it spun. The trick was harder than it looked. If a monkey applied too little pressure, its fingers would be thrown off by centrifugal force; if it pressed too hard, its fingers would revolve along with the disk. But if the animal kept its fingers lightly on the surface without letting them be spun around or off, Jenkins rewarded it with a banana-flavored pellet. (The experiment wasn't easy on the scientist, either; Jenkins had to train hungry monkeys for hour after hour until they understood what was expected of them.) Every day for several weeks, the monkeys underwent hundreds of trials, placing their fingers on the spinning disk again and again. Then it was time to see what their brains had been up to.

First, the scientists carefully exposed a monkey's brain. They then brushed one of its fingertips and determined (with electrodes) which spot in the somatosensory cortex received the signal. Next, they brushed another finger, noting where that signal registered in the brain, and kept on in this way until they had determined which spot in the somatosensory cortex received signals from each finger. They had done the same sort of cartography before training the monkeys on the spinning disk, getting a baseline map. After the monkeys had developed their acute sense of touch, the scientists found, the map changed: the area of somatosensory cortex responding to signals from these fingers increased fourfold.

This wasn't in response to something as radical as a severed nerve. The only thing that had changed in the monkeys' lives was their behavior. They had simply mastered a trick that required their fingertips to be extremely sensitive. The neurons that connected fingers to brain, the experiment proved, are not hardwired.

Jenkins thought the monkeys were capable of even greater dexterity. He and graduate student Greg Recanzone, who had arrived in Merzenich's lab in 1984, taught seven adult owl monkeys to tell when a gentle flutter on a single spot on one finger became faster or slower. At first, the monkeys were able to tell when the frequency changed only when the difference was at least twenty flutters per second. But after seven-days-a-week training for more than two hundred days, six of the seven monkeys could distinguish flutters that differed by only two or three per second, a pretty amazing feat.

And what had happened to the brains of the monkeys whose finger had become so sensitive it could pass for the digital equivalent of the princess who felt the pea under a dozen mattresses? Painstakingly mapping each monkey's somatosensory cortex, the scientists found that the spot that handled messages from the bit of skin that had become sensitive to vibrations was as much as three times larger than the spots handling messages from the comparable bit of skin on the other hand, which had not been trained to detect the tiny changes.

The twin discoveries, from the spinning disk and the fluttering device, showed that the physical layout of the brain—how much space it apportions to which tasks, how strongly one neuronal firing is connected to another—is shaped by experiences and by the life we live. "This machine we call the brain is being modified throughout life," Merzenich said. "The potential for using this for good had been there for years. But it required a different mind-set, one that did not view the brain as a machine with fixed parts and defined capacities but instead as an organ with the capacity to change throughout life. I tried so hard to explain how this would relate to both normal and abnormal behavior. But there were very few takers. Few people grasped the implications."

There was one more obvious place to look for neuroplasticity in response to experience: the motor cortex. This expanse of neurons sends signals to specific muscles with the command "Move!" There was only one problem. The motor cortex was supposed to be hardwired. Neurons that were born to move, say, the right index finger were assumed to always move the right index finger and nothing but the right index finger. The UCSF team had, by the early 1980s, a slew of studies showing that when a monkey's fingers *feel* something repeatedly, such as a flutter or a spinning disk, the finger part of the somatosensory cortex expands. When Randolph Nudo joined Merzenich's lab in 1985, he therefore decided to see what would happen when a monkey *moved* a muscle repeatedly. First, he needed before-and-after shots. That is, he needed to map a monkey's motor cortex before it learned a new trick and then after it had mastered the trick. Only that would show whether experience, and regular, repeated, intensive use, causes the motor cortex to remodel itself.

In an experiment on four squirrel monkeys, Nudo did just that. First he determined the movement maps of each monkey's motor cortex, by the usual method of stimulating each spot with a tiny electrode and seeing what part of the body moved. He concentrated on the neurons that moved the forearm, wrist, and digits, since those were what the monkeys would use for the trick Nudo was going to teach them. Once he had the movement maps—a laborious undertaking that took ten to fifteen hours—it was training time.

Nudo set four shallow cups outside each monkey's cage. The largest was like a dog-food dish, ten inches across, while the smallest was about four inches across. He put a single, tiny banana-flavored pellet into each cup. To eat the pellet from the three largest cups, all a monkey had to do was extend his arm, poke a couple of fingers in, pick up the treat, and get it to his mouth. But the smallest cup presented more of a challenge: it was too small for a monkey to fit two fingers in. At first, the monkeys fumbled around, rarely able to grasp the pellet. But after a few hundred tries over days or weeks, they were palpating the tiny pellets like pros. By extending a single finger into the cup and tapping the pellet until it stuck, a monkey could hold on to it long enough to raise it clear of the cup, get another finger in there to help, and convey the treat to its mouth. Each monkey mastered the trick well enough to get its daily ration of six hundred or so tiny pellets as if it had dined like that all its life.

For that, the monkeys could thank their new brains. When Nudo repeated the arduous process of mapping the motor cortex, he discovered that the maps had undergone something akin to suburban sprawl, he and his UCSF colleagues reported in 1996. The area that moved the fingers, wrist, and forearm—which were getting quite a workout—had doubled, taking over space in the motor cortex that had previously controlled other parts of the body (though evidently without harming those other parts). The motor cortex, they concluded, "is alterable by use throughout the life of an animal."

The UCSF scientists had overturned the dogma that the adult brain cannot change. To the contrary. The somatosensory cortex, which feels touches on the skin, and the motor cortex, which moves muscles, change as a result of experience. The brain is sculpted by life and retains the imprints of the experiences an animal has had and the behaviors it has carried out. "These idiosyncratic features of cortical representation," Merzenich said, "have been largely ignored by cortical electrophysiologists."

It was a contender for understatement of the year. Dogmas die hard. The discovery that normal behavior such as palpating food pellets can change the brain didn't get a much warmer reception than did the earlier work showing that drastic changes such as severing a nerve can change the brain. One problem was that the cortical changes Merzenich and his colleagues reported amounted to only a few millimeters of the brain. To skeptics, this amount of rewiring seemed insignificant, perhaps even an error of measurement. But then two scientists got permission to experiment on what were probably the most famous four experimental animals this side of the astrochimps Ham and Enos. Their names were Billy, Domitian, Augustus, and Big Boy, and they were the last of the Silver Spring monkeys that would give their lives, and their brains, to science.

The Silver Spring Monkeys

The Silver Spring monkeys were named for the town where they were housed, where they were experimented on, where some of them died, and where the raid that launched the animal-rights movement in the United States took place.

In the summer of 1981, Alex Pacheco would silently prowl the darkened rooms at the Institute for Behavioral Research in Silver Spring, Maryland. As his accomplice, close friend, and housemate Ingrid Newkirk stood outside acting as lookout, Pacheco took photographs of caged monkeys. Emboldened after several such forays, in late August, he began to bring with him on these surreptitious tours a number of veterinarians and primatologists who supported animal rights. *Look,* he pointed, making sure they saw the rusty cages encrusted with monkey feces. *There,* he gestured, at cages whose bent and broken wires poked up from the floor like implements of medieval torture. And *there:* sixteen male crab-eating macaques (their name, not their dinner menu), also known as cynomolgus monkeys, and one adult female rhesus monkey. Among them, the seventeen monkeys had gnawed off thirty-nine of their own fingers; their arms were covered with oozing, uncovered, and untreated lesions. Was this standard laboratory practice, Pacheco asked each expert, or was something seriously wrong?

That May, Pacheco, a twenty-two-year-old political science student at

George Washington University, in the District of Columbia, had begun working as a volunteer at the privately owned lab. Although Pacheco told behavioral psychologist Edward Taub, IBR's chief scientist, that he was trying to decide whether to become a researcher, in fact the young man was on a mission. From his undergraduate days at Ohio State University, Pacheco had been an ardent animal-rights activist, organizing protests against the local farmers' practice of castrating their pigs and cattle without anesthetic (something angry agriculture students threatened to do to Pacheco). When he moved east to attend GW, he met Ingrid Newkirk, an experienced animal-rights activist. Together, they formed a group they called People for the Ethical Treatment of Animals. Newkirk, who had exposed appalling conditions at a Maryland animal shelter, pushed Pacheco to infiltrate a bio-medical lab where live animals were experimented on. He chose the Institute for Behavioral Research; it was close to his apartment in Takoma Park.

Edward Taub was an outsider to the elite field of neuroscience, a psychologist whose only knowledge of neuroscience was self-taught. Like many outsiders—and scrappy kids from New York City, which he also was—he was none too infatuated with the conventional wisdom in neuroscience. In particular, he had his doubts about one "fact" dating from 1895 and established by one of the founding fathers of experimental neuroscience, Charles Sherrington, whom we met at the beginning of this chapter. In that year, Sherrington and a colleague, F. W. Mott, reported the results of a now-classic experiment. The scientists had "deafferented" either the upper arm or the lower leg of rhesus monkeys. In deafferentation, a sensory nerve is cut, leaving the animal unable to feel. Mysteriously, although the animals' motor nerves were intact, the monkeys stopped moving the senseless limb—even to reach for a morsel of food when they were hungry.

That seemed odd. There was no obvious reason why an animal would not grasp, support its weight, or walk with the deafferented limb, since all such movements, you'd think, require only motor nerves and the ability to move, not sensory nerves and the ability to feel. After all, if your finger becomes numb from bitter cold, you can still move it even if you cannot feel someone touching it. Sherrington, however, concluded from his deafferented monkeys that one needs to feel in order to move volitionally. (The "volitional" qualifier is important: Sherrington found that when he applied electrical stimulation to the motor cortex of the monkey's brain, the deafferented limb that the animal would not move voluntarily moved reflexively.)

Taub was not impressed. Although researchers as late as the mid-1950s continued to report that deafferentation of sensory nerves left animals unable to move the affected arm or leg—the emerging model, called reflexology, held that all voluntary movement requires sensory feedback—he had his doubts. "Reflexology was the dominant view in neuroscience, even more dominant than the idea that there is no plasticity in the adult brain," Taub told me when I visited his lab. "At this point, it is hard to grasp how incomprehensibly influential Sherrington's views were in psychology and certainly in neuroscience. Since we were psychologists, god help us, we decided that we would . . . reevaluate the Sherringtonian canon."

Lurking in the back of his mind was a long-forgotten experiment he had stumbled across in an old book, from 1909. In it, a German scientist named H. Munk reported results starkly different from Sherrington's. His deafferented monkeys used their unfeeling arm to lift food to their mouth—as long as the intact arm was restrained and if the first clumsy attempts to use the deafferented arm were immediately rewarded. So which was it, Taub wondered: do animals need to be able to feel in order to move or not?

And that is why, when Pacheco began working at the Institute for Behavioral Research, Taub was deafferenting monkeys' limbs. He severed the sensory nerves to both arms of Billy, one of the macaques. In eight macaques, he severed the sensory nerve to a single arm. Seven other macaques, and Sarah, the lone rhesus and the only female, served as controls, undergoing no surgery. As expected, the animals lost all sensation in the part of the body where the sensory nerve was cut. The animal no longer felt its arm or its leg. That was why they were gnawing off their fingers and chewing their senseless limbs raw, and why they seemed unperturbed by their gruesome open sores: they couldn't feel a thing. Billy had chewed off eight of his ten fingers. Paul had torn off all five fingers of one hand. "Deafferented monkeys have a tendency to sustain severe damage to their affected extremities, frequently as the result of self-mutilation," Taub wrote in a scientific paper in 1977. The veterinarians and primatologists Pacheco had sneaked into the lab—Taub had gladly given him the keys, so the enthusiastic young man could work nights and weekends—swore out affidavits testifying to the animals' appalling injuries. Newkirk and Pacheco took the affidavits and photos to the Montgomery County police.

The cops raided Taub's lab on Friday, September 11, 1981, seizing Adidas, Allen, Augustus, Big Boy, Billy, Brooks, Charlie, Chester, Domitian, Hard Times, Hayden, Montaigne, Nero, Paul, Sarah, Sisyphus, and Titus. After an assistant phoned to tell him about the raid, Taub rushed to the lab, incredulous. This just did not happen to federally funded scientists, certainly not to those whose animal facilities had just passed federal inspection, as his lab had. As he told a reporter, "I'm surprised, distressed and shocked by this. There is no pain in these experiments. We surgically abolish pain."

On September 28, the prosecutor charged Taub with seventeen counts of animal cruelty. Taub had the distinction of being the only scientist ever hauled up on criminal charges for how he treated his lab animals. In November, a district court judge found him guilty of six counts of animal cruelty. He was fined $3,000. He lost his National Institutes of Health grant and his job at IBR; his research came to a screeching halt. On appeal, however, Taub was cleared of all but one misdemeanor count of animal cruelty. His fine was reduced to $500. And on August 10, 1983, the Maryland Court of Appeals unanimously overturned even that conviction. A federally funded researcher, it ruled, was not subject to state laws on animal cruelty.

Although Taub's personal legal saga was over, the case of the Silver Spring monkeys would drag through the courts for ten years and do more than any other single incident to launch America's animal-rights movement. But for our purposes, the real milestone came a decade after the raid.

Immediately after the raid, the seventeen monkeys were housed in the basement of the home of a PETA member in Rockville and eventually sent to a primate facility run by the National Institutes of Health, the nation's premier biomedical research agency, in nearby Poolesville. PETA sued in U.S. District Court to have the monkeys transferred to a primate sanctuary called Primarily Primates, in San Antonio, Texas. Although the court ruled that PETA lacked legal standing, the case had become such a cause célèbre that NIH, sensing political disaster, promised that the monkeys would never undergo invasive procedures for research purposes and in 1986 moved the fifteen surviving animals to the Delta Regional Primate Center, located across Lake Ponchartrain from Tulane University's main campus in New Orleans. Brooks died a few months after he arrived. Five of the control monkeys—Chester, Sisyphus, Adidas, Hayden, and Montaigne—were sent to the San Diego Zoo in the summer of 1987. That left Sarah, plus the eight male macaques that had undergone deafferentation—Augustus, Domitian, Billy, Big Boy, Titus, Nero, Allen, and Paul.

But science wasn't done with the Silver Spring monkeys. In a 1988 paper in the *Proceedings of the National Academy of Sciences,* neuroscientists Mortimer Mishkin and Tim Pons of the National Institute of Mental Health and Preston Garraghty of Vanderbilt University had reported results of an unusual experiment. They had surgically damaged the somatosensory cortex of seven macaques. Specifically, they had obliterated the region that registers input from the hand. Although nerves in the monkeys' hands were intact, the animals felt no sensation when their hand was touched or when it touched anything. It was like having perfectly functional phone lines but a broken telephone; no signal registers.

The damage the scientists caused was not the only change in the monkeys' brains, however. A region called the secondary somatosensory cortex receives signals from the primary somatosensory cortex, for further processing. But no such signals were arriving from the hand part of the primary somatosensory cortex; the scientists had destroyed it. The secondary somatosensory cortex, although physically undamaged, therefore rezoned itself. Six to eight weeks after the monkeys' brain surgery, the region in the secondary somatosensory cortex that originally registered sensations from the hand instead responded to stimulation of the animals' feet. The foot-feeling region, which originally occupied only 5 to 12 percent of the secondary somatosensory cortex, had expanded to fill 55 to 75 percent, equal to the combined hand and foot representation in the intact brain. The brain area no longer being used by the hand had been taken over by the foot, in a process called cortical remapping. An area that originally performed one function had switched to another.

Based on these findings, Mishkin and Pons proposed that the Silver Spring monkeys perform one last service for science. When one of the animals was so ill it needed to be euthanized, they said, let scientists first examine its brain in search of evidence that the cortex had reorganized after twelve years of being deprived of sensory input from an arm (that deprivation being the result of having its nerves severed in Taub's experiments).

The Silver Spring monkeys, which had been deafferented when they were three or four years old, were an irreplaceable resource, the scientists argued, since such a large area of the brain—the somatosensory region that registers sensation from an entire arm—had received no sensory input for more than a decade. NIH agreed.

Billy, the only monkey with two deafferented arms, was near death in late 1989. On January 14, 1990, he became the first of the Silver Spring monkeys to undergo neurosurgery before being euthanized. After anesthetizing him, neuroscientists led by Pons and Mishkin gently stroked different parts of Billy's body with a camel's-hair brush or cotton swab. Tiny tungsten microelectrodes recorded the resulting electrical activity in his somatosensory cortex. The goal was to determine which spot in the somatosensory cortex processed each touch. In particular, what was the spot that had originally registered feelings from Billy's arms doing? Since this "deafferentation zone" had not received sensory input for twelve years because the nerves leading to it had been cut, it seemed reasonable to expect it to be as quiet as death.

But no. When the scientists brushed Billy's face, the deafferentation zone tingled with electrical activity. Even gently moving his facial hair produced vigorous neuronal responses in the supposedly silent zone. Apparently, when no signals arrived from the arm and hand for so long, this region of the cortex had gotten tired of waiting. It began picking up signals from the face instead. Indeed, the scientists found that the "face zone" of the somatosensory cortex had taken over the "hand and arm zone." All 124 recording sites in the deafferentation zone were receiving signals from the face. On July 6, 1990, Augustus, Domitian, and Big Boy were also anesthetized, experimented on in the same way Billy had been, and then euthanized.

The researchers reported their findings in the journal *Science* the following June. They had expected the entire deafferented region, which once upon a time had registered feelings from a monkey's fingers, palm, and arm and which every brain book asserted was hardwired to do that and only that, to have become a zone of silence. After all, no signals from the arms were reaching it. You'd think that with no incoming signals to process, the receiver would be silent, like a radio tuned to the frequency of a station that has gone off the air. But this was not what the neuroscientists found. Rather, the entire hand region of the somatosensory cortex crackled with electrical activity—when the researchers brushed the animal's face. The total amount of neuronal real estate the brain zoned for registering feelings from the chin and lower jaw now included not only the area of the somatosensory cortex whose job it had always been to do that but also the area that had originally registered feelings from the arm. Because the entire (original) hand region had been invaded by neurons of the face area, the amount of territory the brain zoned for receiving feelings from the face had grown ten to fourteen millimeters. This, wrote the scientists, was "massive cortical reorganization," "an order of magnitude greater than those previously described."

Pons explained what made the discovery possible. "It was, in part . . . the long litigation brought about by animal-rights activists that [made] the circumstances extremely advantageous to study the Silver Spring monkeys," he told the *Washington Post.* That is, the famous monkeys had been let alone as the case wended its way through the courts. Their brains had reorganized themselves to reflect what input they were receiving, or not receiving, from their body.

Hearing the Lightning and Seeing the Thunder

Scientists who were skeptical about the power of neuroplasticity, about the power of the life one leads and the experiences one has to change the very structure and function of the brain, had one final redoubt. Even the extensive rearrangement of the somatosensory cortex in the Silver Spring monkeys, even the doubling of the neighborhood of the motor cortex that controls a finger in monkeys who mastered a tricky digital maneuver, could be viewed as mere tinkering around the edges. Somatosensory cortex was still somatosensory cortex, faithfully registering signals from one or another spot of skin to produce the sensation of feeling. Motor cortex was still motor cortex, reliably moving a particular muscle. By the mid-1990s, the limits of neuroplasticity remained unclear. Edward Taub was fond of saying "It's all just cortex," implying a brain full of parts as interchangeable as bricks. But the zoning map every neuroscientist carries in his or her head—motor cortex here, somatosensory cortex there, visual cortex back there, auditory cortex over here—would not be overthrown that easily.

Mriganka Sur had never taken a biology course in his life when he earned a degree in electrical engineering from the Indian Institute of Technology and Science, but he had always been interested in the life sciences and, in particular, the brain. That was not quite enough to induce American graduate programs in neuroscience to admit him. His facility with electronics, however, was, at least for Vanderbilt: the university accepted Sur for graduate work in electrical engineering, where he did all his coursework, and didn't protest when he did his research in neuroscience. He knew his way around circuits, which made him a perfect fit for neuroscientists using electroencephalograms, or EEGs, to measure brain activity.

Science has genealogies just as families do, and you can often trace the development of a new idea from one researcher down to his or her graduate students, and to their students, unto the nth academic generation. Sur was one of Jon Kaas's students in 1976 when, as described above, he and Mike Merzenich laid the groundwork for what would be revolutionary discoveries in neuroplasticity. For his Ph.D. thesis topic, Sur chose the sense of touch, and how and where the brain produces it.

"What I wanted to study was change," recalls Sur, now at the Massachusetts Institute of Technology. "There are representations of the body in the somatosensory cortex"—the "feeling map." He was part of the team that conducted the experiment in which the medial nerve from a monkey's hand was severed, resulting months later in the animal's somatosensory cortex rearranging itself so that sensory input from surrounding areas of the hand colonized the region that was no longer receiving its usual signals. "I decided to study the limits of developmental plasticity," he says. "I wanted to ask, how 'native' is the cortex, really? Are functions assigned to different structures and regions in an irrevocable way, or can they change as a result of the input the brain receives?"

To Sur's way of thinking, the most dramatic studies would be what are called gain-of-function experiments. In these, a structure receives an input different from what it ordinarily does, and the scientist probes whether that coaxes a different function from the structure. "We wanted to see if we could cause new functions," he says. "That would provide the sharpest example of how external forces can drive the developing brain."

For the experiments, Sur and his colleagues passed up the usual lab animals and settled on one more commonly found in exotic-pet stores: ferrets. During brain development in ferrets, the optic nerves grow from the eye, and the auditory nerves grow from the ear, just as they do in humans. Both optic and auditory nerves wend their ways through the brain stem and thalamus before reaching their final destinations in the primary visual cortex in the back of the brain or the primary auditory cortex just behind each ear, respectively. The optic nerve from the left eye crosses over and makes connections with the visual cortex in the right cerebral cortex, while the optic nerve from the right eye connects to the left cerebral cortex. The auditory nerves take the direct route, with the left ear connected to the left auditory cortex and the right ear connected to the right auditory cortex. In this, ferret wiring and human wiring are identical. But they differ in their timing. In humans, this basic wiring diagram is present at birth. In ferrets, the auditory neurons do not reach their goal until well after birth.

That delay set the stage for Sur's clever experiments. Soon after baby ferrets were born, the scientists carried out some exquisitely delicate brain surgery. They carefully stopped the auditory nerve from the right ear from reaching the thalamus. They did nothing to the optic nerve, but nature did something for them. When the tip of the growing optic nerve from the left eye arrived at the thalamus a few days later, it found the coast clear: there was no auditory nerve also making a pit stop there. So one branch of the optic nerve grew into the primary visual cortex, as it normally does, but part of it branched off and grew toward the auditory cortex. Now both visual and auditory cortex were receiving signals from the left eye and only the left eye. The scientists left the auditory nerves from the left ear alone, allowing them to follow the normal course of development and reach the auditory cortex. As a result, the optic nerve from the right eye grew only into the visual cortex, not the auditory cortex as well.

How would the ferrets perceive the world? Once they reached adulthood, the MIT scientists trained four of them to respond to sounds and lights. The ferrets learned to turn to a spout on their left if they heard a sound and to a spout on their right if they saw a flash of light. A correct answer earned them a sip of water or juice. After the ferrets got the hang of it, the scientists were ready for the tell-all test. They flashed light in front of the ferrets' left eye. Nerves from this eye, remember, had grown into the auditory cortex. Would the ferrets act as if they heard something—in neurospeak, because their auditory cortex had been stimulated? Or would they act as if they saw something, because the stimulus went into the animals' eye, not their ear? Would they act as if they "heard" the light or saw it?

By the fall of 1999, the scientists had their answer. When the ferrets experienced a flash of light in the left eye (that is, photons landed on their retina and caused electrical signals to travel along the optic nerve), their auditory cortex processed it. The animals *heard* the light. They behaved just as they did when they literally heard something with their intact ear. If the scientists had left the ferrets the way nature had made them, then the patch of cortex that serves as the primary auditory cortex would have processed sounds. But because this patch now received input from the retina, it was processing sights: it was now the animals' de facto visual cortex. "An auditory cortex that grows up with visual input sees rather than hears," says Sur. "Whether function is localized in the brain is one of the deepest questions in neuroscience. We are now seeing that localization is not as fundamental as we once believed. The outside world has the potential to change the brain, and it does. The brain is dynamic; stasis is illusory."

On learning of his former colleague's findings, Mike Merzenich was reminded of a comment once made by William James, the late-nineteenth-century psychologist. James had wondered if, were scientists able to alter neurons' paths so that exciting the ear activates the visual cortex and exciting the eye the auditory cortex, we would be able to "hear the lightning and see the thunder."

The remarkable dynamism Sur had discovered in ferrets, in which the auditory cortex can learn to see, is not a peculiarity of this species. In a series of experiments, he and his colleagues rewired adult mice as they had ferrets, so that neurons from the eye connected to the auditory thalamus rather than the visual cortex. Mice are great learners if you train them with sound. If you let them hear a beep right before you give their feet a mild electric shock, after enough repetitions the next beep makes them freeze instantly, for they have learned that a shock is coming. This is called a conditioned fear response. (The reason sounds are so effective at inducing this kind of learning may be that the auditory pathway snakes through a structure called the amygdala, which is where fear is processed and remembered.) If, however, you flash a light before the shock, the mice require many more lessons before getting the idea; visual signals do not travel through the amygdala. Something about the sense of hearing and its pathway in the brain, it seems, leads to quick learning, but something about the sense of sight and its pathways does not. What Sur wanted to know was, in adult mice he had rewired so that visual signals connected to the auditory part of the brain, would the lesson take more quickly with sight or with sound?

The rewired mice were geniuses when it came to learning what a flash of light meant. After only one lesson—flash, zap—they got it: the next time they saw a flash, they froze like statues. That suggests that the normally auditory pathway, which leads to learning, is activated by vision. Existing pathways, then, can convey novel information. Just as in the rewired ferrets, visual inputs to the auditory cortex convey information that the ferrets' brains interpret as vision, so in the rewired mice, inputs from the eye to the auditory parts of the brain elicit fear and freezing in response to a visual cue much like that caused by sounds in normal mice. These were adult mice, so plasticity was retained well past childhood.

These discoveries of what is now called use-dependent cortical reorganization were the opening shots in a revolution in our understanding of the brain and its essential capacity for change—its neuroplasticity. Increasing activity in part of the motor cortex, such as by mastering the fine art of palpating a banana-flavored pellet from a little dish, causes it to expand. Depriving one part of the somatosensory cortex of input, as happened to the Silver Spring monkeys, causes other parts to move in, so that a region that once "felt" an arm now feels the cheek. The reverse is also true: increasing the input to one region of the somatosensory cortex causes it to expand and become more sensitive, as was the case with the monkeys who felt the spinning disk. Clearly, the hardware of the brain is not fixed at birth. And it is not only fine details that are open to the sculpting hand of experience. It is also major functional assignments, so that neural real estate that is supposed to process vision can be rezoned, through experience, to process a different sense—to hear the lightning and see the thunder.

At least in animals.

Maybe human brains were different. Maybe once a human brain—regarded as the most complex entity in the universe—came into the world, nature knew to leave well enough alone, not to allow the brain to change as a result of something so seemingly insignificant as what its owner did.

Chapter 3

New Neurons for Old Brains

Neurogenesis

The molded-plastic chairs scrape the wooden floor as 119 guests settle in expectantly. They include some of the most accomplished Buddhist scholars in the world—men who have been at the side of the Dalai Lama since shortly after he fled into exile, and monks and former monks equally at home in Western science and Tibetan Buddhism. Taking their places in cushioned armchairs and on sofas flanking a low wooden table covered in a green cloth, they face five of the world's leading cognitive and neuroscientists, invited to spend five mornings and five afternoons describing to the Dalai Lama some of their seminal discoveries in neuroplasticity. Rounding out the audience are some two dozen students from a Tibetan Buddhist monastery, invited by the Dalai Lama as part of his quest to infuse monastic education with substantive courses in science; biologists and physicists who have been part of the Mind and Life Institute's work; philanthropists who helped make the meeting possible; a sprinkling of journalists; longtime friends of the Dalai Lama; and even actor Richard Gere, who has become close to the Dalai Lama through his advocacy of a free Tibet.

Sunshine spills through the French doors and double windows, illuminating the scores of vibrantly colored *thangkas,* traditional Tibetan scroll paintings depicting deities, that hang from the twelve-foot ceiling. A ten-foot-tall tapestry of the Buddha hangs from the back wall of a low wooden stage. The Dalai Lama, in his burgundy robe and amber-tinted glasses, walks onto the stage toward the Buddha from a small anteroom to the right, and everyone rises, some with heads bowed and palms pressed together, others ramrod straight and looking on curiously. The Dalai Lama walks with a bit of a stoop, as do many Tibetan monks, shuffling forward with rounded shoulders in a reflexive posture of humility that, over the years, has become his default gait. After an aide unfurls a prayer rug on the floor before the Buddha, the Dalai Lama kneels for several seconds, bows his head, rises, turns, makes his way to the cushioned armchair at the head of the room, and smiles from ear to ear.

"This is my now second home, more than forty-five years," he says in his unique English. "In these few decades, news from our own home, except for a few occasions, always sad. In the meantime, this [series of formal and informal meetings with scientists] lasts more than four decades, gives me new opportunities, not only myself, but also a number of Tibetans. At the beginning, it was out of my own individual curiosity, eagerness to learn from the scientific explanations. But now, more and more Buddhist students from our monastic institutions carry some systematic study about science. . . . So now we can talk, we can think."

With his feet tucked under him, the Dalai Lama turns expectantly to the meeting's first scientific speaker, Fred Gage, one of the world's most accomplished neuroscientists.

A Family Legacy

As his freshman year at the University of Florida was winding down, Fred "Rusty" Gage was casting about for a summer job. A friend mentioned being hired by one of the university's electrophysiology labs, but something had come up and he couldn't take the job. Was Rusty interested? At that point in his life, Gage had by no means decided to be a scientist, even though his older sister would regularly send him science books. But a summer job is a summer job, so he said yes and never looked back.

In case he needed any further inspiration for a career in neuroscience, Gage got it from an unexpected source. His paternal grandfather was an amateur genealogist, and during Gage's years at Florida, the elderly gentleman made quite a bit of progress with the family tree, tracing Gages all the way back to the Battle of Hastings. But it was one particular branch that his grandfather thought might interest Rusty. One ancestor seemed to be Phineas Gage, who is almost as prominent in the annals of neuroscience as Rusty Gage himself would soon become.

Phineas worked as a railroad foreman. In 1848, his construction crew was building a rail line in Cavendish, Vermont, when an accidental explosion tore through the air. It sent a thirteen-pound, three-feet-seven-inches-long iron-tamping bar flying . . . right into Phineas's brain. Phineas survived the seeming catastrophe with neither memory loss nor cognitive impairment. It seemed like a miracle. But within days, his friends and family noticed a dramatic change. Once modest, reliable, and hardworking, Phineas became erratic and emotional, fitful, and prone to irrational rages and profanity, "manifesting but little deference for his fellows, impatient of restraint or advice when it conflicts with his desires, at times pertinaciously obstinate, yet capricious and vacillating," as an account at the time put it. The region of the brain that the bar penetrated, scientists finally inferred, was responsible for emotional control, reason, and planning. It was one of the first clues that particular brain structures control specific mental functions. This family legacy didn't lure Gage into neuroscience, but "it did perpetuate my early interest," he says.

Today he is an impresario of neuroscience. His lab at the Salk Institute in La Jolla, California, is home to dozens of scientists: graduate students and postdoctoral fellows and junior faculty and professors from other institutions spending a sabbatical year there. He was in Dharamsala to tell the Dalai Lama about one of his most important scientific discoveries, one that suggested that when it comes to change, the brain is not limited to the neurons with which it enters adulthood: even the adult brain can generate new neurons.

Bird Brains

One core corollary of the conviction that the brain is fixed is that people are born with just about all the brain cells they will ever have, Gage began.

Neurons, after all, just aren't like other cells. The liver, to the relief of alcoholics, regenerates. The skin, fortunately for anyone who has gotten a paper cut, regrows. Bone is constantly being remodeled, as new cells are born and old ones are resorbed, at least until middle age catches up with you. But neurons do not divide; one does not become two, and they do not make more of themselves. Because neurons do not divide, Gage explained, "it was inconceivable that one neuron could give rise to another." In what seems, in retrospect, like a serious lapse of imagination, scientists concluded that neurons' inability to reproduce closed off all avenues to the birth of neurons in the adult brain. As the Nobel Prize–winning neuroanatomist Santiago Ramón y Cajal (yes, he of the "fixed and immutable" view of the brain we encountered in chapter 1) wrote about the adult nervous system in 1913, "Everything may die, nothing may be regenerated."

There was another reason why *neurogenesis,* the scientific term for the birth of new neurons, was considered a nonstarter in a brain of any sophistication. "The idea of a brain as a sophisticated, hardwired computer made it difficult to accept the idea that new cells could come into a complicated circuit and become a part of it in a way that would not only not be disruptive but might be beneficial," Gage told the Dalai Lama. "Adding a complete new neuron with ten thousand new connections and thousands of new outputs—it was hard for scientists to believe this could actually happen. It would cause too much disruption." Expecting new neurons arriving from god knows where to make a constructive contribution to the precise circuitry of a mature brain made as much sense as expecting a box of wires to improve an already running supercomputer.

Not even empirical evidence could put a dent in the dogma. In the early 1960s, biologists began using one of those cool new toys that make undreamed-of experiments suddenly feasible. Before cells divide, they make a copy of their DNA. Needless to say, cells can't conjure the double helix out of thin air. Instead, biochemicals snag the requisite ingredients from within the cell and assemble them. It turns out that one ingredient of DNA, called thymidine, is happy to let a radioactive hydrogen molecule glom onto it. When the thymidine becomes incorporated into the brand-new DNA, the DNA has a spot of radioactivity, which can be detected experimentally. Old DNA does not have this glow.

In 1962, when the technique of labeling cells with radioactively tagged thymidine was brand-new, a scientist at the Massachusetts Institute of Technology named Joseph Altman decided to try the new trick on brains. By scanning neurons for telltale glows, he figured, he would be able to detect newborn DNA, and thus newborn cells. This, of course, was at a time when the dogma that neurogenesis did not occur after birth was unquestioned. But Altman gave it a go anyway. To his surprise, he found that neurons in the brains of adult rats, cats, and guinea pigs shone with the thymidine—indicating that they had been born after Altman injected them with the tracer. Altman's papers were accepted and published by leading scientific journals. In 1965, he reported in the *Journal of Comparative Neurology* on "evidence of postnatal hippocampal neurogenesis in rats." In 1967, he published in the prestigious journal *Nature* on "postnatal neurogenesis in the guinea-pig." In 1970, he described in *Brain Research* "postnatal neurogenesis in the caudate nucleus and nucleus accumbens septi in the rat."

It would be charitable to say that the world of neuroscience did not greet Altman with hosannas. His claims were ignored at first and eventually dismissed as the naïve delusion of a not-even-middling scientist. The ridicule did not exactly help his career. Denied tenure at MIT, he joined the faculty at Purdue University and went on to research less likely to torpedo a career, becoming one of science's leading experts on the development of the rat brain.

Michael Kaplan, a graduate assistant in anatomy at Boston University, did not fare much better. Using a technique called immunofluorescent staining, which attaches a luminous tag to thymidine that can be detected under a special microscope, Kaplan used an electron microscope to observe neurons being born in the brains of adult rats. His work, too, was published in leading research journals, including *Science* in 1977, but dismissed as blithely as Altman's papers were.

One scientist, however, was not deterred. Fernando Nottebohm was intimately familiar with brains that seemed to remake themselves. He studies birds. More specifically, he studies birdsongs, and the bird brains that produce them, something that has entranced and obsessed him for more than three decades. Many species have the biological equivalent of a broken record: they sing the same song their whole life, warbling a single melody to attract mates and warn off rivals and claim territories until they die. The songbirds to which Nottebohm was drawn have quite different habits. Canaries and black-capped chickadees and zebra finches adopt and shed new tunes with the fickleness of a teenager turning over her iPod inventory, erasing the previous summer's repertoire and literally singing a whole new tune with the arrival of each new spring. How do they manage it?

Soon after he arrived at Rockefeller University in New York City in 1967, Nottebohm began discovering the bird-brain wonders that make this melodic turnover possible. He identified the clutch of neurons in canaries' brains that create, store, and generate songs and, in 1981, had one of those eureka moments that, Archimedes aside, occur so rarely in science: it dawned on him that, in song-changing birds, the brain cells that encode last season's hit might die and those that will encode this season's might be born. In a paper that year, called "A Brain for All Seasons," he pointed out two facts that were surely not coincidental. First, male canaries are able to learn new songs spring after spring. Second, at that time of year, the regions of their brain that generate melodies are up to 99 percent larger than in the fall.

The very idea that brain neurons might come and go, be born and die like so many flowering annuals, was, of course, anathema to the mandarins of neuroscience and completely at odds with the dogma that the adult brain cannot produce new neurons.

Like the ill-fated Joseph Altman and Michael Kaplan before him, Nottebohm decided to use radioactive thymidine to mark newborn brain cells. Day after day, he and a student injected canaries with radioactive thymidine. A month later, they killed the birds and examined their brains. It was like looking at the neuronal version of the Vegas Strip: there were thousands and thousands of radioactively labeled cells. The canaries were making new neurons. In 1983, he reported the discovery of neurogenesis in adult canaries: the radioactively labeled thymidine technique showed that neuronal precursors are born in the brain's ventricular zone, a sort of reservoir, and then divide and migrate to the song-control regions, differentiating and maturing into full-fledged neurons as they go. As Nottebohm put it, the neurogenesis he had "observed in the adult brain is both provocative and reassuring of the plasticity that may reside in adult nervous systems." The next year, he discovered that new neurons are not the neural equivalent of useless weeds that pop up and serve no function. To the contrary: they hook up into functional circuits. Using radioactively labeled thymidine again, he showed that the new neurons respond to auditory stimuli and are "incorporated into functional neural circuits." Neurogenesis occurred in the adult brain and changed the way the brain behaved.

Nottebohm fared only a bit better than Altman and Kaplan in the court of scientific opinion. Even if he was right about new neurons being born in the brains of his songbirds (and skepticism on that score abounded; maybe those new cells he was seeing were dumb old glia, which are the brain's support cells, not neurons), what relevance did it have for people? Maybe this was just a quirk of canary brains. Cute, but hardly important. And just in case anyone still harbored hopes that what was true for canaries might be true for primates—and for people—only four years after Nottebohm's discovery of neurogenesis in canary brains, one of the nation's foremost neuroscientists, Pasko Rakic of Yale University, unveiled a study that looked as if it would kill off all thoughts of neurogenesis in primates once and for all.

Rakic used the same radioactively labeled thymidine trick in rhesus monkeys, which may be a bit hirsute but still are more relevant to human brains than canaries are. In none of the twelve monkeys was a single neuron born in all the time the thymidine was sloshing around, which ranged from three days to six years. In 1985, Rakic published his findings in a paper titled "Limits of Neurogenesis in Primates." "Not a single [thymidine-labeled] cell with the morphological characteristics of a neuron was observed in the brain of any adult animal," he wrote. The brain of apes and humans, he suggested, "may be uniquely specialized in lacking the capacity for neuronal production once it reaches the adult stage."

The field of neurogenesis got its second wind in the 1990s, when Elizabeth Gould at Rockefeller saw hints that neurons are born in the hippocampus of adult rats as well as New World primates. The hippocampus is the seahorse-shaped region of the brain that is involved in memory. By "involved in," scientists mean that the hippocampus actually stores memories. In that case, germinating new neurons there looked like a good way to mess up the storage system. But it turns out that the hippocampus actually acquires memories rather than stores them, processing incoming information from the senses and parceling it out to other regions of the cortex for long-term storage. With this new understanding of the role of the hippocampus, neurogenesis there didn't seem so far-fetched.

By the 1990s, it had become clear that the objection to neurogenesis based on the model of the hardwired brain was baseless, for three reasons. First of all, Nottebohm had shown that it occurs in birds, and Gould, that it occurs in rats and primates. Second, the fact that neurons do not divide as other cells do turned out not to be an obstacle after all: brains have a reserve of what are now called neural stem cells, precursor cells with the ability to grow and differentiate into neurons and other cells of the nervous system. So even though existing cells cannot make two out of one, the brain has the seeds from which to grow whole new neurons. And finally, the objection that insinuating new neurons into the intricate machinery of a hardwired brain would be like throwing a spanner into the works was shown to rest on a faulty premise. The animal studies discussed in the last chapter had shown that the brain is no more hardwired than is Madonna's appearance. Objection overruled. The search for the causes and extent of neurogenesis in animals beyond Nottebohm's birds and Gould's rats was on.

Enriched Environments

As early as the 1940s, Canadian psychologist Donald Hebb noticed something funny about rats that did not lead the usual boring laboratory existence. From time to time, he would scoop up a couple of the rats he kept in his lab at McGill University in Montreal and take them home as pets. Their littermates remained in the spartan lab cages back at the university. The rats he took home, Hebb noticed, behaved differently from the ones left behind. They showed more curiosity, less fear, and more exploratory behavior.

Hebb did not systematically pursue his observation, and it took more than a decade for other scientists to do so. But in the 1960s, scientists at the University of California–Berkeley, led by Mark Rosenzweig, took Hebb's casual observations and turned them into a rigorous experiment examining the effect of what they began calling an "enriched environment" on crude measures such as total brain weight. The very possibility was as revolutionary as the protests that would soon swirl around the plazas and streets of the Berkeley campus: that experience can change brain structure. If it can, then the assumption that the brain's connections are fixed by our DNA would be out the window. At Harvard, David Hubel and Torsten Wiesel were showing that negative experiences—specifically, visual deprivation—can keep the brains of the cats they studied from developing properly. Could positive experiences, less extreme than being temporarily blinded, alter the brain?

Using an inbred strain of rat called Berkeley S1, which was particularly clever at solving mazes, the Berkeley scientists raised some of the animals in cages in groups of twelve, with toys and mazes and frequent handling by the scientists, some in barren isolation in a dark and almost silent room, and some in spartan cages but with two of their brothers. The rats in the socially and cognitively enriched environment grew bigger brains, with a cortex about 5 percent heavier than those of their littermates in the isolated environment. Brain size is a fairly crude measure, and it wasn't clear how or even whether the rats benefited from their stimulating living conditions. But in follow-up studies, the Berkeley team showed that rats in enriched environments solved mazes better than rats from isolated environments.

At the University of Illinois–Urbana-Champaign, William Greenough showed why. Rats living in an enriched environment with wheels to run on and ladders to scamper up, as well as other rats to interact with, have thicker cortexes than rats raised with neither playmates nor toys. They develop denser synapses—connections between neurons—and their neurons sprout more dendritic branches, the spindly little projections that take in signals from neighboring neurons. Denser synapses and more dendritic branches add up to richer and more complicated brain circuits. This structural difference produced behavioral differences: rats who grew up in an enriched environment were able to find hidden food more quickly than rats from poorer environments.

This is where Rusty Gage came in. It was all well and good that an enriched environment makes the cortex literally bloom with the new connections that underlie learning and complex (for a rat) thinking. But in

1997, Gage and his Salk colleagues discovered that an enriched environment, which resembles the complex surroundings of the wild more than the near-empty cages of a "nonenriched" environment does, causes something even more dramatic than more connections between neurons: it increases neurogenesis in young adult mice. After the mice had spent forty-five days in cages with a posse of other mice, wheels, toys, and tunnels (actually, short lengths of curved pipe; the mice found them immensely engaging), the scientists found that the animals had undergone a dramatic spurt of neurogenesis. The formation and survival of new neurons increased 15 percent in a part of the hippocampus called the dentate gyrus, which is involved in learning and memory. The standard 270,000 neurons in the hippocampus had increased to some 317,000.

"It's not a small number: 15 percent of the total volume can be changed just by switching experience," Gage told the Dalai Lama. Not coincidentally, mice experiencing enhanced neurogenesis also learned to navigate a maze better. It was one of the most striking findings in neuroplasticity, that exposure to an enriched environment leads to a striking increase in new neurons, along with a substantial improvement in behavioral performance.

A year after their discovery that an enriched environment spurs neurogenesis in young adult mice, Gage and his colleagues reported that it happens in old mice, too. Mice with an average of eighteen months (equivalent to sixty-five years for a human) living in an enriched, stimulating environment had three times the number of new brain cells in the dentate gyrus of the hippocampus as peers stuck in spare, bare-bones cages. "It doesn't matter what age they are when they begin to live in the enriched environment," Gage said. The senior-citizen mice got an even greater boost from their stimulating quarters than younger mice did.

"When we published this result, people asked me if it meant that they could increase their brain capacity by having new experiences, like traveling or taking on new challenges," Gage said. "I had to say we didn't know, because neurogenesis had never been shown to occur in human brains, and there were still conceptual objections to its existence."

There is one considerable problem with working with an enriched environment. There's a lot going on in it. There are wheels and toys, tunnels and other mice. If you find an effect of enriched environment, as Gage and his colleagues did, you then have your work cut out for you figuring out what element, or elements, in combination or singly, account for the burst of new neurons. "What is important about that complex environment?" Gage asked rhetorically. "Is it learning? Is it exercise? Is it social behavior?"

An Animal-Rights Interlude

For a tradition that teaches the primacy of compassion, experiments on animals are problematic. Buddhism teaches that the ultimate aspiration is that "all sentient beings be free from suffering." Yet biology has a long track record of falling far short of that. Could the Buddhists condone the use of animals in research when, at the end, they were killed so scientists could examine their brains? Asked how scientists can justify such studies, the Dalai Lama looked straight ahead for several seconds, as he often does while composing thoughts in English. "Treat them respectfully, do not exploit them," he began. "In immediate term, you may lose something, but, long run, you gain much benefit.

"From the Buddhist viewpoint, the moral question of such kind of sacrifice of animals for the benefit of human welfare is very complicated. If the human being for whose welfare the animal was sacrificed, as a result of the benefit that was derived from this, leads a more constructive life, then perhaps there is some justification. But if the human beings who benefit from such results then lead a life that is not constructive, but is destructive, then it has an added difficulty. Now I can give you one example, I think. A Buddhist facing starvation. Some fish are there. He thinks, do I take the life of the fish and survive? If yes, then the rest of your life, devote some sort of beneficial work to others, to pay for that fish. Then, the sacrifice of the fish helped one human to survive, and that human life is now really useful, beneficial to larger set of sentient beings. Then I think there may be some moral justification. But if you lead your life in more negative way, then better to die, instead of taking the fish.

"In the case of scientists, if as a result of experiments the scientists have done and of what the scientists have gained in knowledge, a much larger community of human beings will benefit, in that case there is a beneficial element to this work. To carry out experiments on animals with sincere motivation, and with this sense of compassion, and taking care, full care, of the animals, this has moral justification."

Now that so many of the results of basic biological research have been shown to apply to people, the Dalai Lama suggested, "Time has come now to say to small animal, gratitude and thank you. Goodbye. Not much disturbance. Give them a break. Of course to us, useful, but very sad this happen. We have no special right to experiment on them. If we have no bad feeling at all, then might come to think, yes, it is worthwhile to manipulate some useless human being. And eventually not only useless human being, but most intelligent human being."

"His Holiness's point is that we need to always maintain our sensitivity, a sense of caring, even to the smallest animals, because if we become desensitized, then this desensitization process may extend to bigger mammals," said Thupten Jinpa. "And then the question is, where do you put the line? We may then reach out to human beings that society may deem undeserving or worthless. So we need to be vigilant and always maintain a sense of sensitivity toward other species. If we do not bring ethical values to science, then there is nothing wrong with experimenting on human beings. We need to have ethical constraints."

"Humanity more compassionate species and, particularly, humanity has a unique sort of intelligence, with potential for unlimited, constructive work," continued the Dalai Lama. "So, therefore, from that viewpoint, yes, we have some justification to use another animal's life, but while we are exploiting them, it must be with some feeling, some care."

Human Neurogenesis

Ironically, what would arguably be Gage's most dogma-shattering experiment would not use the "small animal" that concerned the Dalai Lama. "At about the time when there was growing controversy over whether neurogenesis occurs in the frontal cortex of primates [as a result of Pasko Rakic's nay-saying], a bunch of us were sitting around the lab," Gage recalls. "And we basically agreed that the only way to resolve the question was to look for neurogenesis in humans."

That was easier said than done. No form of noninvasive brain imaging can detect the birth of new neurons in an intact, living brain, the way PET scans and fMRI scans can tell which regions of a brain are active. You have to kill the owner of the brain, remove the tissue you want, and study it with sophisticated microscopy and staining techniques, as Gage did the brains of mice in the enriched environments and as Nottebohm did canary brains. Staining was itself an issue. To mark newborn neurons, Gage wanted to use a technique called BrdU, or bromodeoxyuridine to its friends. BrdU is a molecular cousin of thymidine. When BrdU is around, dividing cells slurp it up as athletes do electrolyte drinks, incorporating it into the DNA they are assembling. But no bioethics panel worth its Hippocratic oath would approve an experiment in which healthy human volunteers would be injected with something that could not help them and might harm them. Studies probing for neurogenesis in humans seemed to be blocked before they could even get off the ground.

Even if the researchers could figure out how to look for neurogenesis in humans, it was not at all certain that they would find it. Sure, by the mid-1990s, Fernando Nottebohm had shown that songbirds regularly generate new neurons in their brain. Gage himself had discovered that mice running their little hearts out in exercise wheels produce new brain cells as routinely as human treadmillers produce sweat. And Elizabeth Gould had found that new cells bloom in the brains of some monkeys. That was getting closer and closer to humans on the evolutionary tree. But the hardliners weren't convinced. Human brains are not monkey brains, at least when it came to neurogenesis, they insisted, and they certainly are not mouse brains or bird brains. Everything we know and remember—indeed, everything we are, our beliefs and values and personalities and character—is encoded in the connections that neurons make in our brains. Surely the arrival of new neurons haphazardly trying to push their way into that delicate arrangement would be as disruptive as a pack of Zambonis barging into the delicate choreography of the Ice Capades.

But as the Salk scientists sat around, Swedish neurologist Peter Eriksson, who was spending a sabbatical year in Gage's lab, suddenly realized something. The experiment they were all dreaming of had already been done, at least up to a point. At the time, cancer patients were often injected with BrdU because it marks every newborn cell. Oncologists used it to show how many new cancer cells were being born, how rapidly malignant cells were dividing, and thus how aggressive the tumor was. BrdU, Eriksson reasoned, should be as good at tracking the genesis of new neurons as it is at tracking the proliferation of cancer cells. Both kinds of cells need DNA, and the luminous green molecules that attach to BrdU mark newborn cells as reliably as "It's a girl!" balloons mark the arrival of new babies in a suburban cul-de-sac.

Gage began calling friends at cancer hospitals. Do you have any brains? Can I have some? "I actually got tissue from a couple of places," Gage recalls. One sympathetic colleague sent him some slices of hippocampus that were taken at autopsy to determine whether the patient's cancer had reached the brain; since the patient had been given BrdU, to track malignant cells making more of themselves, there was a slim possibility of detecting newborn neurons in the slices of hippocampus. Although the samples "were in terrible shape," he says, "we thought we had something, some sign of BrdU incorporated into brain neurons. But we couldn't prove it." As his rotating cast of collaborators would go off into the world, returning to their home institutions or graduating to a postdoctoral position in another lab, his parting request to them was, see if you can get involved in a study that will give you access to brain tissue when cancer patients die.

On his return to Sweden after his 1994–1995 sabbatical at Salk, Peter Eriksson managed to do just that. During his time with Gage, he recalls, "I shared lab space with people working on neurogenesis in mice, but I was really skeptical," he recalls. "I didn't believe all the wonderful stuff they talked about all day long, but I realized it was fascinating—and eventually I wanted to study it, too. I made it my mission to know if neurogenesis was occurring in humans." Like Gage before him, he began contacting "almost everyone I could think of who might have autopsy material of a brain that had been treated with BrdU," he says. Then, one night when he was on call in the emergency room at Sahlgrenska University Hospital in Göteborg, he took a 2:00 A.M. coffee break. Joining him was a colleague who was just switching his speciality from internal medicine to oncology. Hey, it was worth a shot, Eriksson figured.

Sure I have cancer patients who have been treated with BrdU, Tomas Bjork Eriksson (no relation) told him. Half a dozen of them are still alive. The patients all had squamous cell carcinomas at the base of their tongue or in their larynx or pharynx, and they were terminal. To track how well the patients were responding to therapy and whether new tumors were forming, they were given injections of BrdU. All the oncologists cared about was whether malignant cells were proliferating and spreading, which BrdU would show. But BrdU isn't fussy. Even though the doctors biopsy only one kind of cell, BrdU tags every newly formed cell—not only cancer cells that arise from the division of an existing cancer cell but also, should there be any, neurons produced by neural stem cells in the brain.

And with that, Eriksson realized the search for neurogenesis in human brains might just be possible after all. He told Gage. And then the scientists found themselves in the awkward position of waiting for the patients to die.

One day in 1996, the phone rang in Eriksson's office at University Hospital. It would be soon, Tomas Eriksson told him. He had just talked to the nurse. Peter should have the neuropathologist, who would remove the patient's hippocampus during autopsy, standing by. Right, Eriksson replied. Putting down the phone, he ran through in his mind the preparations they had made for a moment they had planned and hoped for over two long years. Convincing oncologists that what they had in mind would not require any change in how patients were treated. Getting permission from relatives to take samples of the patients' hippocampus. Even though the care the patients received while alive would be just the same as if the scientists had never found them, what happened to them after they died—and their imminent death was, sadly, a foregone conclusion—would be decidedly unusual.

When the first patient died, Peter Eriksson called the neuropathologist on his team and told him to meet him at the hospital. He arranged with the hospice nurse for an ambulance to pick up the body. Soon after, everyone was assembled and scrubbed and looking at the now-cold body lying before them. The neuropathologist quickly cut through the skull and lifted off the top of the cranium to reveal the still-glossy brain. He sliced down deep through the center to remove part of the seahorse-shaped hippocampus and ventricular zone, which in mice seems to be the reservoir where neural stem cells are born and from which they migrate to the hippocampus, morphing into neurons either along the way or upon arrival.

The neuropathologist placed the tissue carefully in a sterile dish and handed it to Eriksson, who quickly left the room and strode down the corridor to the elevator that would take him up to the pathology lab. He removed the chunk of brain from the dish, placed it in formaldehyde for twenty-four hours to prevent decay, and then transferred it into a sugar solution to preserve it. He made paper-thin slices of the hippocampus, a mere forty micrometers thick, and stored the slices in a solution of ethylene glycol—antifreeze—at minus twenty degrees centigrade. Within hours, the brain samples were in a cargo hold on their way across the Atlantic and on to La Jolla. In all, five of the terminal patients, aged fifty-seven to seventy-two, participated in the experiment. "Participate" is a bit of a misnomer, for all they did was allow their brains to be examined after death. For die they did, all of them from 1996 to 1998, some at home and some at a hospital. And samples of the hippocampus of each of the five made their way to Gage's lab at Salk.

There, the scientists examined the slices of human hippocampus just as they had the brains of the mice in whom they had discovered a spurt of neurogenesis from living in an enriched environment. Bingo. In the first two samples, they found BrdU-tagged cells in the part of the hippocampus called the dentate gyrus. The presence of the glowing BrdU meant that those cells had been born sometime after the patients—all elderly—had been injected with the labeling molecule. After debating how many brains they would need to find neurogenesis in to make a convincing case, they eventually wound up with five.

"I remember bringing in other people, people who were not even working on this, and asking them to look at these brain sections and tell me what they saw," Gage recalls. He knew critics would be ready to pounce, claiming that any BrdU in the brain marked a metastatic brain tumor rather than healthy new neurons or that they had made some other error. "We went back and forth, shipping the microscopy images to Sweden—and this was at a time before the Internet made sending images so fast. We wanted to be right. We had to get to a point where we believed it ourselves."

And finally they did. "All of the brains had evidence of new cells exactly in the area where we'd found neurogenesis in other species," Gage told the Dalai Lama. "And we could prove through chemical analysis that they were mature neurons. The neurons were born in the patients when they were in their fifties and seventies." And they were born at a prodigious rate: neural stem cells, progenitors that are able to morph into any kind of cell in the brain, had created between five hundred and one thousand new neurons—daily—in people who were decades past when neurogenesis in humans was supposed to cease. "And these new neurons stayed alive until the people died," Gage said. "That was the first evidence for neurogenesis in the adult human brain. The physical process of cells being born and developing is happening in the adult brain. So now we know that in some areas of the brain, new neurons are being made all the time. It was a surprise, because we thought the brain was stagnant. But in this region of the hippocampus, there are these little baby cells that are dividing, and over time, they mature and migrate into the circuitry and become a full-blown adult neuron with new connections. And this is occurring throughout life. The finding brought us an important step closer to the possibility that we have more control over our own brain capacity than we ever thought possible."

The discovery overturned generations of conventional wisdom in neuroscience. The human brain is not limited to the neurons it is born with, or even to the neurons that fill it after the explosion of brain development in early childhood. New neurons are born well into the eighth decade of life. They migrate to structures where they weave themselves into existing brain circuitry and perhaps form the basis of new circuitry. And it was the dying cancer patients in Göteborg who made the discovery possible.

Run!

Gage's detour into human neurogenesis was, at the time of his meeting with the Dalai Lama, a onetime excursion. Ironically, just at the time the Swedish patients were spending their final days with BrdU being incorporated into newborn neurons, physicians were becoming concerned about the molecule's toxicity, even in cancer patients, and began phasing it out. That meant there was no obvious way to repeat the study that discovered neurogenesis in the adult human brain. But as Gage told the Dalai Lama, there was no shortage of mysteries to be cleared up. One of the most vexing had to do with those enriched environments. As mentioned above, "enriched" covers a multitude of sins. Gage knew he had to pinpoint just what it was about his mice's fancy toy- and wheel-filled cages that spurred the production of new neurons in the brain.

Although BrdU was becoming off-limits for humans, it was still ko-sher for mice. Gage and his team therefore injected a batch of mice with the neurogenesis-labeling molecule and separated the animals into two groups. One group was housed in the standard barren cages; the other, in cages equipped with a running wheel that they were free to use as much as their little legs desired. (Given half a chance, mice love to run, as anyone trying to catch one in the kitchen knows all too well; in cages, the little guys run something like five kilometers each night.) "Just by allowing the animal voluntary access to a running wheel, they'll spin four or five hours in this running wheel, and that's enough to almost double the number of cells in the brain," Gage told the Dalai Lama: the adult mice produced twice as many new cells in their brain's hippocampus as sedentary mice did. Never mind social interaction and mental stimulation: voluntary running produced the same number of newborn brain cells as the whole-nine-yards' enriched environment, suggesting that physical activity alone can generate new brain cells.

The connection between physical exercise and an enriched environment was becoming clearer. "We think voluntary exercise increases the number of neural stem cells that divide and give rise to new neurons in the hippocampus," Gage explained to the Dalai Lama. "But we think it is environmental enrichment that supports the survival of these cells. Usually, 50 percent of the new cells reaching the dentate gyrus of the hippocampus die. But if the animal lives in an enriched environment, many fewer of the new cells die. Environmental enrichment doesn't seem to affect cell proliferation and the generation of new neurons, but it can affect the rate and the number of cells that survive and integrate into the circuitry."

Indeed, within about a month, the new wires become functionally integrated into existing neuronal circuitry in the mice's hippocampus, forming synapses with already resident neurons, and sprouting the dendrites and dendritic spines with which they reach out and connect to other cells. In this way, they provide the hippocampus with a constantly replenished supply of robust, ready-for-action neurons that might either replace older neurons or augment them. The new neurons that are born in the brain's ventricles and find their way to the hippocampus are more excitable than the neurons that moved into the neighborhood years before and easily form new synapses, too, forging connections with existing neurons that become the basis for new circuitry. "We showed for the first time that new cells born in adult brains are functional," Gage says.

But what function? A clue to the function of the new neurons comes from where they wind up. In the mouse experiments that found an increased rate of neurogenesis, the actual number of additional neurons was on the order of thirty thousand. In a mouse cortex with billions of cells, that's nothing. But all the new neurons go to a spot in the dentate gyrus where they increase the number of cells by 10 percent or so. As a result, "the addition of even a small number of neurons can make a relatively large difference," Gage explained. The exact job of the dentate gyrus is something of a mystery, unfortunately. The best guess is that it somehow encodes information arriving from the senses, figuring out what existing information it belongs with. It's sort of like the assistant who scans incoming e-mails and places them in the right folder for safekeeping. Once the new information has been sorted this way, the hippocampus processes it in such a way that it can be sent to the cortex for storage. Perhaps the new neurons serve as replacements for damaged or aging cells. Because the dentate gyrus is such a madhouse of activity, with sensory perceptions arriving like trains at rush hour, its cells probably sustain a fair amount of damage. The newly arriving neurons can then take their place.

And that seems to have real-world consequences. Gage and his colleagues pitted the runners—whose brains had given birth to new neurons—against genetically identical mice that had been housed in the standard food-and-water-only cages. When the scientists plopped running-wheel mice and sedentary mice into a water tank in which a platform was hidden just below the milky surface, all the animals swam madly until they found solid (if submerged) ground. How long they took to do so reflected nothing but dumb luck, since with no cues to the presence of the platform, the animals can only swim until they happen upon it. But how long they took to find the platform in subsequent dunks reflected much more. It indicated how well they had learned the platform's location, apparently by remembering landmarks scattered around the laboratory ("Ah, the platform is right between that round thing on the wall and that rectangular thing that these annoying two-legged creatures pass through"). With their extra smarts, mice that had leaped into a running wheel at every opportunity managed to find the hidden platform faster than mice housed in standard cages, the scientists reported in 1999. "It suggests that these running mice learned better and got smarter," Gage said.

Curiously, the runners also produced more neurons than mice that were plopped into a water tank and, since it was either swim or drown, paddled around like crazy. That raised the question, of great interest to the Buddhists hearing Gage explain the puzzle, of whether it was the voluntary nature of the exercise that made the difference. "In the running wheel, the mice were free to jump on or off the wheel whenever they liked, but in the water tank, they had no choice but to swim," Gage explained. To test whether the volitional nature of the exercise mattered, the scientists put mice on a treadmill and prevented them from getting off, so the animals had to run or get thrown off the back like a rag doll. After several days of this, the animals' hippocampus contained fewer newborn neurons, and they learned much less quickly, than mice that had run the same distance, for the same time, but voluntarily. Forced exercise, it seems, does not promote neurogenesis, a fact that human couch potatoes can probably exploit.

"Running voluntarily increases neurogenesis and increases learning, even in very, very old animals," Gage explained to the Dalai Lama. "If you put them in a learning test, they're smarter. It seems like the effects of running on neurogenesis and on learning are dependent on volition. It has to be a voluntary act. It's not just the physical activity itself."

Buddhism does not have much to say about the value of exercise or even of staying in shape, as a few of the monks, rearranging their robes over their ample middles, noted somewhat sheepishly. But they were intrigued by Gage's finding that only voluntary exercise stimulated neurogenesis in the mice; forcing the little guys to swim or dropping them onto a moving treadmill had no such effect. The latter might reflect the fact that the prospect of drowning or of being flung off the back of the treadmill can be a mite stressful, and inundating a brain with stress hormones is a good way to kill neurons and rip apart synapses. But voluntary exercise is marked not only by the absence of stress. It is also characterized by the presence of brain rhythms called theta waves. These waves, which have a frequency of six to twelve cycles per second, are also present when you pay close attention to something but not when you eat or drink or are otherwise on automatic pilot. "Because theta activity can occur without physical activity," Gage told the monks, "the voluntary component could be the key to the promotion of neurogenesis."

In studies announced just weeks after the scientists' meeting with the Dalai Lama, at the 2004 annual meeting of the Society for Neuroscience, Brian Christie of the University of British Columbia found that individual neurons in the wheel-running mice "are dramatically different" from those in more sedentary mice in two important ways. For one thing, they have more dendrites, the little bushy projections through which a neuron receives signals from other neurons. Dendrites are the very parts of a neuron that tend to deteriorate with age. It has become a truism that the better connected a brain is, the better it is, period, enabling the mind it runs to connect new facts with old, to retrieve memories, and even to see links among seemingly disparate facts, the foundation for creativity. Not only are there more dendrites in the neurons of wheel-running mice, Christie found, but each of these bushes has significantly more spines on it. "Each of these spines represents a site at which neuronal communication can occur," Christie explained at the meeting. "In effect, we are showing that there are structural reasons for the enhanced learning and memory capacities we and others have observed in animals that exercise." The experiments, he said, "lay the foundation for establishing exercise-induced changes in brain structure as a viable [way] to combat the deleterious effects of aging" and might explain the beneficial effects on brain functions of leading an active life.

Neurogenesis and Depression

By the time Gage sat down with the Dalai Lama, it was clear that, in the adult human brain, new neurons arise from neural stem cells, which persist and support ongoing neurogenesis. The discovery suggests that the possibilities for neuroplasticity are greater than initially suspected: the brain may not be limited to working with existing neurons, fitting them together in new networks. It might, in addition, add fresh neurons to the mix. The neural electrician is not restricted to working with existing wiring, we now know: he can run whole new cables through the brain.

In mice, new neurons seem to help with learning. But in humans, the new neurons might serve another function. Gage's discovery of neurogenesis in the hippocampus of the adult human brain came just when neuroscientists were discovering that the hippocampus plays another role—in depression. It turns out that in many people suffering from depression, the dentate gyrus of the hippocampus has shrunk to a mere shadow of its former self. It is not clear whether that is cause or effect—that is, whether another factor caused the hippocampus to shrink, leading to depression, or whether depression caused the shrinkage. But in the first decade of the new millennium, scientists also saw hints that popular antidepressants such as Prozac, Zoloft, and Paxil exert their therapeutic effect through neurogenesis: in lab animals given the drugs, when neurogenesis is blocked, the animals show no behavioral effect from the medication.

That intrigued Gage, who saw links between the neurogenesis-depression discovery and his own work on the birth of new neurons in the adult hippocampus. Emerging evidence suggests that people who are suffering from depression are unable to recognize novelty. "You hear this a lot with depressed people," Gage said to the Dalai Lama. " 'Things just look the same to me. There's nothing exciting in life.' It turns out these individuals have a shrunken hippocampus. It may be that depression is the inability to recognize novelty. And this inability so see things as new, as fresh, as different, this is what elicits the feeling of depression. That may be why you want this reservoir, this cache of young cells in the hippocampus. It's able to recognize novelty, to recognize new experiences. Without that, you will have these fixed connections unable to recognize and acquire new information." There is also evidence, he said, that "if you can get someone with depression to exercise, his depression lifts." Neurogenesis may be the ultimate antidepressant. When it is impaired for any reason, the joy of seeing life with new eyes and finding surprises and novelty in the world vanishes. But when it is restored, you see the world anew.

It is also clear that chronic stress impairs neurogenesis, at least in mice. Peter Eriksson, Gage's colleague in the study that led to the discovery of neurogenesis in people, suspects that that holds lessons for how we live our lives, too. "In lab animals, chronic stress dramatically decreases neurogenesis as well as spatial memory," he points out. "When people under stress experience severe memory problems—forgetting their way to work, going into the kitchen and then not remembering why they went in—it's likely that what they're experiencing is the very negative effect of stress on the function of the hippocampus due to decreased neurogenesis."

The Changing Self

To the Dalai Lama and other Buddhists listening to Gage that day, the idea that even a part of the brain blooms with new neurons struck a chord. As Gage told them, "The environment and our experiences change our brain, so who you are as a person changes by virtue of the environment you live in and the experiences you have." Richie Davidson called that discovery "a point of intersection with Buddhism."

For science, as well as for ordinary people steeped in the traditions of Western religion and its notions of a soul and a self, the existence of neurogenesis—and the implication that the brain is both changeable and constantly renewed—poses a challenge. "How can we reconcile the sense of continuity or immutability and a relatively fixed notion of self with the notion that the brain is continuously turning over, cells dying, cells being born?" asked Davidson. Buddhism has no such trouble. "The question of how the self can remain intact despite neuroplasticity and neurogenesis is not a problem so far as Buddhism is concerned because of the idea of no self," said Thupten Jinpa.

The Buddhist concept of self is not simple. Some scholars say that the self is simply the continuum of mental consciousness. "But even if you take that as the basis of designation of the self, that stream of mental consciousness also is in a constant state of flux," said Alan Wallace. "So there's nothing stable there. Or in another school of Buddhist philosophy, they speak of the *Alyah Vijana*, the substrate or foundational consciousness. But even if you take that as the basis of the self, that, too, is in a constant state of flux. No matter what basis you have for the self, they're all in a state of flux. There is simply no basis at all that is static and therefore no possibility of the self as being static and immutable."

In stark contrast to the Judeo-Christian tradition, Buddhism therefore denies the existence of a fixed, unchanging, personal self or soul that imbues a living being for life and beyond. In rejecting the concept of *ātman*, as the self was called in the Indian traditions of two thousand years ago, the Buddha emphasized the changeability of all beings and the sheer impossibility of defining, much less finding, a timeless and unchanging self. A Buddhist work called *Questions of King Milinda,* written around the second or first century B.C., offers an analogy. In this text, a monk named Nagasena compares humans to chariots, which are made of many elements—wheels and chassis and axle and seat and walls. But none of these elements can be said to embody the essence of the chariot. Similarly, a person can be viewed as an amalgam of five elements—the physical body, feeling or sensations, ideation or mental activity, mental formations or perceptions, and consciousness.

The five aggregates "are in a constant state of flux, never, never static even for a moment, and the self is simply imputed upon the basis of these psychophysical aggregates," Wallace pointed out. "There's no possibility, then, of the self being any less in a state of flux than that upon which it's imputed. The notion that somehow the self will be less mutable is completely an illusion."

Although consciousness comes closest to the idea of a self or soul, in fact it undergoes subtle shifts as each new sensation arrives and as each new thought is born and becomes a part of that consciousness. The Buddha believed that relinquishing the notion of self would free people from the attachments that lead to craving and thus suffering and that therefore prevent them from transcending the cause of suffering. The recognition of non-self, in contrast, was a step toward an end to personal suffering.

Gage had demolished the dogma that the human brain leaves the womb with all the neurons it is ever going to have and that neurogenesis is a gift we left behind deep in the evolutionary past. The adult brain can add neurons to a structure crucial for memory and for retaining the sense of wonder, the sense that the world is bursting with novelty and surprise. It is said that half of what medical schools teach is wrong; the hard part is figuring out which half. With the discovery of human neurogenesis, the assertion that we are born with all the neurons we will ever have and that it's all downhill from there was finally outed as an assumption as gloomy as it is wrong. But the birth of new neurons is only one foundation for neuroplasticity.

Chapter 4

A Child Shall Lead Them

The Neuroplasticity of Young Brains

Esref Armagan has never seen a ray of light, a shadow, or a mountain. To him, color is a property that, people have told him, objects have, and perspective something he has learned from the casual conversations of friends. When he was born in a poor neighborhood of Istanbul in 1951, one of his eyes remained undeveloped and the other was damaged, with the result that he has always been functionally blind. Armagan received no formal education, and although he tried to play with the other street kids, his blindness set him apart, leaving him to find his own amusements. When he was little more than a toddler, he began scratching lines in the dirt and, by six, was sketching with pencil and paper. As a young man, he took up oils and eventually became a professional artist. Armagan's canvases are not abstract swirls and shapes, not stark geometrics or flat primitives. They show windmills and flying dragons, vibrant landscapes with shadows and three-point perspective. The sort of images you would think possible only with vision.

But Armagan has developed a unique compensation for his handicap. Using a special rubberized stylus, he draws lines that he can feel as tiny bumps and creases, so as one hand sketches a scene, the fingers of the other trail behind, feeling the lines and "seeing" the drawing as it develops. To depict objects receding into the distance, he relies on a seemingly innate sense of perspective. When he is satisfied with a sketch, he transfers it to canvas and applies oils with his fingers, one color at a time so the hues do not smear, waiting two or three days for blue to dry before applying yellow, for red to dry before applying black. Armagan has achieved some measure of success in the art world. But in the world of neuroscience, he is a veritable rock star. His visual cortex, the structure in the back of the brain that normally processes signals from the eyes, has never received a message from his eyes. According to the dogma of the hardwired brain, that should be that; a structure destined by genetics to handle visual signals should, in their absence, face a lifetime of unemployment. Scientists exploring neuroplasticity had other ideas.

The Brain You Are Born With

The role of experience in the development of vision and other senses has puzzled scientists for centuries. In 1688, an Irish philosopher named William Molyneux wrote a letter to John Locke, posing this hypothetical: if a man born blind learns to distinguish a cube from a sphere by touch, and if his sight is suddenly restored, if he were to see a cube and a globe on a table in front of him, could he tell by sight which is the globe and which the cube? Molyneux thought not. Locke, too, concluded that "the blind man, at first, would not be able with certainty to say which was the globe, which the cube."

From her earliest years as a neuroscientist, Helen Neville was drawn to a modern version of Molyneux's question, one that has long occupied the minds of parents and educators, no less than philosophers and scientists: how, and to what extent, do the experiences a child has interact with the brain with which he or she was born? Yes, the brain certainly seems to be hardwired, she told the Dalai Lama at the 2004 meeting. In virtually everyone ever born, the back of the brain receives and processes signals from the eye into a sense of sight, and a strip across the top of the scalp receives and processes signals from each point on the outer body from toes to head into a sense of touch, and a region arcing from just above the temples receives and processes signals from the ears into a sense of hearing. Structure seems to determine function.

But when you think about it, there is no compelling reason for that specialization. No matter where in the brain a neuron lives, from the visual cortex to the somatosensory cortex, it is basically identical to neurons in any other neighborhood. Why, then, is one clump of neurons visual and another tactile or auditory? As Neville put it to the Dalai Lama, "The question is, does the visual experience arise out of intrinsic properties of this tissue, or is it instructed, educated by the eyes to become visual? This is an age-old question." What if, Neville wondered, the kind of input a brain receives matters . . . and matters as much as the instructions it receives from its genes? What if the specialized functions of different regions of the brain—the basis for those brain maps with "visual cortex" and "auditory cortex" labeled so authoritatively—are not hardwired at all, by DNA or anything else? What if, instead, environmental inputs, and thus the experiences a person has, shape the development and specialization of the brain's regions and circuits?

As she told the Dalai Lama, "The motto of my university, the University of Oregon, is *Mens Agitat Molen:* Minds Move Mountains. And that's the bottom line of my research. Virtually every brain system that we know about—visual systems, auditory systems, attentional systems, language systems—is importantly shaped by experience. This is what I mean by neuroplasticity. But this ability of the brain to change with experience is not monolithic. Some brain systems are much more plastic than others. Some are plastic only during limited periods, while some are capable of change throughout life. Our job is to figure out which are which."

Since earning her undergraduate degree in psychology from the University of British Columbia and her Ph.D. in neuropsychology from Cornell University, Neville has been driven by the conviction that by discovering which brain systems can be sculpted by experience and when, scientists will be able to tell parents, teachers, and policy makers the best ways to help young brains blossom. "We want to know who we are and where we come from," she told the Dalai Lama. "How do we work? But we also study brain development because we want to optimize human development. On a practical level, what we learn about how a young brain develops, and how experience influences it, can tell us how to design our schools. If we know which brain systems are the most sensitive to the environment and to the experiences the person has, as well as when those systems are most modifiable, then we can do the most good. It's basic research, but it can make a difference in the world. I think if people just knew more about the brain, it could help make the world a better place. We have made some discoveries that make us want to go to policy makers and say, we should put more resources into the education of children. People who hold the purse strings might say that what a brain becomes and how it develops is genetic. We're showing that it's not."

It had been clear for some time that the brain of a child is remarkably plastic. This much was conceded even by scientists who insisted that the adult brain is as fixed as cement. Consider the children who have undergone operations that remove an entire cerebral hemisphere, a procedure called hemispherectomy. By the mid-1980s, this radical operation had become the treatment of choice for children suffering from uncontrollable and often life-threatening seizures due to developmental abnormalities or strokes. Neurosurgeons routinely describe the children's recovery as nothing short of amazing. If they remove a child's left hemisphere, and thus (supposedly) all of the brain's language regions, for instance, as long as the operation occurs before the child is four years old, he still learns to talk, read, and write. The worst a child typically suffers from losing half a brain is some impairment of the peripheral vision and fine motor skills on one side of the body, opposite the side of the surgery.

One possible reason for the resilience is that in brains this young, structure is not inextricably tied to function. As a result, tissue left intact after a hemispherectomy can take on jobs ordinarily assigned to tissue in the half of the brain that was removed. After a left hemispherectomy, for instance, the brain reassigns language function to the intact right hemisphere. Plasticity of this magnitude wanes with age, however. After six or seven, loss of the language regions due to surgery or injury can leave a severe and lasting language deficit.

As far as scientists can tell, the basis for the plasticity of the young brain is its extreme redundancy: a one-year-old has twice as many neuronal connections as her mother. Much as a sculptor starts with much more marble than will eventually make up the finished work, so the human brain, too, starts with a plethora of connections. Each of the 100 billion or so neurons in the newborn brain connects to, give or take, an average of 2,500 other neurons, though the number of connections can range from a few thousand for less-sociable neurons to 100,000 for those that embrace the "reach out and touch someone" maxim. The young brain doesn't stop there. For the next two or three years, most of its neurons continue on a connectivity rampage, until they form an average of 15,000 synapses each at age two or three. And regardless of how much that brain goes on to learn, regardless of how many rich experiences it has, how many languages it masters or mathematical algorithms it memorizes—all of which are encoded in synapses—that is as connected as the brain gets.

After age two or three, the brain starts losing synapses in a process called pruning. "We lose about half the connections that we make in early childhood," Neville told the Dalai Lama. They vanish like baby fat, melting away so that neurons that once met at the synapse no longer communicate with one another. In the visual cortex, the loss of synapses starts even earlier, just before a child's first birthday. By one estimate, some 20 billion synapses are pruned every day from childhood to early adolescence. If we take 1,000 as a conservative mean for the number of connections each neuron makes, then the adult brain has settled back to an estimated 100 trillion synapses, less than half as many as at the synaptic peak.

The synapses that endure are those that carry traffic; those that melt away are like unused railroad lines, going out of business. The dramatic shift from a newborn brain endowed with an entire world of possibility to an older brain whose circuits are less malleable reveals itself in ways both dramatic and subtle. If a baby is born with cataracts, she can develop normal visual acuity even if her eyes remain clouded until she is five months old. As long as the cataracts are removed by then, the brain can regroup, taking the clear visual inputs that finally start arriving and fine-tuning the visual cortex to process them. Similarly, if a baby's eyes are misaligned, the brain does not receive the input required to develop the ability to perceive depth and distance. (Cover one eye and look around: the world looks flat.) As long as surgery restores the requisite convergent input to the two eyes by eleven months of age, this "stereopsis" develops as if there had been no delay at all; again, the young brain is still malleable enough at eleven months to assign circuits to construct three-dimensional vision out of the input the eyes receive. If the eyes remain misaligned later into childhood, however, the brain no longer has the plasticity required to develop stereoptic vision.

Other systems retain their plasticity longer, but again with a dramatic falloff. Infants can hear every sound in every one of the thousands of human languages, from the French *u* in *du* to the Spanish *ñ* in *niño* to the English *th* in *thin*. By "hear," I mean they can distinguish, say, English's *th* from *t*: the phonemes sound different. Each phoneme that the infant brain hears often enough, such as those of his native language, becomes represented in the brain's auditory cortex by a tiny cluster of neurons that come alive with electrical activity when and only when the sound of that phoneme enters the child's ear and gets passed into the brain. This auditory map is like the somatosensory map I described in connection with the animal studies that first proved the neuroplasticity of the adult brain. Just as there is a cluster of neurons in the somatosensory cortex that represents the right forefinger and another that represents the left knee, and so on to all the spots on the skin, so there is a cluster in the auditory cortex that represents *gr* and another that represents *sh*, through all the sounds of your native tongue.

The auditory cortex has limited storage space, however. After a few years, something changes. Either space is literally used up, with no spare neurons that can be drafted to represent a new phoneme, or else the process by which oft-heard sounds claim such a cluster becomes sclerotic. Whatever the reason, the result is that the brain loses its ability to hear every new phoneme that comes its way. In one now-classic experiment, seven-month-old Japanese babies had no trouble discriminating the sound of an English *r* from the sound of an English *l*. But ten-month-olds were deaf to the difference. The auditory cortex apparently loses the ability to encode new phonemes, especially if they sound anything like a phoneme that has already staked a claim to territory in the auditory cortex. It's as if this chunk of the brain sprouts "Sold" signs all over, and once every parcel is claimed, the neural land rush is over. "If you don't hear the sounds of your second language before the age of ten, you will never learn a native accent," Neville told the Dalai Lama. He smiled in recognition.

The dogma that the human brain cannot change therefore came with an asterisk: adult brains may be fixed, but young brains retain their malleability. If the human brain has the ability to change its structure and function, the smart money was on finding it in the brains of children. That's where Helen Neville decided to look.

Hearing Sight, Seeing Sound

She had heard all the folk wisdom about people who are blind or deaf from early childhood. For as long as there have been myths, there have been myths about the blind and deaf, tales of their almost supernatural ability in another realm of the senses. Especially in people who are blind from birth, according to a long-held view in both science and folklore, the surviving senses supposedly develop far beyond those in people with normal vision, with the result that blind people's sense of touch becomes highly acute and their hearing so sharp they are able to discern the presence of obstacles merely by listening to echoes. Folklore saw this as a compensatory gift from the gods.

Studies with lab animals suggested there is something to the legends. Rats that are blinded at birth run mazes better than sighted rats do, for instance. That may seem paradoxical, but rats do not run mazes by looking around. Instead, they feel their way by brushing their whiskers against the walls of the labyrinth. In blind rats, the whiskers are more sensitive than in sighted rats. More intriguing, the region of the brain that receives signals from the whiskers (it's called the barrel cortex) is larger and has better angular resolution—the ability to tell where the touch came from—than does the barrel cortex of sighted rats. Blindness had indeed changed the rats' brains and, in so doing, sharpened a surviving sense.

Trouble was, humans did not seem to follow the rats' script. Most studies had found that blind people do not hear better, in the sense of perceiving softer sounds, than sighted people do. Nor do deaf people see better than hearing people do, as measured by their ability to detect minimal contrasts, perceive the direction of motion of a barely moving object, or see in dimmer light. As Neville puzzled over the failure to find experimentally what blind people and deaf people themselves reported, and what animal studies suggested should exist, she realized that one problem might have been that scientists were measuring the wrong things. Maybe, she thought, compensatory improvement in the sensory ability of the blind or deaf appears in subtler aspects of perception.

Her first clue to how dramatically deafness can alter the brain came when she conducted a small study in people who had been deaf since birth. Because a genetic glitch had kept the cochlea from developing normally, no electrochemical signals from the ears ever reached the primary auditory cortex, which ordinarily receives and processes auditory signals. It is stuck in an eternal waiting-for-Godot moment, anticipating auditory signals that never arrive. Is the brain's hardwiring so powerful, Neville wondered, that this region becomes the Vladimir and Estragon of the brain? Or does it assess the bleak situation and remake itself?

It was 1983, and the tools of the brain game were pretty limited, with widespread use of fancy imaging techniques such as PET (positron-emission tomography) scans and fMRI (functional magnetic resonance imaging) still on the horizon. But one thing Neville could measure was the strength of the brain's response to a stimulus, by gluing electrodes all over volunteers' scalps. The stimulus she used was a simple flash of light, over to the side, so her volunteers—some with normal hearing and some who had been deaf since birth or early childhood—could see it only with their peripheral vision. Look straight ahead, she told them. Flash. Flash. Flash.

Then she compared the response of the deaf brains to the response of the hearing brains. The evoked potential—roughly, how many neurons fired in response to the flash—in the brains of the deaf was two or three times larger than in people with normal hearing. It was a hint that something was different in how the deaf *saw*, something different about their peripheral vision. The strength of the evoked response, however, was not the real surprise. The electrodes that registered the response of the hearing brains were right over the visual cortex, which is where any well-behaved brain should be registering flashes of light. But the electrodes that registered the response of the deaf brains were over the *auditory* cortex. It was a preliminary but tantalizing answer to Neville's waiting-for-Godot question. It looked as if auditory regions do not wait patiently for a signal that never comes. When the ears transmit only silence, the brain's auditory regions somehow begin picking up signals from the retinas.

It seems like the setup to a bad joke—what does the auditory cortex do in the brains of people who are completely deaf?—analogous to "What does a eunuch do at an orgy?" But as Neville began to see, the answer is not the obvious "nothing." And with that realization would come some of the most dramatic evidence that the functions of the brain's primary structures, even those supposedly so hardwired they practically have "visual cortex" or "auditory cortex" embossed on them, remake themselves in response to experience.

It was years before neuroplasticity would capture the imagination of neuroscientists, but it was the neuroplasticity of some of the brain's basic sensory cortices that Neville would discover. In a series of studies, she explained to the Dalai Lama, she tried to pin down what visual functions the auditory cortex of deaf people performs. In one experiment, she had volunteers pay close attention to a white square on a video screen and detect in which direction it was moving. Sometimes the square was in the center of the visual field, sometimes on the periphery. As the volunteers tracked the square, electrodes on their scalps measured millisecond-by-millisecond changes in electrical signals that meant neurons had registered the motion. When the square occupied the center of the visual field, the strength of the brain signal was the same in deaf people and hearing people. But when the square meandered around in their peripheral vision, the brain signals were several times stronger in the deaf. That signal strength had real-world consequences: the deaf people were much faster and more accurate than people with normal hearing at detecting in which direction the square in their peripheral vision was moving.

The brain registers signals from the center of the visual field and from the periphery along different neuronal highways, one a sort of high road and one a low road. When light falls on the edge of the retina, Neville explained, the signal zips down to the primary visual cortex in the back of the brain and then up to the parietal cortex just above the ears, which plays an important role in integrating information from various senses. This peripheral-vision highway also carries information about motion and location and is colloquially known as the "where" pathway. But when light falls on the center of the retina, it travels from the primary visual cortex along a different highway, toward a clump of neurons at the front of the brain called the anterior inferior temporal cortex (some of whose neurons are so specialized they respond only to faces). This central-vision highway carries information about color and form and is known as the "what" pathway. Since deaf people had better peripheral vision, Neville realized that the "where" pathway might actually benefit from deafness. That is, it might be plastic and malleable, responding to experience.

Neville therefore decided to investigate how deafness alters the brain's visual highways. Is the "where" pathway, which carries information about motion and peripheral vision, more strongly shaped by deafness than the "what" pathway, which carries information about color, shape, and the central visual field? She and her colleagues had volunteers, some deaf and some with normal hearing, watch a screen on which patterns of dots changed color. The brains of the deaf and the hearing responded in essentially the same way. That supported her hunch that the "what" visual pathway, which handles color, is not affected by deafness. But when volunteers watched moving streams of dots, hearing brains and deaf brains acted differently. In the deaf, the strongest signal occurred in a region that specializes in detecting motion and is located along the "where" pathway. Losing the sense of hearing, it seems, produces a very specific compensation in the brain, sharpening the ability to see changes in motion.

"All the functions of the 'where' pathway are enhanced," Neville told the Dalai Lama. "The deaf people have better detection of motion, better peripheral vision. But none of the functions of the 'what' pathway—color vision and central vision—are changed." People who have normal hearing but who learned sign language to communicate with their deaf parents and siblings do not show this enhancement, suggesting that "this effect is due to auditory deprivation, not to learning sign language," she added.

It was not only the strength of the brain's "where" signal that differed between the deaf and the hearing. Its location was different, too: there was a spike in activity in the auditory cortex. Even though genetics constrains the auditory cortex to hear, if this structure has different sensory experiences than what nature expected—that is, silence rather than sounds—it can apparently take on an entirely different job, processing information about movement. As the millennium turned, she had pretty clear evidence that deaf people are better than hearing people at peripheral vision and at detecting motion, thanks to the plasticity of neuronal highways in the brain.

Much of her work had been done with electrodes, which detect the electrical activity of neurons right under the scalp where they're glued. But that's a fairly imprecise way to locate a brain signal. Neville therefore turned to fMRI, the imaging technique that can pinpoint an active region of the brain to within a millimeter or so, to nail down just where deaf people were processing sights.

For these studies, she and her team recruited eleven congenitally deaf adults who had learned sign language from their deaf parents starting in infancy, five adults with normal hearing who had learned sign language from their deaf parents starting in infancy (they grew up to be interpreters for the deaf), and eleven hearing people who did not know sign language. Each volunteer looked at the center of a video monitor. In one test, they saw 280 dots splayed across the screen, sometimes static and sometimes moving radially like an exploding star. The task was to press a button when they noticed any of the dots becoming dimmer. The dimmings were infrequent, perhaps three in each twenty-second run. In the next test, they saw the same field of dots but were to detect if they sped up or slowed down. Sometimes the change—dimming or acceleration—occurred only in the dots in the center of the field, sometimes it occurred only in dots around the edges, and sometimes it occurred in both.

The deaf signers did better than any of the hearing volunteers, signers or nonsigners, when either acceleration or dimming occurred in the periphery. A hint of what accounted for the sharper perception showed up on the fMRI. In the deaf, when they were paying attention to dots in their peripheral vision, a larger area of the brain around the motion-detecting region on the left side of the visual cortex was activated compared to the analogous region on the right side, an asymmetry that did not occur in people with normal hearing. In addition, only the deaf showed extra activity in the part of the brain that receives input about multiple senses, including the parietal cortex. That suggested that multisensory regions become more sharply attuned to visual information when deafness deprives the brain of auditory information. This was the first demonstration that connections between brain structures that first receive visual input and those that assemble that input with information from other senses are remodeled by the experience of deafness. As a result, people who are deaf from birth or early childhood have superior peripheral vision. For that, they can thank neuroplasticity.

To nail down the basis for differences in ability, Neville and colleagues asked eleven normal adults and eleven congenitally deaf adults to watch a video monitor that was divided into five panels, one in the middle and four at the corners. In one test, the volunteers were to pay attention to a series of vertical blue and green bars in the four corner panels and determine when any of them turned red, which they did for only one-tenth of a second. In another task, they had to notice when fuzzy light-gray and dark-gray bars moved from left to right, also for only one-tenth of a second. The room was dark and quiet, and the participants, sitting in comfortable chairs, were to push a button when they noticed a change in color, in the first test, or a change of motion, in the second test.

The brain activity when the volunteers were on the lookout for color changes was virtually the same in the deaf and the hearing. But the brain responses to motion were noticeably different. Brain activity was greater in the deaf adults, and occurred over a more extensive area, Neville and her colleagues reported in 2002. In deaf people, it seems, the brain compensates for the absence of hearing by tinkering with the circuitry that handles particular aspects of vision. Unable to monitor the world around them by sound, they devote greater areas of the brain to processing peripheral vision and motion. Movement, after all, is more likely to signal a change or a danger than, say, color. It helps to be able to quickly notice a truck that is suddenly barreling down on you from the side.

"Among the deaf, the visual pathway is greatly enhanced, with a stronger response to peripheral signals and greater sensitivity to motion," Neville explained to the Dalai Lama. "The brain's *auditory* regions can be recruited to process at least two aspects of *vision*—peripheral vision and the perception of motion. This was some of the first evidence that brain specializations such as auditory cortex are not anatomically determined. It's not an inherent property of the tissue."

As recently as the 1990s, neuroscientists believed that if the ears do not send signals to the auditory cortex, then the neurons there eventually wither and die, making it as quiet as in a butcher shop on an island of vegetarians. They were wrong. Through neuroplasticity, the brain's structures are in no way stuck with the career their DNA intended.

What the Braille Readers Showed

Some of the most revolutionary discoveries about the malleability of the brains of children emerged from a lab that intended to probe the brains of the elderly—in particular, those who had suffered a stroke. When Mark Hallett began working at the National Institutes of Health in 1994, his research plan was clear: he intended to study how people recover from stroke. And recover they do, at least some of them. Although stroke looms in the public mind as a life sentence of partial paralysis, loss of speech, and other tragic impairments, in fact an estimated one-third of stroke victims recover spontaneously, regaining fairly quickly most or all of the function they lost in the immediate aftermath of the stroke—the ability to move the left arm, for instance, or the ability to speak. Another one-third recover after physical therapy. Those were the patients Hallett wanted to study. What was the neurological basis for their recovery?

His thoughts turned to neuroplasticity. If the brain regains the power of speech after its language region has been damaged, for example, or can move an arm even though the strip of motor cortex that controls it has been knocked out by stroke, then maybe a different region of the brain has taken over for the damaged region, like a fellow soldier taking over from a buddy lost in action. "Neuroplasticity as the basis for recovery from stroke was only hypothetical then," Hallett recalled in 2005. "The belief was that the adult brain doesn't change. Nevertheless, Mike Merzenich's work raised it as a possibility. So we began doing studies in people that mimicked what he had done in monkeys. Almost immediately, we began to find plastic changes in the brain." Research that began with the goal of discovering the basis for recovery from stroke would provide some of the strongest evidence for the plasticity of the young brain.

Among the bright young scientists Hallett attracted to his lab was Alvaro Pascual-Leone. Born in Spain in 1961, Pascual-Leone quickly became a citizen of the world, earning his M.D. and Ph.D. degrees in neurophysiology from Albert-Ludwigs University Medical School in Germany, and continuing his training in neurology at the University of Minnesota in the late 1980s. There, he became intrigued by Merzenich's experiments, especially that in which the UCSF scientists trained monkeys to keep two fingers in contact with a spinning disk, pressing just hard enough to maintain contact but not so hard that their fingers got whirled around as if on a merry-go-round. After weeks of this training, there was a fourfold increase in the area of the somatosensory cortex that processes signals from these fingers, as discussed in chapter 2. This expansion came at a cost to the representation of adjacent fingers, which got smaller. "I wondered if the same thing might happen in people who use a single finger a great deal," Pascual-Leone says. Who might such people be? Blind people who read Braille with the tip of their index finger.

Braille has its roots in the French army. In the early eighteenth century, a soldier named Charles Barbier de la Serre invented a code for military messages that could be read in the trenches at night without light; it used patterns of twelve raised dots to represent phonemes. The system was too complicated for the beleaguered soldiers to master, but when Barbier met Louis Braille, who had been blind since boyhood, the latter simplified the system into the six-dot version used ever since. Braille is not a language per se but rather a code by which other languages, from English to Japanese to Arabic and Hebrew, can be read and written. The raised dots are arrayed in "Braille cells": each cell contains two columns of dots, each column having zero, one, two or three dots. There are thus sixty-three possible combinations, allowing each cell to represent either a letter of the alphabet, a number, a punctuation mark, or a full word. Since the dots within a cell are only 2.29 millimeters apart, and the cells themselves are just 4 millimeters apart, reading Braille requires extremely fine tactile acuity.

With help from a local association for the blind, Pascual-Leone found a group of Braille experts happy to volunteer for research. He also recruited people with normal sight to serve as controls. To determine how the Braille readers' brains handled the tactile barrage, he used a technique called somatosensory-evoked potentials. The basic idea is to administer weak electrical shocks to the tip of the reading finger, while a Medusa's net of electrodes glued to the scalp above the somatosensory cortex records which spots register the feeling. In other words, the skin sends signals; where in the brain are they received? That would reveal the extent of the cortical representation of the reading finger.

The somatosensory cortex contains a map of the body, though apparently one drawn by a cartographer with a sense of humor. These twin strips of gray matter, one for the right side of the body and one for the left, run from the top of the head to just above the ear. Every spot on the skin is represented by a spot on the somatosensory cortex, much as the corner of Twelfth and Vine is represented by intersecting lines on a street map. It was Canadian neurosurgeon Wilder Penfield who found, in experiments in the 1940s and 1950s, just what a joker the mapmaker was. When patients were about to undergo brain surgery, Penfield stimulated (with a mild electric shock) one spot after another on the surface of the exposed brain. The brain has no sensory receptors itself and so does not feel the little zaps. But they have an effect nonetheless, triggering electrochemical activity. Penfield asked his conscious subjects what they felt. It was uncanny: the patients were sure that Penfield had touched their fingers, their lips, their leg, or their arm. All he had done, however, was cause neurons to fire in the region of the somatosensory cortex that receives signals from the fingers, lips, leg, or arm. The brain can't tell whether the neurons are firing because a signal races up to the brain from the point that was touched or because a curious neurosurgeon has set them abuzz. In this way, Penfield was able to determine which spots in the somatosensory strip correspond to which spots on the body.

And that's when he discovered how odd the map was. It is not like a street map, where the line representing First Avenue intersects Forty-second Street just south of where it intersects Forty-third Street and north of where it meets Forty-first Street, equidistant from each. If the somatosensory map were similarly faithful, it would be a little homunculus, a minuscule but accurate representation of the body laid along the strip of cortex, head above neck above shoulders above trunk . . . down to the toes. Instead, the somatosensory representation of the hand sits beside the face. The genitals lie directly below the feet. The lips dwarf the trunk and calves. The hands and fingers are huge compared to the puny shoulders and back. The reason? The more cortical real estate a body part claims, the greater its sensitivity (compare the sensitivity of your tongue to the back of your hand: the tip of your tongue can feel the ridges of your front teeth, but the back of your hand feels them only as a dull edge). This is the strip of cortex Pascual-Leone was probing.

What he found was that the area of the brain that processes what the reading finger of an expert Braille reader feels is much greater than the area handling the nonreading finger, or either index finger in non-Braille readers. The extra stimulation that a Braille-reading finger regularly feels— stimulation to which the person pays attention—causes an expansion of the region of somatosensory cortex devoted to processing that input. Just as in Merzenich's monkeys, that expansion comes at the expense of other fingers, Pascual-Leone reported in 1993. "The thumb and the middle finger got crowded out of their usual place in the somatosensory cortex," he says. The somatosensory cortex, it turns out, is not all that strongly wedded to how it represents parts of the body. In response to injury or amputation (as Merzenich discovered in the monkeys he studied), to behavior or activity (such as reading Braille), it rearranges or it enlarges or it shrinks the cortical territory it assigns to this or that part of the body.

To Pascual-Leone, that finding was the start, not the end, of a saga that would lead him to some of the most dramatic discoveries in neuroplasticity. As soon as he had that one in the books, he started wondering about something else. Sure, it makes sense that the representation of a Braille expert's reading finger in the somatosensory cortex should expand and elbow out (finger out?) the representations of the less-used thumb and middle finger. But touch is only one part of Braille reading. Movement is equally crucial. To read Braille, you do not just slide your finger across the dots in a single pass. Instead, the finger quickly moves side-to-side over each cell, as many times as necessary to figure out what the character is, and only then moves on to the next cell. It all happens in a blur, but the smaller side-to-side motions embedded in the overall left-to-right motion require precise motor control. "Braille readers move their reading finger exceedingly precisely," says Pascual-Leone. "We wondered if that might show up in the motor cortex." That would be his first project when he joined Mark Hallett's lab at NIH, probing how a motor cortex responds to all that Braille reading.

Neuroscientists had recently invented a new toy. Called transcranial magnetic stimulation (TMS), it produces short bursts of a strong magnetic pulse from an electromagnetic coil of wire, shaped like a figure eight and placed on the scalp. The bursts induce an electric current to flow in the region of the brain directly below the coil, temporarily exciting or inhibiting that area. When TMS inhibits activity, the effect is like a momentary stroke: that region of the brain briefly stops functioning. Transcranial magnetic stimulation can therefore be used to pinpoint which regions of the brain are necessary for particular tasks. If the volunteer can't do something when that part of his brain is off-line, you can infer that that region is necessary to the task. In this way, you can "map" the motor cortex: if zapping one point causes the index finger to become immovable, and zapping a point adjacent to it has the same effect, but zapping a third spot leaves the finger's mobility unhampered, then the region including points one and two, but not three, constitutes the motor cortex's representation of the index finger.

This is what Pascual-Leone did with his blind Braille readers. Using TMS, he and his colleagues discovered that, in proficient Braille readers, the motor representation of the reading digit is notably larger than the representation of the corresponding finger in the nonreading hand or of the pinkie in either hand. And the representation of the pinkie of the reading hand is considerably smaller than in the nonreading hand. The reading finger has usurped what was rightfully the pinkie's. When they performed the same cartography in the brains of people with normal vision, they found that the right and left index fingers took up roughly equal space. And the territory claimed by the pinkie of the reading-finger hand was not especially shrunken compared to the territory of the pinkie on the other hand. Pascual-Leone had discovered, in people, what Michael Merzenich and his team at UCSF had discovered in monkeys: when an animal uses a finger repeatedly, the brain region that controls that finger expands. In blind Braille readers, the representations of the reading finger in both the motor cortex and the somatosensory cortex are notably larger than they are in non-Braille readers. Experience had wrought dramatic changes in the brain with which the blind person was born, rewiring the cortex in response to the demands placed on it by reading Braille.

The conclusion was clear, said Mark Hallett: "The cortical representation of the reading finger in proficient Braille readers is enlarged at the expense of the representation of other fingers." After all, the brain has boundaries just as a city does. If you are going to increase the zoning allotted to one thing—to moving the reading finger or to parkland, for instance—then it has to come at the expense of other things. And the closest place for a cortical landgrab is the motor cortex's representation of the pinkie on the same hand as the reading finger.

In 1993, a Japanese scientist, Norihiro Sadato, joined Hallett's lab as a postdoctoral fellow. Ten years earlier, he had graduated from Kyoto University Medical School, and although he completed a residency in diagnostic radiology (as well as internal medicine and general surgery), he had been bitten by the research bug. "As a clinician doing diagnostic neuroradiology, I learned much about the structural detail of the brain, but I wanted to know more about its functions, by visualizing them," he says. His timing could not have been better. The 1980s had seen an explosion of research in what has been called (not always kindly) "the new phrenology." The discredited phrenologists of centuries past felt for bumps on the skull as a way of diagnosing personality, intelligence, and other mental traits. With neuroimaging, sophisticated scanners detected active regions of the brain. The first such "functional neuroimaging" device to emerge from the lab was positron-emission tomography, or PET, which was developed in the 1980s. PET scanners detect regional blood flow in the brain. Blood carries glucose, which brain cells devour more of when they're active; glucose metabolism rises in parallel with neural activity. By detecting regions of greater blood flow, PET infers which regions are active and, by default, which are relatively quiescent.

That is the tool Sadato used when he joined Hallett's lab. He was interested in the neural substrates of hand movement—what characteristics of the brain underlie the fine motor control of, say, a pianist or a knitter, and how does the brain change as someone learns greater and greater manual dexterity? Building on Pascual-Leone's discovery that the motor cortex of proficient Braille readers changes, Sadato expected to find something pretty straightforward: when someone becomes adept at reading Braille, the side of the motor cortex responsible for controlling the reading finger should be more active, and have much finer resolution, than the other side. (The right motor cortex controls the left side of the body, including the left index finger, and the left motor cortex controls the right side of the body, including the right index finger, which most blind people use to read Braille.)

The clinical center at NIH's parklike campus in Bethesda, Maryland, has a registration system through which patients can volunteer for studies.

Sadato found his control subjects, people with normal vision, in this pool. For his blind subjects, he contacted support groups for the blind. His lab didn't have a Braille printer, so he got a sympathetic soul at the Department of Education downtown to print out Braille cells for him. Then he was ready to run his first experiments.

He had his Braille-reading volunteers read a series of words in Braille as well as strings of characters that were not words (*grxlto,* for instance) while PET detected regions of heightened activity in the brain. Based on Pascual-Leone's discovery that the representation of the reading finger in the motor cortex expands, Sadato figured the PET scan would show greater activity there, too.

PET has one big advantage over transcranial magnetic stimulation. With TMS, you induce a temporary short circuit, as I mentioned, only in a tiny region of the brain, directly below where you place your magnets. It's like a powerful telescope. Point it at some tiny porthole of the sky and you will see that tiny region in glorious detail. But if the comet of a lifetime is streaking across a region where your telescope is not pointed, you are out of luck; the guy who is gazing at the whole celestial vault with just a pair of crude binoculars will make the discovery. Similarly, with TMS, what's happening in other regions of the brain is not on your screen. But PET sees the whole brain, showing activity everywhere, and when the numerical readings are transformed into colors for easier reading, the spots of high and low activity practically scream at you. "Even if our interest was focused on one specific part of the brain, still we could detect changes in other areas of the brain," says Sadato.

As he completed a preliminary analysis of data from three participants, in the spring of 1994, he was dismayed to see something that looked all wrong. He was getting activation in the wrong place. "I thought there might have been some error in the analyzing process, so I checked carefully and repeatedly," says Sadato. But there it was, and no matter how he checked and checked and analyzed and reanalyzed the data, he couldn't get rid of the strange signal. He went to Mark Hallett, his boss, with the bad news. "He came and told me that the visual cortex is activated when the volunteers read Braille," says Hallett.

"We were astonished," Sadato recalls more than a decade later. If he was right, it would be a seminal discovery, that a region of the brain supposedly hardwired to see is, instead, feeling. Hallett and Pascual-Leone showered him with congratulations.

That was not a universal reaction, however. When Sadato wrote up the study and submitted it to the Washington, D.C.–based journal *Science,* the reviewers—scientists whom the editors ask to read the manuscript and advise on whether the experiment was sound enough and the analysis robust enough to justify publication in this very-choosy journal—were decidedly skeptical. You can see their point. There was not a whole lot of reason to expect the visual cortex to have anything to do with tactile information. For one thing, if your primary visual cortex is destroyed, you can't see, but you can still feel things on your skin. For another, when the eyes send sights to the brain, and when the skin sends feelings, those two streams of signals travel along physically separate, distinct pathways. And they arrive at physically separate, distinct destinations: the primary visual cortex in the back of the brain, and the primary somatosensory cortex along the top of the head, respectively. They're not even close neighbors.

Sadato redid the analysis to make sure that only the blind volunteers and not the sighted ones had activation of the primary visual cortex during Braille reading. But *Science* still wasn't interested. The NIH researchers then submitted their paper to the London-based journal *Nature, Science*'s arch competitor, in the summer of 1995. The study was published the following April. Now the world knew that when people who have been blind from birth feel Braille dots, their brain's visual cortex—not just their somatosensory cortex—lights up with activity. "These findings suggest remarkable brain plasticity," Sadato observed when looking back on the dramatic findings.

The discovery upended a long-standing belief that, in people blind from birth or a young age, the visual cortex is like a Morse code operator in the twenty-first century: because the signals it is programmed to process and translate and hand off for further analysis never arrive, it has nothing to do. For almost as long as there has been a science of the brain, researchers assumed that, in the absence of signals from the retina, the visual cortex would close up shop. Sadato showed how wrong they were.

"That, of course, got us very excited, so we began to investigate further," says Mark Hallett. First, he and Sadato confirmed the PET finding with fMRI. They also sorted their volunteers by age, to see whether the capacity for cross-modal plasticity—recruiting a brain region that usually handles information from one sense, such as vision, to instead process information in another sensory channel, such as touch—varies depending on when the person became blind. After all, someone blinded later in life has had years in which his or her visual cortex got used to, well, seeing.

Just as Hallett suspected, the capacity for this extreme form of plasticity declines with age, and fairly abruptly. It seemed that people who lose their sight after age eleven to fifteen (as in everything about the brain, there are individual differences) cannot make the radical transformation of rezoning the visual cortex to process the sense of touch. It is not clear what happens, at the cellular or molecular level, to prevent this career switch. "The capacity for neuroplasticity does diminish with age," says Hallett. "But it doesn't disappear completely. There is some neuroplastic ability at any age. You don't lose it 'til you die."

There was one nagging question about the discovery that the visual cortex is active when blind people read Braille. PET reveals which regions are active when the brain carries out some task; it cannot tell you whether those active regions are *necessary* for the task. If a nervous person always clears his throat before speaking, we don't conclude that throat clearing causes speech. The relationship between throat clearing and speaking is correlational, not causal. Or, to take a brain analogy, imagine that the cortex is carrying out some mind-numbing task such as reciting the alphabet over and over. A PET scan shows that the brain's "boredom" region becomes active. If you interpret that as evidence that this region is necessary for alphabet reciting, you will be way off base.

The NIH scientists knew they needed a way to tell whether activation of the visual cortex during Braille reading was correlational or causal. Hallett suggested that his colleague Leonardo Cohen carry out a study using transcranial magnetic stimulation over the visual cortex. TMS, you will recall, induces a temporary, virtual lesion in the part of the brain at which it is aimed. Cohen figured, if the visual cortex is just along for the ride—active, sure, like the boredom area of the brain during a monotonous task but not at all necessary to the task—then a temporary lesion would not affect the blind volunteers' ability to read Braille. But if the visual cortex is necessary for reading Braille, then knocking it out would have noticeable effects.

So Cohen and his colleagues used TMS to temporarily disable the visual cortex in people who had been blind from birth and who were proficient Braille readers as well as in people with normal vision. Then they tested the volunteers' tactile ability. In sighted people, there was no difference in the acuity of their sense of touch whether or not their visual cortex was briefly out of commission: they could feel an embossed roman letter and tell what it was even when the TMS temporarily disabled their visual cortex. (An interesting finding in itself apart from its implications for neuroplasticity, since it suggests that when we feel something and try to identify it, presumably by conjuring up a mental image, we don't need our visual cortex.) With normal vision, the brain has no need to tap its neuroplastic potential and turn the visual cortex into a processing center for the sense of touch. And why should it? Those tactile signals are being received, processed, and decoded perfectly fine, thank you, by the somatosensory cortex. The visual cortex has no more to say about it than do eyes when you smell lavender.

It was a different story for the blind Braille readers. When TMS knocked out their visual cortex, it was as if their fingers were roving over nothing more meaningful than bumps on a log. The raised dots they felt meant nothing to them. The blind people could no longer tell what their fingers were feeling, the scientists reported in 1997. The blind knew perfectly well that their fingers had brushed over Braille dots, but the TMS had left them unable to read them. The dots felt "different," "flatter," "less sharp and well-defined," they told the scientists.

"This was the difference between showing that the visual cortex is *involved* and showing that it is *necessary*" to process the tactile sensations from the raised dots of the Braille, said Mark Hallett. The visual cortex didn't just happen to be activated during Braille reading; it was required for Braille reading. When no signals from the eyes reach the visual cortex, neuroplasticity enables that region to start a new job, becoming a specialist in the sense of touch. This cross-modal plasticity, the scientists suggested, "may account in part for the superior tactile perceptual abilities of blind subjects." After all, if blind people are calling on two powerful brain structures (somatosensory cortex *and* visual cortex) to decode the feeling of touch, small wonder they are more sensitive than the poor souls who, with their visual cortex fully booked decoding what the eyes send it, can tap only their somatosensory cortex to figure out what the fingers feel. Think of it as a consolation prize. If a child is blind, the brain partly makes up for the lost sense by giving a surviving sense greater acuity.

Reliance on the visual system to handle tactile input from the fingers can also cause problems, however. In 2000, scientists described the case of a woman who had been blind from an early age and who became a proficient Braille reader, working as a proofreader for a Braille newsletter. When she was sixty-two, she suffered a stroke in her visual cortex. According to the old way of looking at the brain, for a blind person to have her visual cortex damaged is like a paraplegic suffering a broken leg. The site of the injury wasn't doing her any good, so an additional injury should have had few ill effects. In fact, however, although she could still identify everyday objects by touch, the stroke left her unable to read Braille. She could feel the raised dots just fine, she told scientists, but could not "make sense" of them. Her visual cortex had assumed the job of feeling the raised dots and translating them into language. When it was damaged, she could no longer feel Braille.

Eyes That Hear

Neuroplasticity is not without its ironies. In people with normal vision, the visual cortex is so busy handling sight that it has no spare processing capacity to do anything else (or, at least nothing else that scientists have been able to detect). In people with normal hearing, the auditory cortex is so busy handling hearing that it has no spare capacity for anything but. It is only in the blind and the deaf that these primary sensory cortices become unleashed from their genetic destiny, and as the millennium turned, Neville was about to add to what Hallett's team had discovered about the plasticity of the visual cortex.

An old wives' tale about the blind says they have sharper hearing than the rest of us. But as mentioned earlier, experiments had failed to validate that. The blind cannot hear softer sounds than sighted people can, for instance. But as part of her hunch that neuroplasticity is more likely to affect subtler or more sophisticated functions in the brain, Neville decided to test the blind on the aural analogue of the peripheral-vision superiority she had discovered in the deaf: processing peripheral sounds.

In a study with colleagues in Germany, sixteen volunteers—eight congenitally blind, eight with normal sight but blindfolded—took turns in a special soundproof chamber. Before them stood four speakers, one directly in front and the others to the right, the last one opposite the person's right shoulder. The volunteers had to tell when a tone coming from the central speaker or the far-right speaker had a higher pitch than previous tones. They were to ignore the other two speakers. If they pressed the button when the higher tone came from the speaker they were focusing on, it counted as a correct response. If they pressed the button when the higher tone came from a different speaker from the one they were supposed to be paying attention to, it counted as incorrect. To gauge what was happening in the volunteers' brains during all this, the scientists wired up their scalps with electrodes to measure activity in neurons.

When the task was to tell when the tone from the central speaker was higher-pitched, all sixteen volunteers did well. Neither group did as well when they were asked to monitor the tones from the peripheral speaker— but the blind people did better than the sighted controls. They were faster at detecting the change in tone, and the brain signals associated with this perception were also nimbler, returning to the rested-and-ready state more quickly than did those of sighted people, the scientists found in this 1999 study. Loss of vision during early childhood or before had made peripheral hearing sharper, just as loss of hearing had made peripheral vision sharper.

More curious was where in the brain neurons became active in response to the peripheral sounds. When sighted people listened intently to a speaker in their peripheral hearing, the strongest neuronal activity was around their auditory cortex, as you'd expect. In the blind, however, the response occurred in the visual cortex. This showed that their brains had a different organization from the sighted people, a "compensatory reorganization," as Neville called it. "The blind can detect peripheral sounds much better than people with normal vision can, and they actually activate the primary visual cortex during hearing," she told the Dalai Lama. She had discovered the human equivalent of Mriganka Sur's work in his rewired ferrets, in whom the auditory cortex saw and the visual cortex heard. His results reflected forced rewiring, since surgery had redirected neurons, as described in chapter 2. In the blind people Neville studied, cortical reorganization was the result of the lives they led, lives in which vision was absent.

The notion that people who are blind from birth or shortly after can localize sounds more accurately than people with normal vision is no myth. When you think about it, it makes sense for the visual cortex to read the writing on the wall—the absence of signals from the eyes—and switch jobs. After all, the visual regions take up about 35 percent of the brain's volume. That's an awful lot of gray matter to remain unemployed.

"Seeing" Language

Until the turn of the millennium, studies of what the auditory cortex can do in the deaf, and what the visual cortex can do in the blind, had focused on sensory processing—an auditory cortex that sees and gives the deaf greater peripheral acuity, a visual cortex that hears and gives the blind greater sensitivity to where sounds are coming from. The next round of studies would uncover something even more startling. A sensory cortex, which neuroscientists always assumed specializes in taking in one or another kind of information from the outside world, can be smarter than anyone thought. A sensory cortex is not limited to handling one of the five senses.

Teachers and physicians had long noted that children who have been blind from birth are slower at acquiring language than peers with normal vision. They lag behind in learning pronouns as well as locational terms such as *here* and *there,* for instance, and deictic terms such as *this* and *that.* That seemed odd, since babies rely on hearing and not vision to learn language. You'd think that a blind child's language development would be accelerated, not delayed, thanks to superior hearing. Even odder, although blind adults do not have a lower threshold for hearing than sighted adults, they are better at recognizing voices and understanding speech against a noisy background—the cocktail-party effect. That suggests that their auditory superiority occurs not at the level of detecting when a sound has arrived but in higher-order processing of language, sorting out a conversation they're paying attention to from background chatter.

Searching for how blindness affects language activity in the brain took Neville down a new path. For one thing, language is a step up the ladder of neurological complexity from mere sensory perception. For another, at first glance, there is no particular reason why being blind should trigger neuroplastic changes in how the brain makes sense of sounds and turns them into language. Still, reading Braille activates the "visual" cortex. Might spoken language do the same?

A young graduate student at Hebrew University in Jerusalem had read about the discovery that blind people use their visual cortex to feel Braille dots. "I loved it," recalls Amir Amedi. He asked his mentor if he, too, could study the neuroplasticity of the visual cortex in the blind and got all the encouragement of an atheist at a revival meeting. "Everyone told me no, no, you'll never get anything out of this," Amedi recalls. "You'll waste a year and risk not getting a Ph.D. thesis." The notion that the visual cortex not only hangs in there, rather than going silent, in people whose eyes had not sent it any signals for decades, but also switches to the sense of touch was still regarded as borderline ludicrous. But Amedi insisted, and when his professors saw how stubborn he intended to be, they gave him a year and helped him design an experiment to test the plasticity of the visual cortex. The NIH scientists had shown that the visual cortex can change jobs and handle the sense of touch. Amedi and his mentor, Ehud Zohary, suspected it had other, undiscovered, talents.

The scientists found ten blind students willing to participate in their study. The volunteers did three things: remember a list of abstract words, read Braille, and think of a verb that goes with a noun they heard on a recording. During each task, the volunteer would lie in a hammering fMRI tube and have his or her brain scanned to find out what regions turned on.

The first thing Amedi found was a reprise of the discovery that the visual cortex glows with activity when blind people read Braille. So far, so good. The test of verbal memory produced more of a surprise. When blind volunteers were recalling as many words from the list as they could, their visual cortex spiked with activity, the scientists reported in 2003. No such activation of the visual regions occurred when volunteers with normal sight recalled lists of words. What was striking about the activation of the visual cortex when blind people recalled words was that, unlike in earlier experiments, there was absolutely no sensory input. All the volunteers did was sit and try to remember. They neither felt nor heard anything, so the visual cortex activity did not reflect its propensity to change which sense it handled once visual signals no longer arrived. Neuroplasticity, it seems, is not limited merely to reorganizing the brain so that one sensory region handles a different sense; it can reshape the brain so that a sensory region performs a sophisticated cognitive function.

It's not as if the primary visual cortex is just along for the ride, either, like the throat-clearing public speaker. Amedi and another member of Zohary's lab, Noa Raz, showed that, as a group, the blind volunteers had superior verbal memory compared to sighted controls. A closer look at their brains suggested why. Individually, blind people who recalled the most words from the list also had the greatest activation of their visual cortex. That correlation—better verbal recall with more active visual cortex—was a strong hint that the activity in the visual cortex was functional, not incidental. Adding to the plausibility of that inference, the left side of the visual cortex was more active than the right during verbal memory. It is the left side of the brain—though, ordinarily, the left side in regions far from the visual cortex—that specializes in language. Somehow, the visual cortex, having abandoned the career laid out for it from birth and making its way in the world as a language specialist, adopted the left-leaning tendencies of traditional language regions.

That became even more striking with the final task, when the volunteers listened to a noun and generated an appropriate verb (hearing *ladder,* one might come back with *climb,* while *hammer* might elicit *hit*). Just as in the word-recall task, the visual cortex burst into activity. Such activation was nowhere to be seen in people with normal sight carrying out the identical task. In them, only the expected language regions of the brain were humming. Amedi's stubbornness and insistence that there was something important to be discovered probing the neuroplasticity of the visual cortex had paid off.

"There was growing evidence that the visual cortex plays a more important role in nonvisual tasks in blind people than it does in people with normal sight," NIH's Leo Cohen said shortly after the results were announced. "Which sensory inputs it becomes sensitive to seems to be activity-dependent. Amir's 2003 study had shown that the visual cortex becomes active when blind people generate verbs, recall words, and do other language tasks, but these were only correlational—there was no proof of a causal link." Maybe the primary visual cortex was just along for the ride—active, yes, but not really contributing much to the cause.

To find out, Amedi spent part of 2003 and 2004 in Cohen's lab at NIH. This time, they were determined to resolve whether activity in the visual cortex when the blind students remembered words and thought up verbs was correlational or causal. They recruited nine volunteers who had been blind from birth or early childhood and nine with normal sight to play name-that-verb. Immediately after the volunteers heard the noun for which they were to come up with a verb, the scientists used transcranial magnetic stimulation to create a transitory virtual lesion in the left side of the primary visual cortex, briefly putting it out of commission.

Those who had been blind from birth generated off-the-wall verbs. *Apple* elicited something like *jump* or, more rarely, *green* or *eap,* the scientists reported in 2004. When they made such mistakes, the volunteers explained that they were having trouble "coming up with the right word." In sighted people, temporarily knocking out the primary visual cortex produced no such nonsense. (The sighted volunteers made similar semantic errors only when their prefrontal cortex, which other brain-imaging studies had implicated in verb generation, got zapped.) That clinched it. In people who are blind from a young age, the left side of the visual cortex grabs hold of the golden ring of neuroplasticity and takes on the exalted task of processing language.

That the primary visual cortex can do something as advanced as language came as a shock to neuroscientists. For more than a century, their theories had held that the brain is organized in a hierarchy, with crude sensory information first arriving in the primary visual cortex, the primary auditory cortex, or the primary somatosensory cortex. Only then, once those regions had determined that the arriving signal meant, say, that there were a bunch of horizontal lines and a few verticals and a diagonal; with colors here, here, and there; and a brightness pattern like so . . . only then did that information get kicked upstairs to a so-called association area. The association area is the real brains of the operation. It takes crude sensory data and comes up with, say, "porcupine!" According to this idea, Christian Büchel of the University of Hamburg observed, "areas involved in verbal processing should be placed high up in the hierarchy, given the complexity of verbal material. However, exactly the opposite was observed in [Amedi's] study. Some of the most complex functions (verbal memory and verb generation) were located in a primary sensory area," the primary visual cortex. It seems that the functional hierarchy of the brain, he added, "is not carved in stone." To the contrary. The visual cortex "is recruited to be part of the network involved in a high-level cognitive function, processing speech and remembering words," said Leo Cohen. That a usually low-level region such as the visual cortex can handle such a sophisticated task was as astounding as finding a granite worker leaving the quarry and sculpting pietàs instead.

Painting Blind

But what about the blind Turkish painter? Esref Armagan never learned Braille. He is illiterate, he told Amedi and Pascual-Leone when they invited him to Boston so they could study his brain, and has poor verbal memory. Ironically for someone who lives in perpetual darkness, his is a purely visual world, not a verbal one. The life he led was strikingly different from that of the well-educated, Braille-fluent blind Americans whose visual cortex felt, heard, and generated language. Would Armagan's visual cortex be different, too? To find out, the Harvard scientists had him perform various tasks while fMRI detected regions of heightened activity in his brain. He sketched coffee mugs and cats and hammers. He listened intently to a list of words. He heard those words again as well as words he had not heard before.

When the scientists analyzed the fMRI scans, they were brought up short. Armagan's visual cortex was alight with activity when he drew. Scientists have known for several years that when people conjure up a mental image in their mind's eye, the visual cortex is active just as it is when people see something in the real world. But the activity is much quieter when you imagine seeing something than when you actually see it. In Armagan's case, activity in his visual cortex when he conjured an image in order to draw it was as intense as when a sighted person sees, and anyone looking at the fMRI would conclude that it showed someone with normal vision gazing out at the world. Amedi said, "It suggests that by becoming so expert, he was able to recruit visual cortex for the mental imagery he needs to recall the shapes of objects and how perspective and shadows look."

But when Armagan tried to recall words, his visual cortex was mostly quiet. "This was unlike every other blind person we tested," Amedi said.

"They all showed visual cortex activity during verbal memory. This suggests that environmental influences determine what a blind person's brain recruits the visual cortex to do. Mr. Armagan uses his visual cortex for the mental imagery he needs to create his paintings. He never learned Braille. It may be that learning Braille creates an association between touch and language and that that is a prerequisite for recruiting visual cortex for verbal memory." But when a person puts no such demand on his or her visual cortex, there is opportunity for the visual cortex to choose another career. Many of the blind people who so graciously volunteer to be zapped and scanned and tested by neuroscientists are well-educated, functioning participants in American society. And that means they are highly verbal as well as proficient in Braille. These are the demands they place on a visual cortex that would otherwise go to waste, and it rises to the challenge. But Armagan places different demands on his visual cortex, ones of visual imagery. And his, too, responds to those demands.

The bottom line is that, in the blind, the seeing part of the brain is no longer seeing. As Sadato puts it, the primary visual cortex becomes "unbound from visual perception." When it does, it turns to the processing of other senses, notably the sense of touch, as well as nonsensory tasks such as language. Just as the mind is, as they say, a terrible thing to waste, so is the brain. And the brain is not going to let a little thing such as the lack of the expected visual signals keep the visual cortex—which, as mentioned above, accounts for an impressive 35 percent of the brain's space—from being gainfully employed. Neuroplasticity sees to that.

Rewiring Dyslexia

One of Neville's strongest messages to the Dalai Lama was that there are, as she put it, "two sides to neuroplasticity." Systems and structures that display the greatest plasticity are those under the weakest genetic control and most subject to the whims of experience and the environment. That can be beneficial, allowing the otherwise out-of-work visual cortex in the blind to enhance the ability to localize sounds in space. But it is also a risky way to make a brain. "The same systems that display the greatest plasticity and are enhanced in the deaf are more vulnerable in development and will display the greatest deficits in developmental disorders such as dyslexia," Neville says. Specifically, "blind people can process *fast* auditory stimuli much faster than people with normal vision can. In most people, if we present sounds really fast, the neural response is very small. But in blind people, it's big. They're really good at fast auditory processing." If brain circuits that detect fast staccato sounds are plastic, as this suggests, and if plasticity and vulnerability go hand in hand (or perhaps we should say neuron in neuron), then circuits that process fast sounds will also be more vulnerable to disruption. It is no coincidence, Neville said, that "people with developmental disorders are very bad at fast auditory processing."

By the mid-1990s, Mike Merzenich had a pile of studies on neuroplasticity in the brains of adult owl and squirrel monkeys. He was itching to apply the findings to people, and one study offered a way to do that. It was a relatively obscure one, but it stuck in Merzenich's mind. The scientists had piped sounds through headphones into monkeys' ears. The auditory cortex has what is called a tonotopic map, akin to the map in the somatosensory cortex. In the latter case, the map is the little homunculus with dinner-plate lips and hypertrophied hands and fingers. In the tonotopic map, clumps of neurons in the auditory cortex each specialize in a different pitch. You can probably guess what Merzenich discovered. Whichever frequency the monkeys heard most, the region of the tonotopic map that processed that frequency expanded. Regions devoted to unheard frequencies shrank. Add sound to the kind of input that can reshape the brain.

Around this time, scientists were trying to understand a condition called specific language impairment (SLI). In this condition, a child has great difficulty reading and writing, and even in comprehending spoken language, despite normal intelligence. The best-known form of specific language impairment is dyslexia, which affects some 5 to 17 percent of the U.S. population and accounts for the majority of learning disabilities. For decades, educators had blamed dyslexia on deficits of visual processing. According to the stereotype, a dyslexic child sees *p* as *q* and vice versa, and *b* as *d*.

Paula Tallal of Rutgers University in New Jersey didn't buy it. She suspected that many cases of dyslexia arise not because kids confuse the appearances of letters but because they can't hear the sounds for which letters stand. In particular, some people with dyslexia may be unable to process certain speech sounds—fast ones.

She was right. Some dyslexics struggle to break words into their component phonemes, the smallest units of speech. They have particular trouble distinguishing the sounds of *b, p, d,* and *g,* all of which explode off the lips or tongue and vanish in just a few milliseconds. In these dyslexics, the auditory cortex literally cannot hear staccato sounds, much as an ordinary digital camera on Earth cannot resolve the rings of Saturn. The brains of these children do not hear short phonemes. In *ba,* for instance, the explosive *b* lasts a mere forty milliseconds. The difference between the *b* sound in *bay* and the *d* sound in *day* comes in that initial instant. If your brain cannot resolve sounds that take so little time, then trying to fathom what a teacher is drilling into you about the difference between these two sounds is a real problem. *Bay* is therefore mistaken for *day,* and vice versa, because all the kids hear clearly is the *aaa.* Since learning to read requires matching letters to sounds, if *ba* sounds like *da,* it's tough to learn to read phonetically. (In contrast, the *mmm* in *mall* takes about three hundred milliseconds. Children with specific language impairment hear *mall* just fine.) Merzenich suspected that a brain unable to process rapid-fire sounds, and thus to recognize the difference between *dip* and *pip,* might be different—physically different—from a brain that can.

He and Tallal decided to collaborate. His experiments on monkeys had shown that the auditory cortex can be remodeled as a result of distinctive input. Might kids' brains also be remodeled? If some cases of dyslexia arise because the auditory cortex lacks the circuitry for detecting explosive phonemes, then that circuitry would have to be created—by exposing a child over and over to those phonemes just as Merzenich's monkeys were exposed over and over to certain frequencies. But the phonemes could not come in their usual fast form, which the children cannot hear. They would have to be artificially stretched out so the children could hear them.

Using special software, the UCSF scientists synthesized phonemes that still sounded like spoken English but that stretched out the duration of *b* before *aaa,* for example. To people with normal hearing, it sounded like someone shouting underwater. But to the children, the scientists hoped, it would sound like *baa,* a sound they had never before heard clearly. In the summer of 1994, seven school-age dyslexic children spent five mornings a week in Tallal's lab. They listened to tapes of the stretched-out speech, hearing instructions to "point to the boy who's chasing the girl who's wear-

ing red" and the like. *Point* and *boy* and *girl* were all intoned so that the initial explosive consonant lasted many times longer than it does in normal
speech. The children also played computer games using processed speech at
home. Over several weeks, the phoneme would creep up ever so gradually
to its proper sound, so that what began as ultra-drawn-out phonemes became progressively less-drawn-out ones and finally speech that was almost
normal. The following summer, twenty-two more children played computer games that spoke to them in that funny stretched-out speech. The
computer asked the kids to, for instance, click the mouse when a series of
spoken *b*'s was interrupted by a *p*. Once a child learned to tell the difference
between *b* and *p* when the initial phoneme was stretched to three hundred
milliseconds, the software shortened the phoneme by a couple of dozen
milliseconds at a time, aiming for a sound that was not stretched out at all.

The results were remarkable. After twenty to forty hours of training, all
the children could distinguish fast phonemes as correctly as kids who did
not have dyslexia. After one month, all had advanced two years in language
comprehension. Fast ForWord, as the scientists called the program, was
rewiring the children's brains. "You create your brain from the input you
get," said Paula Tallal.

She, Mike Merzenich, and other colleagues eventually formed Scientific
Learning Corporation to sell Fast ForWord. It has not helped every child
with dyslexia, to be sure. If the problem is caused by something other than
an inability to process fast phonemes, the intervention has no effect. But by
2005, almost half a million children in twenty-seven school districts in
twenty-five states had been trained on Fast ForWord. After six to eight
weeks, 90 percent of the children who practiced on it for the recommended
one hundred minutes a day, five days a week, had improved their reading
skills the equivalent of 1.5 to 2 years. "Most children who adequately complete one or more Fast ForWord language or reading programs make sub-
stantially more rapid improvement in a variety of language and reading skills than control children receiving standard language or reading
intervention," Paula Tallal told the 2005 annual meeting of the Society for
Neuroscience. Thanks to the brain's neuroplasticity, feeding it specialized
input—acoustically modified speech—coaxes new circuits in regions important for language.

Scientific Learning had its critics in academia, with one professor telling a reporter that inducing neuroplasticity was "an absurd stunt" that would not help anyone learn to read. To see whether Fast ForWord truly rewires the brain, Tallal and Merzenich teamed up with John Gabrieli, then at Stanford University, whose "Gab Lab" studies everything from memory to fear. He recruited twenty dyslexic children and twelve children with normal reading ability, and used fMRI to image their brains while they figured out whether two letters rhymed. *C* and *D* rhyme, for instance, but *P* and *K* do not. The dyslexic kids struggled with the task as well as with other language and reading challenges. Normal readers breezed through them. Moreover, the brains of the dyslexic kids were strikingly quiet in two interesting regions: the left temporoparietal cortex, which is involved in oral language and handles phonics, and the left inferior frontal gyrus, which is involved in processing words. In the good readers, these regions blazed with activity during language and reading tests.

The dyslexic children then underwent training with Fast ForWord for one hundred minutes a day, five days a week, for eight weeks as part of their regular school day. At the end of the eight weeks, their brains had changed. The phonemes to which their brains had responded with silence before the training now triggered activity in the temporal lobe's language regions just as they did in the brains of normal readers. Fast ForWord "resulted in changes in brain function that include left hemisphere language regions," the scientists reported in 2003. The dysfunction that characterizes the left temporal region in many dyslexics "can be at least partially ameliorated through behavioral remediation." This was the first study to show changes in the brain activity of dyslexic children after training and to show where brain plasticity targeted by the training had occurred. And it confirmed Helen Neville's suspicion that brain circuits that display the greatest plasticity are also the most vulnerable to disruption during development. But the same plasticity that lets them be disrupted can be harnessed to repair them.

Attention Must Be Paid

Neville has made a big push to extend her scientific findings into the world of schools and families. Her work shows that auditory attention, or the ability to focus on one stream of sound in a sea of noise, develops through-out childhood and into adolescence, for instance, as does the ability to shift attention quickly and effectively. There is also a long window of opportunity for learning a second language. "There are different plasticity profiles for different aspects of language," she told the Dalai Lama. If you do not learn a second language before the age of ten, "you will never learn a non-native accent. But we have the ability to learn the meaning of words throughout life." The ability to judge whether a sentence in your nonnative language is grammatical decreases if you learn the second language after the age of six, whereas the ability to judge whether a sentence is semantic decreases only if you learn it after age sixteen or so. "Delays in learning a second language have more pronounced effects on grammatical than on lexical-semantic aspects of language," Neville says.

"But what about music? What about math? What about compassion? What about social skills? What about the theory of mind, the ability to know what another person knows? When are these brain systems most malleable under the influence of various environmental inputs, both good and bad?" she continued. "We don't know anything about the development of those systems. Plus, we have to determine the mechanisms that allow greater or less plasticity. We want to determine which interventions can enhance plasticity. We have to design and implement the educational and support programs that will optimize human development. People have spent a lot of money to enable us to do this research. But society is not reaping any benefit from it."

Even the neuroscientists sitting with the Dalai Lama had a greater appreciation for the brain's plasticity after Neville's presentation, for her work and that of other scientists had overturned a long-standing neurobiological dogma. You might think that if you were designing a human brain, you would make darn sure that the structures to which you're assigning crucial senses such as seeing and hearing are hardwired to within an inch of their life, with no possibility of drifting off into another line of work. You'd design all sorts of fail-safe mechanisms to keep the visual cortex and the auditory cortex from being usurped by one of those pushy other senses.

That's not how nature did it.

Instead, the key sensory cortices are, for the first decade of life and per-haps longer, like a flighty new college graduate hopscotching from job to job, responding to the best offer. No signals from the eyes arriving? No problem; the visual cortex will handle a different sense and even a nonsensory job such as language. No transmissions from the ears? The auditory cortex will be happy to help out with peripheral vision. By the early years of the millennium, it was clear that these structures should really be referred to as the "visual cortex" and the "auditory cortex," in quotation marks. "Visual information is going into the auditory cortex, and auditory information is going into the visual cortex," Neville told the Dalai Lama as she ended her presentation. "This isn't supposed to be how our brain is wired. But what this research has shown is that the primary visual cortex is not inherently different from the primary auditory cortex. Brain specialization is not a function of anatomy or dictated by the genes. It is a result of experience. Who we are and how we work comes from our perceptions and experiences. It is the outside world that determines the functional properties of the brain's neurons. And that's what our work has been about: how experience shapes the functional capabilities of the brain."

As of 2006, the best explanation for the ability of the visual cortex to hear and feel, and of the auditory cortex to see, is that, at birth, the brain is shot through with redundant connections. In one of Neville's earliest studies, when she played musical tones for normal adults, there was a spike of brain-wave activity in the auditory cortex. The visual cortex was, as expected, quiet. When she played tones for six-month-olds, however, the resulting brain waves in the visual region were just as large as in the auditory region. That dual response disappears between the ages of six and thirty-six months. But its fleeting existence suggests that, in the young brain, supposedly specialized regions have not really decided what they want to be when they grow up and are full of redundant connections. Sure, neurons connect the retina to the visual cortex and the ear to the auditory cortex. But some wayward neurons from the retina also meander into the auditory cortex, and some from the ear reach the visual cortex. "In the immature brain, there are many more connections than in the adult," she told the Dalai Lama. "In adults, neurons from the ear project only to the auditory cortex. But in a newborn, they also project to the visual cortex."

Usually, the pathways from ears to visual cortex and from eyes to auditory cortex remain sparsely traveled if traveled at all, like back roads. In people with normal vision and hearing, superhighways carry signals from the eyes to the visual cortex and the ears to the auditory cortex just fine, swamping any activity along the back roads of the brain. As a result, the wayward connections fall away soon after birth, when the brain figures out where signals are supposed to go. But in the absence of normal sensory input, as when neurons from the retina are unable to carry signals to the visual cortex or neurons from the ears to carry signals to the auditory cortex, the preexisting but little-used connections become unmasked and start carrying traffic. The "visual" cortex hears, and the "auditory" cortex sees, enabling the brain to hear the lightning and see the thunder. ("In Buddhism," Thupten Jinpa added, "there is a claim that an advanced meditator can transfer sensory functions to different organs, so that visual activity can be performed by something other than the eyes and hearing by something other than the ears. In this case, a meditator can read with closed eyes.") In what Alvaro Pascual-Leone and colleagues call "the intrinsically plastic brain," more permanent structural changes then kick in, as neurons grow and sprout more connections to other neurons. This may be how the visual cortex adds higher cognitive functions to its repertoire, too.

So pick your proof: the ability of the visual cortex of a blind person to abandon all hope of seeing and assume a new job hearing, feeling, or even processing language; the malleability of the brain of a deaf person to rezone the auditory cortex to see; the plasticity of the brain of a child that learns to hear normally, overcoming dyslexia. The discoveries of Helen Neville, Alvaro Pascual-Leone, and their colleagues showed conclusively that when the brain is deprived of one sense, the cortex undergoes radical reorganization. In every case, it is a young brain that has shown this remarkable neuroplasticity; the brains of people who become blind or deaf later in life do not show this dynamism.

Or so it seemed. As the next round of discoveries would show, even a brain that has been around the block a few times can adapt to change and to experiences, rolling with whatever punches the environment throws its way. It is not just the young brain that is plastic.

Chapter 5

Footprints on the Brain

Sensory Experience Reshapes Adult Brains

But what about adults?

Discoveries of the brain's plasticity came with an asterisk. Yes, the auditory cortex of the deaf could see, and the visual cortex of the blind could hear or feel or even become a language expert. But from the very first, when Norihiro Sadato was astonished to see the visual cortex of blind people light up on PET scans when they felt the raised dots of Braille and realized that this supposedly hardwired region had changed in response to the experience of blindness, there was usually a difference between brains. In people who had been blind from birth or a very young age, activity in the visual cortex when they felt or heard or processed language tended to be greater than it was in the visual cortex of brains of those who had become blind later in life. That suggested that young brains have greater, and perhaps significantly greater, neuroplasticity than older brains, since the former seemed to slide much more readily into new roles.

In one typical experiment, for instance, Mark Hallett at the National Institutes of Health and his colleagues probed for when the window of opportunity for the brain's primary sensory cortices to become rewired slams shut. They recruited eight people who had lost their vision after the age of fourteen. As in other studies, the scientists used PET imaging to pinpoint which regions of the brain become active when blind people read Braille. And to make sure that the activity they found was necessary rather than just a coincidence, they used transcranial magnetic stimulation to induce brief neuronal hiccups that interrupt the functioning of the active regions, to see if the blind could still read Braille despite that region's being temporarily furloughed. With people who had been blind from birth, as described in the previous chapter, the visual cortex had not only been rewired to process the sense of touch but was *necessary* for the blind people to read Braille. This was true plasticity, in which a basic brain structure had been induced, through new and repeated sensory experiences—long-term Braille reading—to take on a new job.

In contrast, the brains of volunteers who had lost their vision later in life showed no such activity in the visual cortex. When they read Braille, their visual cortex was as dark and quiet as a cave, the NIH scientists reported in 1999. And when transcranial magnetic stimulation knocked the visual cortex out of commission, the volunteers kept right on reading Braille. They clearly did not need their visual cortex to feel Braille dots or translate them into words.

That gave scientists pause. People who lose their sight as teenagers or later have enjoyed many years of normal vision, with signals arriving from their eyes to the visual cortex as nature intended. That gives the visual cortex endless opportunities to learn its job. Maybe it learns its job so well that it has no interest in a career change. Like a lonely lighthouse keeper who stays at his post long after the last great ships have passed into history, and who has no intention of retraining himself for, say, a nice job in retail, so a visual cortex that has spent years and years handling input from the eye and turning it into vision has no inclination to begin handling touch or hearing. Perhaps the window of opportunity for the visual cortex to become rewired slams shut by age fourteen, when the riotous neuroplasticity that enables the young brain to send new neurons snaking into regions that DNA never intended seems to peter out. After that, the visual cortex can no longer be recruited to process the sense of touch.

Neuroscientists even had a handy explanation for the loss of neuroplasticity. Older brains, they said, can neither unmask dormant "back road" connections that would let the visual cortex process other senses nor sprout new neurons and new connections. "This is a mechanism that is not available throughout life," Helen Neville told the Dalai Lama during her morning in the spotlight.

That conclusion was well grounded in what was known about brain development. As far as neuroscientists knew, there is a burst of synaptic sprouting and pruning during infancy and toddlerhood, as described in the previous chapter. But it doesn't last, scientists believed. When you reach the ripe old age of about two, you have pretty much the brain you're going to be stuck with for the rest of your life. Sure, synapses still form; these connections are, after all, the basis for memory and learning, and neither stops until we die. But that's retail brain change. Wholesale change, the kind that begins with newborn neurons and weaves them into functional assemblages, was supposedly a thing of the brain's past.

Teen Brains

When scientists examined the living brains of tweens and teens and twentysomethings, there was therefore no reason to expect the brains of twelve-year-olds to be different, structurally, from the brains of twenty-five-year-olds. By twelve and even ten, the brain was thought to be long past its youthful spurt of growth and pruning, so whatever it was like then should be what it was like a dozen years later.

But two groups of scientists, one at UCLA and one at NIH, found otherwise. Between ages ten and twelve or so, they discovered, the frontal lobes (the seat of such high-level functions as judgment, emotional regulation and self-control, organization, and planning) experience a growth spurt, with gray matter proliferating almost as exuberantly as it did during gestation and infancy: the volume of gray matter increases noticeably, reflecting the formation of new connections and branches. And then, in a person's twenties, there is another reprise of the neurological events of early childhood, as unused synapses are eliminated so the networks that remain are more efficient. Other brain regions also remain under construction through adolescence. The parietal lobes, which assemble information that arrives from distant neighborhoods of the brain, are works in progress through the midteens. They continue to add gray matter until age ten (in girls) or twelve (in boys), after which underused synapses are pruned just as they are in childhood. Similarly, the temporal lobes, which contain regions responsible for language as well as emotional control, pack in gray matter until age sixteen and only then undergo pruning.

Contrary to the belief that wholesale neuronal birth and synapse formation occur only during gestation and infancy, then, the brain gets a second wind just before puberty. Describing these discoveries to the Dalai Lama, Neville said that "we've learned an astonishing thing in the past few years, and that is that the human brain—in terms of the hardware, the number of synapses, the number of dendritic branchings—doesn't look adultlike until twenty to twenty-five years after birth." Even a brain this ancient has the raw material for neuroplasticity. That suggests that those raw materials could be put to one of the same uses they were in childhood—namely, giving the brain the malleability to respond to experience.

The fact that the brains of adolescents and young adults undergo such extensive synapse formation and pruning means that kids have a second chance. It's great to take up the piano or violin in early childhood, to develop the hand-eye coordination required to hit a curveball, to cultivate the habits of mind that let you think logically or construct a geometric proof. The neural circuits that underpin such skills will flourish, staking near-permanent claim to neural territory. But if a child gets to the ripe old age of ten without establishing such neural circuits through diligent and focused practice of some cognitive or physical skill, nature is kind enough to offer a second chance. During the second decade of life, the brain has another opportunity to create the neural foundation for the flowering of cognitive and other skills. As Jay Giedd of NIH, who discovered this second wave of proliferating and pruning of synapses, says, if you spend your young-adult years playing video games, circuits underpinning those will become dug-in; if you fail to nurture before age twenty or so circuits that support sight-reading music, it will be difficult to recruit them later on; if you read and read and grind through logic and math exercises, those are the synapses that nature will spare. Synapses that support unused skills will wither like rosebushes targeted by a zealous gardener.

As the next round of discoveries would show, neuroplasticity is not a gift bestowed only upon the brains of the very young. To the contrary. You can teach an old brain new tricks.

The Blindfold Experiment

Something bothered Alvaro Pascual-Leone about the patients who had lost their vision after age fourteen. True, PET scans showed that their visual cortex had not reshaped itself to process tactile sensations, as the visual cortex of brains blind from birth had done. But these late-blind people differed from those with congenital blindness in more than the age at which they lost their sight. For one thing, most retained a little bit of vision, such as the ability to tell light from dark. Maybe even these rudimentary signals were enough to make the visual cortex hang in there and persevere in its original job of processing signals from the retina, Pascual-Leone speculated. Also, their blindness came on gradually, often as a result of diabetes, a slow process that unfolds over many years. He wondered if the more limited plasticity of late-blind people, which seems to leave the visual cortex unable to process sensations or language, is a reflection not of the age at which they became blind but of how quickly they became blind. Maybe that old lighthouse keeper didn't notice when, one by one, the great ships went into permanent dry dock and so did not realize until too late that his livelihood was vanishing. Perhaps, Pascual-Leone mused, the visual cortex is like that, too: only a sudden loss of vision, or never having any in the first place, enables it to make the career switch.

Pascual-Leone and his colleagues therefore decided to see what would happen if sighted adults suddenly lost their vision. They recruited people with normal vision and blindfolded them. This was not a brief, pin-the-tail-on-the-donkey sort of lark, however. The volunteers wore their blindfolds all day, every day, from a Monday morning to a Friday evening. A piece of photographic paper attached to the inside of the blindfold served as the tattletale, since if it were exposed at the end of the study, that would indicate the volunteers had cheated. Although they did not exactly try to navigate the Boston subway system with their temporary disability, they did manage to get around their rooms at Beth Israel Deaconess Medical Center in Boston, by touch and by sound, without too many bruised knees. They spent their days learning Braille and having their brains scanned by fMRI while they performed various tactile and auditory tasks: they heard a series of tones and indicated whether each tone had the same pitch as the previous one, for instance, and they felt pairs of Braille cells to determine whether they were the same or different.

Before their five days of enforced blindness, the volunteers' visual cortex behaved according to the textbooks, showing activity when they looked at something. It was quiet, as expected, when they listened, touched something, or thought about words. It was behaving as nature intended. While the volunteers were blindfolded, though, the visual cortex seemed to get bored, what with no signals arriving from the eyes and all. Even though it had spent decades handling visual information and only visual information, after a mere five days of enforced unemployment, it got a new gig.

According to the fMRI, it was now handling tactile and auditory information: when the volunteers listened to tones to determine whether their pitch was the same or different, and when they fingered Braille symbols, their "visual" cortex became active. Moreover, as the week went on, their somatosensory cortex became quieter and quieter when feeling the Braille dots, and their visual cortex became more and more active. The "seeing" brain was now feeling and hearing. Just as Mriganka Sur's rewired ferrets came to "hear the lighting and see the thunder," so the blindfolded volunteers had undergone changes in one of the most basic regions of their brain. And these were adults who for twenty years or more had used their visual cortex to see and only to see.

It is highly improbable that the visual cortex established brand-new connections to neurons from the ears and fingers. Five days wasn't time enough for that. Instead, Pascual-Leone says, "some rudimentary somatosensory and auditory connections to the visual cortex must already be present," left over from brain development when neurons from the eyes and ears and fingers connect to many regions of the cortex rather than just the ones they're supposed to. The connections went unused when the visual cortex had input from the retina. But when that input ceased, due to the blindfold, the other sensory connections were apparently unmasked, or unrepressed, brought back online after a lifetime of having their message drowned out by the much more voluminous signals that visual neurons carry to the visual cortex. The capacity of the visual cortex to feel and hear was always there, probably from before birth, when the brain was forging connections all over the place. The blindfold experiment suggests that even connections that remain silent for decades can be brought into the game in time of need. If the new connections are used repeatedly—if the blind-folds had stayed on for years rather than days—maybe those rudimentary changes would become more firmly established, changing the most basic zoning map of the brain in an adult just as they did in the brains of the very young.

Faced with sensory deprivation such as blindness or deafness at any age, the brain taps its power of neuroplasticity to reorganize, using the sensory inputs it does have. "When vision is normal, visual input is the ideal input for the visual cortex, so much so that input from other senses is suppressed or masked," says Pascual-Leone. "But when visual input is absent, the visual cortex turns to the next-best inputs. I mean, it has to use something; that's too much brain to lie dormant."

The fact that these were adult brains that had so quickly given the visual cortex a new assignment was one clue that neuroplasticity does not vanish with childhood. Indeed, as studies turn up more and more examples of the plasticity of the adult brain, the idea that there is a significant difference be-tween the brains of people who become blind in early childhood and those who lose their sight later has been called into question.

The Cost of Neuroplasticity

Before we turn to the new worlds of possibility opened up by discoveries of the adult brain's neuroplasticity, it is important to mention a significant downside. One hope for restoring the sight of the blind is what's called arti-ficial vision, in which some sort of microcamera captures images of the out-side world, transforms them into electrical impulses, and sends those impulses down the optic nerve to the visual cortex. The premise is that the visual cortex has been sitting around for years, or even decades, waiting eagerly for a missive from the outside world.

But work such as Pascual-Leone's suggests that the visual cortex is not quite the long-suffering martyr that that scenario suggests. In all the years that visual input has been AWOL, the visual cortex has not sat idly by. It has been unmasking connections carrying other senses, of feeling and hearing. As these preexisting but rudimentary connections become reinforced with use, they become strong, firmly established new pathways, robust and heavily trafficked, taking up all the "visual" cortex's processing capacity. As a result, when "neuroprostheses" carry visual input to the visual cortex, the result is disappointing: the person still cannot see. "The visual cortex has already undergone profound plastic changes and has basically changed jobs," says Pascual-Leone. "Previously suppressed inputs have been brought online, and that's what the 'visual' cortex handles."

Similarly, deaf people whose brains have already reorganized so that the auditory cortex becomes the receiving station for visual input hardly benefit from cochlear implants. These devices send electrical signals to what had been the patients' auditory cortex, but that area has already changed functions. It is like a radio antenna that had once been tuned to frequency A but that got tired of waiting and waiting for signals that never arrived; it retunes itself to frequency B. When frequency A resumes broadcasting, the receiver cannot pick it up. So it goes with brains that have not received auditory input from birth: the auditory cortex gives up on sound signals and, rather than remain silent and idle, begins processing visual signals. If auditory signals suddenly show up, the auditory cortex is otherwise engaged.

As that understanding sets in, scientists have realized that if they are to restore sight to the blind, they will have to work with the visual cortex as it is, not with the visual cortex of the textbooks. That means sending it the kind of signals to which neuroplasticity has tuned it, tactile and auditory ones. One such system, called a "sensory substitution device," captures visual images with a camera but then transforms them into tactile stimulation or sound. In the sound version, the device encodes key aspects of a scene, such as brightness and locations and shapes, using auditory information. The work is only beginning, but early results suggest that the brain of a blind person can turn these "soundscapes" into visual images.

Phantom Limb

As soon as neurologist V. S. Ramachandran read the Silver Spring monkeys study, he recalled, he thought, "My god—might this be an explanation for phantom limbs?" Touching the faces of the monkeys, as described in chapter 2, caused activity in the part of the somatosensory cortex that once processed signals from the arm, showing that an area of the brain that originally performed one function—in this case, processing feelings from the arm—had changed to a different function. That much was clear enough. But the monkeys, being monkeys, were never asked what that felt like. Did they feel as if their cheek was tickled—which it was—or as if their arm was, since that was what this region of the somatosensory cortex originally "felt"? The monkeys couldn't say. But human amputees, Ramachandran knew, could.

"Phantom limb" is not the most respected idea in neurology. It has been around since just after the Civil War, when it was coined by one Dr. Silas Weir Mitchell to connote the feeling that a lost arm, hand, leg, or foot continues to feel pressure, pain, warmth, cold, tingling, or other sensations. An estimated 70 percent of amputees experience phantom limb. Psychiatrists often ascribed it to wish fulfillment.

Ramachandran invited Victor Quintero, seventeen, to participate in a little experiment. Victor had recently lost his left arm just above the elbow in a car crash. He swore that he could still feel the missing arm. Ramachandran had Victor sit still with his eyes closed tight and lightly brushed the boy's left cheek with a cotton swab just as Tim Pons's team did to the Silver Spring monkeys.

"Where do you feel that?" Ramachandran asked. On his cheek, Victor answered—and the back of his missing hand. Ramachandran stroked another spot on the cheek. "Where do you feel that?" On his absent thumb, Victor replied. Ramachandran touched the skin between Victor's nose and mouth. "And that?" he asked. His missing index finger was being brushed, Victor said. A spot just below Victor's left nostril caused the boy to feel a tingling on his left pinkie. And when Victor felt an itch in his phantom hand, scratching his lower face relieved the itch. (Now whenever his missing fingers itched, Victor knew where to scratch.)

People who have lost a limb, Ramachandran concluded, experience brain reorganization similar to that in the Silver Spring monkeys: brain neurons that originally received input from a hand become rewired. Specifically, the little homunculus undergoes a metamorphosis. His face invades what had once been the hand, since the two are adjacent. And because the feet and genitals abut in the homunculus—or, put another way, the representation of a foot lies adjacent to the representation of the genitals—some people who have suffered the loss of a leg report feeling phantom sensations in the missing limb during sex.

The Silver Spring monkeys, being somewhat less verbal than your typical amputee, had not been able to say what the brain reorganization felt like. Ramachandran's was thus the first report of a living being knowingly experiencing the results of his own brain rewiring. Like the experimental animals, amputees who lose a limb after childhood and experience this cortical remapping show that the adult brain, and not only the supposedly more malleable developing brain, is capable of wholesale reorganization.

Other studies of amputees show that neuroplasticity allows the brain to remodel itself like a sculptor who's never content. Christina Saccuman of the San Raffaele Scientific Institute in Milan, Italy, studied three men who had lost their right hands in accidents. Many years after the trauma—five, ten, or twenty-two years after, to be precise—the men were scheduled to receive hand transplants, an operation that has achieved good rates of success thanks to advances in microsurgery. But before the operation, the scientists scanned the men's brains with fMRI to determine which regions were active during specific tasks. The scientists had the men do several things: open and close the fingers of the left hand, flex and extend their arms, open and close their mouth, and imagine—merely imagine—moving the fingers of the lost right hand. After the transplant, which enabled the men to recover pretty good functionality, the scientists had them repeat all of the original tasks plus an additional one: open and close the fingers of the transplanted hand in reality, not only in imagination.

Before the transplant, the men's somatosensory cortex looked pretty much as expected. The hand area had been invaded by the arm and the mouth, much as the studies of the Silver Spring monkeys and Ramachandran's amputees had found. Soon after the surgery, however, the original hand area of the somatosensory cortex was back to its designated job, registering feelings from the transplanted hand. Even though it had been as long as twenty-two years since the hand part of the somatosensory cortex had heard anything from the hand, Saccuman told the 2004 meeting of the Society for Neuroscience, "Normal organization was regained."

One possible explanation lay in what the fMRI caught when, before the transplant, the men imagined moving their missing hand. The original hand region of the somatosensory cortex as well as the hand region of the premotor cortex (which plans movement) became active. That suggests that even if the brain has not received electrical missives from a part of the body for many years, it does not abandon hope. The representation of the hand action "persists years after the amputations," says Saccuman. "Functional changes induced by long-lasting hand amputation are reversible." Like an abandoned lover who keeps her heartthrob's room just as he left it, the brain retains the wisp of a memory of what the hand region of the cortex used to do, the better to do it again when a hand is restored.

Stroke Is Not Forever

Edward Taub, too, found inspiration from the Silver Spring monkeys. From the first time he wondered about the effects of deafferenting a monkey's arm, he was driven by one hope: that what he learned would help people recover from stroke and other brain lesions.

Every year, some 750,000 Americans suffer a stroke. A clot in a blood vessel, or a ruptured blood vessel, shuts off blood flow to part of the brain. Because blood carries the oxygen that brain cells need to survive, cells in that region are at risk of dying. Cells, however, can hold their breath longer than people can, so there is a window of about eight hours in which doctors can minimize the damage by administering the drug TPA (tissue plasminogen activator) or even by cooling the brain, which reduces its oxygen demands much as a person can survive for longer without oxygen in a frigid lake than in a warm one. But many stroke victims fail to get medical help quickly enough, often because they do not even realize they have suffered a stroke. As a result, stroke is the country's leading cause of disability, with roughly one-third of those who suffer a stroke becoming permanently and seriously disabled—unable to walk, to use their arms, to speak.

Taub argued that his work with deafferentation pointed the way toward testing whether *learning* not to use an affected arm accounted for much of a stroke patient's disability. He then outlined a possible way around that maladaptive learning. The therapy he had in mind would exploit the discovery that a region of the Silver Spring monkeys' brains that originally had one job could be trained to perform another. From this, Taub inferred that people in whom a stroke had knocked out one region of the brain could undergo training that would coax a different region of the brain to assume the function of the damaged part.

The therapy came to be known as constraint-induced movement therapy. By putting a stroke patient's good arm in a sling and her good hand in an oven mitt so she could not use either, Taub reasoned, she would have no choice but to use her "useless" arm if she wanted to hold something or feed herself or get dressed or do the laborious rehabilitation exercises through which he put patients. It was an uphill battle from the start. "The rehab community was united in opposition to the idea that therapy after a stroke could reverse the neurological effects of the infarct," Taub told me. "The official position of the American Stroke Association was that rehab for patients with chronic stroke only increases a patient's muscular strength and confidence" but does nothing to address the brain damage.

After the legal problems from the Silver Spring monkeys were behind him, Taub joined the University of Alabama–Birmingham. There, in 1987, he and some open-minded colleagues began working with four stroke patients who were in the top quartile of stroke survivors in their ability to move their affected arm. Taub had the patients wear a sling on their good arm for about 90 percent of waking hours for fourteen straight days. On ten of those days—two five-day weeks—they spent six hours at UAB undergoing intensive training. They threw balls. They played dominoes. They held cards. They picked up sandwiches and laboriously delivered lunch to their mouths. They tried again and again to extend their arm far enough to pick up a peg, to hold it tightly enough to keep from losing their grip on it, to pull their arm back toward the hole in the pegboard, and to slip it into the right hole. It is painful to watch. You hold your breath as when a gymnast attempts a particularly tricky move. The reward for successfully inserting a peg, of course, was getting to do it again . . . and again and again. If the patient could not reach a peg at first, the therapist took her by the hand, guiding her arm to the peg, and then back to the hole, all the while offering encouragement.

After just those ten days of therapy, Taub found, patients regained significant use of an arm they thought would always hang uselessly. They could put on a sweater, unscrew a cap on a jar, and pick up a bean on a spoon and lift it to their mouth. They could perform almost twice as many of the routines of daily living as patients who, serving as controls, did not receive the therapy. And these were not patients whose stroke was so recent that they might have regained movement spontaneously, as many do. No: these patients had suffered their stroke more than a year before beginning therapy and so were long past the period when, rehab wisdom held, either spontaneous or therapy-aided recovery takes place. Two years after treatment ended, Taub's patients were still brushing their teeth, combing their hair, eating with a fork and spoon, and picking up a glass and drinking from it.

Science doesn't work the way newspapers might have you believe. One study, especially one that overturns decades of conventional wisdom, doesn't change the orthodoxy. To the contrary. Although constraint-induced therapy brought dramatic improvements in his patients, Taub was still regularly turned down for funding by NIH. But as the number of patients helped by constraint-induced therapy grew, it became clear that his hunch was right: the old brain, even the damaged brain, retains some of its early neuroplasticity—enough, at least, to rezone the motor cortex so that the functions of a damaged region can be assumed by a healthy region.

The crowning achievement for constraint-induced therapy came in early 2006, when Taub and colleagues reported the results of the most rigorous trial ever conducted of it. They recruited forty-one stroke patients who had suffered their stroke an average of four and a half years before. Twenty-one of the patients received constraint-induced movement therapy. Six hours a day for ten days, they received training in tasks using their stroke-affected arm, while their good arm was strapped down. The other twenty patients served as controls, undergoing training in strength, balance, and stamina, as well as games that challenged their mind and relaxation exercises, but nothing specifically targeting their "useless" arm.

At the end of the two weeks, the constraint-induced therapy group showed large improvements in the quality and amount of use of their impaired arm, compared to the control group. Even two years later, the constraint-induced group had retained their edge and were able to use their impaired arm—which was hardly impaired by this point—significantly more and better than those who did not receive this training. The patients had overcome what Taub calls learned nonuse, in which patients (understandably) simply stop trying to use their impaired arm. But something else accounted for the improvement: the therapy, the scientists reported, generated "a large use-dependent brain reorganization in which substantial new areas of the brain are recruited" to take over the function of the region that had been knocked out by the stroke. The study showed that "activity-dependent brain plasticity can be harnessed through appropriate behavioral or rehabilitation techniques to produce a clinically meaningful therapeutic effect on chronic motor deficits after neurological damage." Just to emphasize, these patients were all older adults. Yet their brain had changed.

These stroke studies have toppled the dogma that when a brain region is damaged by a stroke, the function it used to perform is forever lost. Instead, the brain is able to recruit healthy, usually nearby, neurons to perform the function of the damaged ones. It doesn't happen with every patient, for reasons neurologists are still puzzling out. But it is now clear that neuroplasticity enables the brain to shuffle the job descriptions it had originally assigned to neurons. What remains unclear, however, is the neurological basis for the improvement brought about by constraint-induced movement therapy. Neurons that previously had nothing to do with moving an arm or a leg must be recruited, called up to send signals to the spinal motoneurons, which, in turn, send electrical signals to move the once-paralyzed limb. Experiments on visual cortices that feel and auditory cortices that see strongly suggest that those alternative inputs have been there all along, like reservists keeping in shape but seeing no action as long as the frontline troops are available. Similarly, when a stroke incapacitates neurons in the primary motor cortex that had controlled the movement of an arm or a leg, these reservists are activated. The question is, from where?

In theory, the new recruits might come from any of several places. They might come from the primary motor cortex in the opposite and undamaged hemisphere. Although the right motor cortex ordinarily moves the left side of the body, and the left motor cortex moves the right side of the body, perhaps a few wayward neurons from the right motor cortex maintain tentative connections to the right side of the body, and the left motor cortex to the left. Or perhaps other regions of the brain involved in movement step up—neurons from the premotor and supplementary areas (which ordinarily just plan and initiate movement rather than executing it, as the primary motor cortex does), neurons from the basal ganglia (which seem to encode habitual, repeated movements), neurons from the cerebellum (involved in the visual guidance of movement).

To find what exactly in the brain was changing, Taub and German colleagues used transcranial magnetic stimulation on thirteen chronic stroke patients whose injury had left one of their arms and hands almost useless. The magnetic pulse temporarily disabled one spot after another in both the right and the left motor cortex, in regions that control the hand, to see which regions were involved in the very weak hand movements they could manage. The scientists repeated the zapping after the patients had received twelve days of constraint-induced movement therapy.

Treatment caused the area of the motor cortex controlling the affected hand to enlarge significantly. Even in stroke patients who had suffered their injury seventeen years before, neuronal networks in the damaged hemisphere had become more active—in particular, those adjacent to the ones that originally controlled the arm, the scientists reported in 2000. Taub called it "use-dependent cortical reorganization." Through constraint-induced movement therapy, the brain had drafted the healthy motor cortex to do what injured tissue no longer could. "The area responsible for producing movements of the affected arm almost doubles in size, and parts of the brain that are not normally involved, areas adjacent to the infarct, are recruited," Taub said. This was the first time an experiment had demonstrated the rewiring of the brain as a result of physical therapy after a stroke. For Taub, who had been working toward such a result for some three decades, it was both a scientific triumph and, after his Silver Spring monkeys debacle, a personal vindication.

Recruiting healthy tissue adjacent to the tissue damaged by a stroke is not the only way patients can recover movement, however. At NIH, Mark Hallett began to suspect that right around the lesion, if not too much tissue is damaged, there is what he calls local reorganization: neighboring neurons take over for the group that used to move, say, the right arm. This is what Taub had found. But if the damage is more extensive, Hallett says, then a region farther afield can be recruited to assume the function of the damaged motor cortex: the premotor cortex. Ordinarily, the premotor cortex is like the green room of a talk show, its occupants waiting to be called on. The main route out of the premotor cortex—the neuronal connections that transmit signals it generates—leads to the motor cortex, so the premotor cortex can be thought of as the place where a plan of movement first takes tangible form. But apparently, the premotor cortex keeps some outbound lanes in reserve for an emergency such as a stroke that disables a spot in the motor cortex. In that case, its signals can travel directly to the spine, where they race down the nerves until they reach the muscle that is to be moved. "It looks like the premotor cortex can take over," says Hallett. "It was somewhat of a surprise, because the understanding had been that the premotor cortex only plans movements, not carries them out."

But that is not the end of the neuroplasticity that can come to the aid of a stroke-damaged brain. In some cases, the opposite hemisphere steps in. If the damage is in the right motor cortex, which controls the left side of the body, then the left motor cortex might take over moving the left side of the body. It doesn't do as good a job as the original, so movement is less controlled, weaker, more spastic. Still, it's better than paralysis. "I'm convinced, myself, that adjacent tissue and even the premotor cortex in the original hemisphere is the main contributor to recovery," Hallett says. "But in some cases, we find that the opposite hemisphere has been recruited." What is clear, however, is that "the earlier and more intensive the therapy, the better the outcome" for stroke patients, he says. "The brain tries to repair itself."

With two clinical trials and numerous lab studies under his belt, all showing the value of constraint-induced movement therapy, Taub faced a thorny practical question. Although the technique had been shown to increase patients' use of their impaired arm, even many years after the stroke and even when the damage was moderately severe, it was not reaching many stroke patients: it is extremely labor-intensive, requiring hours and hours of one-on-one time with a therapist. That put it out of reach of many patients and deterred rehab centers from sending their staff for training in it, much less offering it widely. So Taub and his colleagues developed what he calls AutoCITE, for automated constraint-induced therapy extension. In 2004, they reported that six chronic stroke patients had successfully used the remote system: practicing three hours a week for two weeks, their good arm kept out of commission by the padded mitt they wore on that hand for a target 90 percent of their waking hours, they experienced improvements in mobility as good as patients treated one-on-one. That opened the door to making the therapy available to stroke patients who could not get to a center with expertise in constraint-induced movement therapy, and to the homebound.

The Musical Brain

Even as he kept refining constraint-induced movement therapy for stroke patients, Edward Taub had broader questions about the neuroplasticity of the adult brain. In the spring of 1995, he and his wife were visiting Germany to meet with some of his scientific collaborators. At dinner one night with Thomas Elbert of the University of Konstanz, Taub asked, is there any normal human activity in which you get a big increase in the use of one hand and not the other hand? Taub's wife, Mildred Allen, a lyric soprano who had been a leading singer at the Santa Fe Opera, piped up, "Oh, that's easy: the left hand of string players."

When a right-handed musician plays the violin, the four fingers of the left hand continuously dance across the strings, which is why they are called the fingering digits. The left thumb grasps the neck of the violin, undergoing only small shifts of position. The fingers of the right, or bowing, hand, make almost no fine movements. If any part of the body was demanding more than its fair share of cortical space, then, it was the four digits of the fingering hand.

To see if this were so, Taub and his colleagues recruited six violinists, two cellists, and one guitarist, each of whom had played his or her instrument for seven to seventeen years. For comparison, they enlisted six nonmusicians. Each volunteer sat still while a device applied light pressure to their fingers; it was sort of a static version of the fluttering-bird-wing device on which Michael Merzenich had trained monkeys. A magnetoencephalograph recorded neuronal activity in the somatosensory cortex. The spatial extent of the activity when, say, the left index finger was stimulated would indicate how much cortical real estate had been zoned to receive feelings from that finger.

There was no difference between the string players and the nonmusicians in how much space the brain allotted to registering feelings from the digits of the right hand. But there was a substantial difference in how much brain space was zoned for the fingering digits, the scientists reported.

The cortical space devoted to registering feelings from the digits of the left hand in string players was much greater than that in the nonplaying controls. The difference was greatest in those who took up the instrument before the age of twelve.

The study attracted a great deal of media attention, and to Taub's dismay, almost all of the reporters emphasized that last finding, that brains exposed very early to the demands of playing the violin undergo more extensive alterations than brains exposed later. Taub considered that unsurprising and almost trivial. The point, he said, was that the cortical area devoted to the fingering digits had expanded even in people who did not begin playing until they were adults. "Everyone knew" that the brain of a child is plastic, Taub said, so the finding that children's brains change when they repeatedly use their fingers to coax the right note from an instrument was to be expected. The real news, he said, was that "even if you take up the violin at forty, you still get use-dependent cortical reorganization."

To a stickler, of course, there was an equally possible conclusion to be drawn: that people who were born with more cortical space given to what would be the fingering digits in a string player had a natural head start, as it were, and were therefore more likely to gravitate toward playing a violin, or at least more likely to stick with it, than someone whose brain didn't zone extra space for these fingers. But when taken in conjunction with what Merzenich had found in monkeys—that extra sensory stimulation expands the brain region that specializes in processing this tactile input—Taub's interpretation makes sense: the more you use fingers in a way that puts a premium on sensitivity, as when you play a violin, the more the brain responds by reallocating precious cortical space. That reallocation occurs even in musicians who take up the instrument after childhood, showing that use-dependent reorganization is not confined to the young brain. Regardless of when the musicians start, the more years of training, the larger the representation.

Retraining the Seeing Brain

With the popularity of brain imaging, neural cartographers have identified not only the regions responsible for general functions such as seeing or hearing or feeling, but for almost ridiculously specific jobs, such as recognizing faces, playing Tetris, generating verbs, solving math problems, creating metaphors.

With such specificity, you'd think the brain would be pretty resistant to rezoning. But it isn't. Dramatic changes can still occur when the input to the cortex changes drastically. Taub's violin players showed such "use-dependent reorganization," as did Ramachandran's amputees. In the first case, an increase in sensory input to the fingers of the left hand, which get a tremendous workout dancing up and down the strings, causes the brain region that registers the sense of touch to those fingers to expand. In the second case, a decrease in sensory input—indeed, an elimination of it, in the case of amputation—lets the hand and arm areas of the somatosensory cortex be invaded by the adjacent face areas.

Although the first discoveries of the neuroplasticity of the adult brain came in studies of people who had lost a limb or suffered a stroke, there was no reason to think that the motor cortex or the somatosensory cortex—the regions of the brain that change in these cases—is unique in its malleability. As Taub was fond of saying, "It's all just neural tissue." Given the discoveries about the plasticity of the visual cortex, as shown by studies of blind people in which this "vision" region hears or feels or processes language, it made sense to see whether it, too, could be reshaped in a way that would help patients.

In macular degeneration, the center of the retina—the fovea—becomes seriously impaired, leaving patients with no central vision. They have to rely exclusively on peripheral vision, with the result that reading, driving, and even recognizing people become difficult or impossible. At the cellular level, the damage to the fovea means that no electrical signals travel from the central part of the retina to the visual cortex.

The visual cortex, like the somatosensory cortex and the motor cortex, is not one big undifferentiated blob but rather an impeccably zoned neighborhood. It "contains a detailed map of visual space," says Chris Baker of the Massachusetts Institute of Technology, who presented the work to the annual meeting of the Society for Neuroscience in 2004. Neighboring spots in the visual cortex respond to neighboring spots on the retina. Put another way, signals traveling from two specific spots on the retina reach spots in the visual cortex that mirror precisely their spatial relationship back where they came from. With the fovea out of commission, the region of the visual cortex that once received signals for central vision is like a quiet, empty lot devoid of activity.

Other regions of the visual cortex seem to consider that an invitation. Like developers spying an underused parcel of land, they swoop in. Using fMRI to measure activity in the visual cortex, scientists had two volunteers with macular degeneration look at photos of faces, objects, and scenes in their peripheral vision and then their central vision. The damage to their fovea kept them from seeing anything straight-on, so when a photo was directly in front of them, they turned their heads to position it in their peripheral vision. "We found that the part of the brain that would only respond to central visual information in people with normal vision was now responding to peripheral visual information," says Baker: the part of the brain that used to handle signals from the fovea was now handling those from the peripheral vision. It had not remained an empty, useless lot but had been taken over by the next-door neighbors and rezoned for peripheral vision. This had occurred in people well into their adulthood. "The visual brain is modifiable even late in life," says Baker. "The fact that brain reorganization occurs in people with macular degeneration suggests that we may be able to develop better strategies for rehabilitation of people suffering from this devastating disease."

It is important to emphasize what neuroplasticity is not: a glam name for the cellular changes that underlie the formation of memory and hence learning. New synapses, connections between one neuron and another, are the physical manifestation of memories. In this sense, the brain undergoes continuous physical change. But neuroplasticity goes beyond that. It produces wholesale changes in the job functions of particular areas of the brain. Cortical real estate that used to serve one purpose is reassigned and begins to do another. The brain remakes itself throughout life, in response to outside stimuli—to its environment and to experience. As Taub's violin players and stroke patients, and Pascual-Leone's Braille readers, and Ramachandran's amputees showed so dramatically, many brain systems retain well into adulthood their ability to respond to altered sensory inputs and reorganize themselves accordingly. "Plasticity is an intrinsic property

of the human brain," says Pascual-Leone, whose work on blind Braille readers and blindfolded volunteers did so much to show that plasticity enables
the visual cortex to soar far beyond its nominal destiny. "The potential of
the adult brain to 'reprogram' itself might be much greater than has previously been assumed," he and his colleagues concluded in 2005.

As he sees it, neuroplasticity is evolution's way of letting the brain break
the bonds "of its own genome," escaping the destiny that usually causes one
region to process visual input and another to process auditory input, one
stretch of the somatosensory cortex to process feelings from the right index
finger and another to process input from the thumb. Genes set up all that.
But genes can't know what demands, challenges, losses, and blows the
brain will encounter, any more than parents can know what slings and ar-
rows the child they send out into the world will meet. Rather than set strict
rules of behavior, wise parents teach their children to respond to each situation that presents itself, adapting their behavior to the challenges they
meet. So, too, has nature equipped the human brain, endowing it with the
flexibility to adapt to the environment it encounters, the experiences it has,
the damage it suffers, the demands its owner makes of it. The brain is neither immutable nor static but is instead continuously remodeled by the
lives we lead.

But there is a catch. These changes occur only when the person (or the
monkey) is paying attention to the input that causes them. As we shall see,
if I ran the fingers of your left hand over the strings of a violin while you
were sleeping, and did it again and again, the region of the somatosensory
cortex that registers sensations from these fingers would not expand. This
was one hint, seen even in Michael Merzenich's early monkey experiments,
that mental activity affects, and perhaps even enables, neuroplasticity. That
is, neuroplasticity occurs only when the mind is in a particular mental
state, one marked by attention and focus. The mind matters. The question
was, what power does it have over the brain?

Chapter 6

Mind over Matter

Mental Activity Changes the Brain

The Long Shadow of Descartes

During a visit to an American medical school, the Dalai Lama was invited to watch a brain operation (with the permission of the patient's family). Afterward, he sat down with the neurosurgeons to chat about science's understanding of the mind and the brain. He recalled the hours of conversations he had enjoyed with neuroscientists over the years, and how they had explained to him that perception, sensation, and other subjective experiences reflect chemical and electrical changes in the brain. When electrical impulses zip through our visual cortex, we see, and when neurochemicals course through the limbic system, we feel—sometimes in response to an event in the outside world, sometimes as a result of a thought generated by the mind alone. Even consciousness, he recalled scientists explaining, is just a manifestation of brain activity, and when the brain ceases to function, consciousness vanishes like the morning fog.

But something had always bothered him about this explanation, the Dalai Lama said. Even if one accepts the idea that the mind is what the brain does, and that feelings and thoughts are expressions of brain activity, isn't two-way causation possible? That is, maybe in addition to the brain giving rise to the thoughts, feelings, and other cognitive activity that together add up to this thing we call mind, some aspects of the mind might also act back on the brain to cause physical changes in the very matter that created it. In this case, the arrow of causality would point both ways, and pure thought would change the brain's chemistry and electrical activity, its circuits, or even its structure.

The brain surgeon hardly paused before answering. Physical states give rise to mental states, he patiently explained. "Downward" causation from the mental to the physical is not possible. The Dalai Lama, out of politeness, let the matter drop. This wasn't the first time a neuroscientist had dismissed the possibility that the mind can change the brain and that consciousness might not be reducible to matter.

But "I thought then and still think that there is yet no scientific basis for such a categorical claim," he wrote in his 2005 book *The Universe in a Single Atom.* "The view that all mental processes are necessarily physical processes is a metaphysical assumption, not a scientific fact."

The classic Buddhist texts include very little discussion of the brain. The discovery that this three-pound orb with the consistency of soft tofu is the locus of our mental and emotional life is only a few centuries old, while many Buddhist texts date back more than a millennium. There was no more reason to focus on the brain than to muse about the left eyebrow. Buddhism does explore the five senses, and their relationship to the mind, explains Thupten Jinpa, the Buddhist scholar who has long served as the Dalai Lama's English translator. "There is a recognition in the Buddhist texts that the sense organs are the basis of physical sensations and the means by which these outside sensations are transformed into the mental," he says. "Discussions of how the mental might affect the physical come in the context of healing, of how thought processes might affect the body, and of how meditation can affect the body and bring about its healing." With the discovery by Western science that the brain is the organ of cognition and emotion, it was not a big leap to apply these traditional Buddhist beliefs to how the mind might act back on the brain.

The Dalai Lama had no quarrel with the fact that brain activity gives rise to mental activity. But he felt it premature to reduce the latter to the former. There might be aspects of consciousness that cannot be explained by pulses of electrical current and the release and absorption of neurotransmitters in the brain. In these cases, brain would fall short of explaining mind. That implies that something about mind remains separate and apart from brain. As he told scientists visiting him in Dharamsala during the 2000 Mind and Life meeting, "I am interested in the extent to which the mind itself, and specific subtle thoughts, may have an influence upon the brain. In that case, it would not be a one-way correlation of brain to mental activity but a correlation of mental activity to brain." And not just any old correlation, but a causal one, in which mental states affect the very neurons and circuits that give rise to them. As soon as the Dalai Lama raised this, neuroscientist Francisco Varela jumped in: "The mental state must also be able to modify the brain condition," he said. "This is necessarily true. However, it's not an idea that has been explored very much because it seems counterintuitive to Western assumptions. But it is logically implicit in what science is saying today."

"Logically implicit" is a far cry from widely and explicitly recognized, however. The closest scientists come to acknowledging that the mind can shape the brain is by interposing an intermediary—the brain itself. According to the accepted wisdom, brain states give rise to mental states. A particular pattern of neurons firing *here* and neurotransmitters docking with neurons *there* gives rise to some mental state; let's say it's intention. Like every mental state, intention has a neural correlate, a corresponding brain state marked by activity in a specific circuit such as that detected by fMRI. The neural correlate of intention is different from the brain state that caused intention, and it can and does give rise to subsequent brain states. So while we might naïvely think that intention is causing the brain to change, what is really happening is something pretty mundane: the brain state that corresponds to intention is affecting another aspect of the brain in a perfectly Newtonian way, with something electrical or chemical over *here* altering electricity and chemistry over *there*. And that's all you need to explain brain changes—one brain state giving rise to another. The intervening step of a mental state to which we give the name "intention" is a mere sideshow, an epiphenomenon, with no causal power of its own. Brain and only brain affects brain. Or so scientists told the Dalai Lama.

The idea that only brain acts on brain reflects a view that philosophy calls "causal closure." It holds that only the physical can act on the physical. A baseball bat can move a ball, a hand can lift a cup, air molecules can move the leaves of grass. But a nonphysical phenomenon is powerless to affect anything made out of tissues, molecules, and atoms. In this view, something nonphysical, such as intention, is not what moves your body out of bed. It is the physical manifestation of that intention, the ensemble of electrical signals pulsing through the brain, that moves the body out of bed.

Buddhism rejects the reducibility of mind to matter, and this belief acts as no small impediment when it comes to finding common ground between Buddhism and neuroscience. At the 2004 Mind and Life meeting, it was the elephant in the room. The scientists were so certain that everything of the mind is reducible to brain, and that mind is just what the brain does, that they didn't even bother to engage the Buddhists on the topic. But in his innocent question to the brain surgeon, the Dalai Lama had, as it happened, hit upon something with which neuroscience itself had recently begun wrestling, after more than a century of treating the very idea of dualism as a quaint relic of a prescientific era.

It was the seventeenth-century French philosopher René Descartes who posited dualism as a scientific principle. Descartes believed that the mental realm of fleeting thoughts and evanescent feelings, and the material world of rocks and rocking chairs, are two parallel but distinct domains of reality, what we today call mind and matter. That was perfectly consonant with the ideas of his era, when scientists had no idea how the brain worked. As the English philosopher Henry More wrote, the brain "shows no more capacity for thought than a cake of suet or a bowl of curds." To imagine the slimy flesh within the skull as capable of thought, faith, genius, and love was ridiculous. But by the middle of the seventeenth century, a group of natural philosophers—alchemists and physicians and men of faith—known as the Oxford Circle, led by one Thomas Willis, had undertaken the first scientific investigation of the brain and the rest of the nervous system.

Considered the father of modern neurology, Willis was convinced that the brain's myriad folds and fissures brewed thoughts and memories, feelings and insights. Everything the mind does, he insisted, reflects that intricate dance of chemicals along the nerves he so painstakingly dissected. Willis called his work neurologie. It raised the curtain on a materialist, reductionist way of thinking about thinking, which persists to this day: that everything we call "mental" (including "emotional") is just a manifestation of brain activity and that everything in the mental realm can be reduced to physical events. Mind and brain, the mental and the physical, are seen as identical. It is not simply that neural processes *cause* conscious processes, as philosopher Colin McGinn puts it in describing the reigning view in neuroscience: "Neural processes *are* conscious processes. Nor is it merely that conscious processes are an aspect of neural processes; it is rather that there is nothing more to a conscious state than its neural correlate." Believing otherwise—that there is any merit to the dualist idea that mind has any independence from brain—is enough to get you disinvited from the better neuroscience parties.

But in the 1990s, a whiff of uncertainty about the identity of mind and brain began to creep in around the edges of neuroscience. Philosopher John Searle, who has probed the mysteries of mind and brain as deeply as any contemporary scholar, described the problem this way: "As far as we know, the fundamental features of [the physical] world are as described by physics, chemistry and the other natural sciences. But the existence of phenomena that are not in any obvious way physical or chemical gives rise to puzzlement. . . . How does a mental reality, a world of consciousness, intentionality and other mental phenomena, fit into a world consisting entirely of physical particles in fields of force?"

That puzzle, of how patterns of neuronal activity become transformed into subjective awareness, "remains the cardinal mystery of human existence," neurobiologist Robert Doty argued in 1998. For although scientists have gotten remarkably adept at understanding the physiological mechanisms of perception, their work fails to explain why that perception *feels* the way it does. I could give you the most detailed neurophysiological account of what the brain is doing when you feel sad, and if you have never felt sad, this explanation would fall short of enabling you to understand sadness. Similarly, if you have the form of color blindness that makes shades from pink and scarlet through maroon and rust all look the same muddy shade of brown, my showing you neuron-by-neuron how the perception of red arises in the brain would leave you as ignorant as ever of the *feel* of red. A mental state, be it a sense of the color red or the sound of B-sharp or the emotion of sadness or the feel of pain, is more than its neural correlates. This is what neuroscientists call the explanatory gap, and it has never been bridged. As McGinn put it, "The problem with materialism is that it tries to construct the mind out of properties that refuse to add up to mentality."

Some iconoclasts have begun taking that "problem" seriously. While they start from the basic premise that mind arises from brain, they part company with the mainstream by arguing that there is something more to the mind than the brain's physical activity. For our purposes, it is the corollary to that position that is particularly interesting: that what the mind does can change the brain. According to "emergentists," a high-order property such as the mind can affect lower-order processes that created it. What emerges has the power to act back on what it emerges from.

Nobel Prize–winning neuroscientist Roger Sperry, who taught at the California Institute of Technology from 1954 until his death in 1994, developed the most scientifically rigorous form of this position, which he called "mentalism" or "emergent mentalism." Uneasy with the ascendancy of what he saw as "exclusive 'bottom-up' determination of the whole by the parts, in which the neuronal events determine the mental but not vice versa," he theorized that there is "downward control by mental events over the lower neuronal events." Mental states can act directly on cerebral states, he suggested, even affecting electrochemical activity in neurons. In contrast, as mentioned above, the mainstream view then as now holds that mental states are able to influence other mental states only because they are really brain states.

Sperry took pains to acknowledge that consciousness cannot exist without the brain and that the "mental forces" he considered causally efficacious are not "any disembodied supernatural forces independent of the brain mechanism" but are "inseparably tied to the cerebral structure and its functional organization." But it did not help his cause (or his reputation) much. As a visiting professor at Caltech said of Sperry in 1970, if he "goes on in this vein it is likely to diminish the impact of his many marvelous achievements." He went to his grave convinced that "higher-level" mental activity exerts a causal effect on "lower-level" neurons and synapses and that the stuff of the brain can change in response to the whispers of the mind. As discoveries in the 1990s and the first years of the new century were to show, he was ahead of his time—and the Dalai Lama's question to the brain surgeon about the mind affecting the brain was spot-on.

Quieting the OCD Circuit

As discussed in the two preceding chapters, scientists were piling up examples of how *sensory* input—signals carried into the brain from the outside world—can alter the structure of the adult human brain. Thanks to neuroplasticity, the extra sensory input a violinist experiences causes the brain's representation of the fingering digits to expand, and the extra sensory input a stroke patient experiences in constraint-induced movement therapy causes the brain's representation of the injured arm and hand to move to healthy tissue. Thanks to neuroplasticity, depriving the visual cortex of visual signals causes it to seek other employment opportunities, such as handling sounds or touch or even language. All of these changes arose from the world outside the brain. Neuropsychiatrist Jeffrey Schwartz of the University of California–Los Angeles suspected that signals capable of changing the brain could arrive not only from the outside world through the senses. They could come from the mind itself.

Schwartz and colleague Lewis Baxter had launched a behavior-therapy group to study and treat obsessive-compulsive disorder. In this neuropsychiatric disease, patients are barraged by upsetting, intrusive, unwanted thoughts (obsessions) that trigger intense urges to perform ritualistic behaviors (compulsions). Depending on the patient, the compulsion can be to wash hands, to check door locks or stove burners, to count stop signs or windows or blackbirds or anything else on which he or she has fixated. Together, the obsessions and compulsions can become all-consuming, making leaving the house, holding a job, or forming meaningful relationships just about impossible. Oddly, however, in all but the most severe cases, the intrusive thoughts and fixations feel as if they are arising from a part of the mind that is not the real you. Sufferers describe feeling as if a hijacker has taken over their brain's controls. As a result, OCD patients who feel compelled to wash their hands know full well that their hands are not dirty; those who feel compelled to dash home to check that the front door is locked know that it is securely bolted. OCD has a lifetime prevalence of 2 to 3 percent. In round numbers, it affects an estimated 1 person in 40, or more than 67 million Americans, typically striking in adolescence or early adulthood and showing no marked preference for males or females.

According to brain-imaging studies, OCD is characterized by hyperactivity in two regions: the orbital frontal cortex and the striatum. The main job of the orbital frontal cortex, which is tucked into the underside of the front of the brain, seems to be to notice when something is amiss. It is the brain's error detector, its neurological spell-checker. When overactive, as in OCD patients, it fires repeatedly, bombarding the rest of the brain with the crushing feeling that something is wrong. The second overactive structure, the striatum, is nestled deep in the core of the brain just forward of the ears. It receives inputs from other regions, including the orbital frontal cortex and the amygdalae, twin structures that are the seat of fear and dread. Together, the circuit linking the orbital frontal cortex and striatum has been dubbed "the worry circuit" or "the OCD circuit."

Until the mid-1960s, psychiatrists thought of OCD as "treatment intractable." They tried all sorts of therapies, from electroshock and brain surgery to drugs and lie-on-the-couch talk therapy. In the late 1960s and early 1970s, however, psychiatrists noticed that when OCD patients who were also suffering from depression took the tricyclic antidepressant clomipramine, some experienced relief from one or more of their OCD symptoms. Newer antidepressants, including Prozac, Paxil, and Zoloft, also help some patients: about 60 percent respond at least a little, and among these responders, there is a 30 to 40 percent reduction in symptoms, measured by how often the patient feels an urge to carry out a compulsion. But with some 40 percent of patients not helped at all, and with those who are helped left with 60 percent of their symptoms, there is clearly room for improvement.

At about the same time that researchers found that antidepressants helped some OCD patients, a British psychologist working in a London psychiatric ward began to develop what would become the first effective behavioral therapy for the disease. In what he called "exposure and response prevention," or ERP, Victor Meyer had patients face their fears. He first exposed them to the "trigger" of their obsessive thoughts. For instance, he would have a patient who was convinced the world is covered with germs touch all the doorknobs in a public building but would not let her wash her hands afterward (the "prevention" part of ERP can be anything from gentle coercion to physical restraint). Although Meyer reported improvement in his patients, a number of them—estimates run from 10 percent to 30 percent—are so distressed by the treatment they never complete it and never improve.

By the late 1980s, UCLA's Schwartz had another objection to ERP: its cruelty. "I just couldn't see myself hauling patients to a public restroom, forcing them to wipe their hands all over the toilet seats, and then preventing them from washing," he recalls. As he cast about for alternatives that were both more humane and more effective, Schwartz, a practicing Buddhist, became intrigued with the therapeutic potential of mindfulness meditation. Mindfulness, or mindful awareness, is the practice of observing one's inner experiences in a way that is fully aware but nonjudgmental. You stand outside your own mind, observing the spontaneous thoughts and feelings that the brain throws up, observing all this as if it were happening to someone else. In *The Heart of Buddhist Meditation,* the German-born Buddhist monk Nyanaponika Thera described it as "the clear and single-minded awareness of what actually happens to us and in us, at the successive moments of perception. It . . . attends just to the bare facts of a perception as presented either through the five physical senses or through the mind . . . without reacting to them by deed, speech or by mental comment which may be one of self-reference (like, dislike, etc.), judgment or reflection."

Schwartz decided to see if mindfulness could help his OCD patients. He had two goals for them: to experience an OCD symptom without reacting emotionally and to realize that the feeling that something is amiss is just the manifestation of a wiring defect in the brain—overactivity in the OCD circuit. Mindfulness practice, he thought, might make OCD patients aware of the true nature of their obsessions and therefore better able to focus their attention away from them. "It seemed worth investigating whether learning to observe your sensations and thoughts with the calm clarity of an external witness could strengthen the capacity to resist the insistent thoughts of OCD," says Schwartz. "I felt that if I could get patients to experience the OCD symptom without reacting emotionally to the discomfort it caused, realizing instead that even the most visceral OCD urge is actually no more than the manifestation of a brain wiring defect that has no reality in itself, it might be tremendously therapeutic." If so, then mindfulness-based cognitive therapy, in which patients learn to think about their thoughts differently, might succeed where drugs, plain-vanilla cognitive therapy, and exposure and response prevention had failed.

The mental note-taking central to mindfulness would go something like this. When an obsessive thought popped up, the patient would think, "My brain is generating another obsessive thought. Don't I know it is not real but just some garbage thrown up by a faulty circuit?" He would think, that's not really an urge to wash; that's a brain-wiring problem.

In 1987, Schwartz launched a group-therapy session in conjunction with an ongoing study of OCD's underlying brain abnormalities. Patients came in for therapy, and scientists tracked their progress using the brain-imaging technique positron-emission tomography (PET). Schwartz began showing patients their PET scans, to emphasize that their symptoms arose from a faulty neurological circuit. One patient got it right away: "It's not me, it's my OCD!" she exclaimed one day. Soon other patients, too, saw that their obsessions and compulsions were not really "them" but were instead the electronic detritus of brain circuitry. Schwartz wondered, could getting patients to respond in a new way to the obsessive thoughts characteristic of their OCD actually change their brains? He therefore taught patients to use mindfulness to sharpen awareness of the fact that they do not truly believe that they left the stove on or that their hands need washing. Instead, he said, tell yourself you are just experiencing the arrival of an obsessive thought. Start saying to yourself, this thing that feels like an urge to check is in reality just a brain-wiring problem.

"The week after patients started relabeling their symptoms as manifestations of pathological brain processes, they reported the disease was no longer controlling them, and that they felt they could do something about it," says Schwartz. "I knew I was on the right track."

To find out whether the benefits the patients were reporting were accompanied by brain changes, the UCLA scientists launched what would be a landmark study in how the mind can shape the fundamental biology of the brain. They performed PET scans on eighteen OCD patients before and after ten weeks of mindfulness-based therapy. None of the patients took medication for their OCD, and all had moderate to severe symptoms.

Twelve improved significantly. In these, PET scans after treatment showed that activity in the orbital frontal cortex, the core of the OCD circuit, had fallen dramatically compared to what it had been before mindfulness-based therapy.

"Therapy had altered the metabolism of the OCD circuit," says Schwartz. "This was the first study to show that cognitive-behavior therapy has the power to systematically change faulty brain chemistry in a well-identified brain circuit." The ensuing brain changes, he said, "offered strong evidence that willful, mindful effort can alter brain function, and that such self-directed brain changes—neuroplasticity—are a genuine reality." Calling it "an avenue to self-directed neuroplasticity," he reached a conclusion that Roger Sperry, not to mention the Dalai Lama, would applaud: "Mental action can alter the brain chemistry of an OCD patient. The mind can change the brain."

Thinking Depression

Just as the UCLA scientists were discovering that a mind-based, cognitive therapy can change the brain—that thinking about your thoughts in a certain way can alter the electrical and chemical activity of a brain circuit—science was embroiled in a bitter debate over whether psychotherapy has any effect whatsoever, let alone on the physical structure and activity of the brain. The controversy centered on depression. On December 29, 1987, the U.S. Food and Drug Administration had given the pharmaceutical giant Eli Lilly and Company approval to sell fluoxetine hydrochloride as a treatment for depression. Marketed as Prozac, the drug was featured on the covers of magazines, starred in newspaper stories, inspired bestselling books, and was soon racking up $2 billion in annual sales. Prozac was not just another drug for depression. It was hailed as a compound that specifically targeted the disease's underlying neurochemical cause, supposedly a paucity of the neurotransmitter serotonin in the brain's synapses. The rise of Prozac coincided with the continuing fall from grace of psychotherapy. Expensive, time-consuming, and the subject of more jokes than rigorous scientific studies, psychotherapy was starting to have the whiff of something as antediluvian as Freud's couch.

Which is not to say that psychotherapists were throwing in the towel. To the contrary. In 1989, scientists reported the results of the most ambitious study ever undertaken to examine the effectiveness of psychotherapy compared to medication in treating depression. Called the Treatment of Depression Collaborative Research Project, this two-year study was funded and organized by the National Institute of Mental Health. Two hundred and fifty outpatients with major depression were randomly assigned to receive one of four treatments: interpersonal psychotherapy, cognitive-behavior therapy, imipramine (a common antidepressant), or an inert pill. In the last two cases, patients also received what is called clinical management, which essentially means they saw a psychiatrist to receive their medication.

Cognitive-behavior therapy, which was developed in the 1960s, does not dwell on causes of depression. It focuses instead on teaching patients how to handle their emotions, thoughts, and behaviors. The idea is to reappraise dysfunctional thinking, to see the fallacy of thoughts such as "The fact that I was not offered that job means I am doomed to be unemployed and homeless." Patients learn to think about their thoughts differently and not to ruminate endlessly about minor setbacks. Instead of seeing a failed date as evidence that "I am a total loser, and no one will ever love me," patients learn to view it as just one of those things that didn't work out. Instead of seeing a leaky roof as a sign that "nothing will ever go right for me," they think of it as "Stuff happens." They learn to recognize their tendency to magnify disappointments into calamities and mishaps into tragedy, and to test the accuracy of their extreme beliefs. If they are convinced that no one will ever like them, the therapist encourages them to join a social group and strike up a conversation and possibly a friendship. Such reality testing will show patients that they are unrealistically pessimistic. With their new-found cognitive skills, patients can experience sadness and setbacks without being sucked into the black hole of depression.

Interpersonal therapy, on the other hand, recognizes that although depression may not be caused by interpersonal relations or experiences, it affects them. It therefore targets interpersonal disputes and conflicts, role transitions such as becoming an empty nester, and complicated and persistent grief.

In all four groups, patients suffered fewer symptoms of depression over the sixteen weeks of the study. Imipramine produced the greatest improvement in the most severely depressed patients, placebo the least, with the two psychotherapies in between. For patients whose depression was mild to moderate, however, the two psychotherapies produced results on a par with those of the medication. "The power of the cognitive behaviour therapies in [depression] is considerable, certainly equal to the power of the standard drug treatments for depression," Gavin Andrews, professor of psychiatry at the University of New South Wales in Australia wrote in the *British Medical Journal* in late 1996. "If these psychological treatments had been drug treatments they would have been certified as effective and safe remedies and be an essential part of the pharmacopoeia of every doctor. As they were not developed by profit making companies, and thus are not marketed or promoted, their use often languishes." Despite this and subsequent studies validating the efficacy of psychotherapy for depression, it has been tough to shake the perception that psychotherapy is ineffective and inferior to medication.

While the NIMH study was under way, a young psychologist named Zindel Segal was studying depression. He recalls of the drugs-versus-psychotherapy debate that "the sides were drawn very sharply. There was a productive fractiousness, with psychologists saying there was good evidence for the efficacy of therapy" but many scientists convinced that psychotherapy has no place in a Prozac world. Rather than attacking the efficacy question straight on, Segal decided to study whether psychotherapy has an effect on a different, but arguably even more important, aspect of depression: the rate of relapse.

Depression is notorious for its frequent and cruel relapses. A patient may finally feel she has broken the chains of her illness, only to plunge back into the abyss of despair, as 50 percent do. Because of the high relapse rate, patients suffer an average of four major episodes of depression lasting about five months each over the course of their lives. "Many people continue to become ill," says Segal. "The typical progression, unfortunately, is that treatment brings relief, but the risk of relapse or recurrence remains high. Sustained recovery from depression is not the rule." Indeed, doctors and patients had begun noticing that antidepressants come with a dark side: unless patients continue taking the medication, they are very likely to suffer a relapse within two years of the initial treatment. Most patients, says Segal, "require treatment beyond the point when their symptoms disappear."

That was disappointing, of course. But it was also interesting for the possibilities it suggested about the relative benefits of psychotherapy and antidepressants. "The thinking at the time was that psychotherapy, especially cognitive therapy, might produce lasting changes in people's attitudes and beliefs about themselves, which would protect them well after the end of the therapy," says Segal. "Some beliefs make people vulnerable to relapse, like the idea that asking for help is a sign of weakness or that always being right is the way to get others to respect you. If a person with these attitudes suffers a minor setback, even after successful treatment for depression, their explanations for what this means about them—they are weak, they will never be respected—make them more likely to spiral down into depression. What we proposed was that if cognitive therapy could modify these attitudes, then the risk of relapse would be reduced."

That hunch was based on the fact that cognitive therapy is, in essence, a form of mental training. It teaches patients a different way of approaching their thoughts. In the case of depression, those thoughts are, all too often, sad, glum, bleak, or otherwise "dysphoric." Everyone gets those thoughts now and then, of course. What's different in patients with depression is that the thought tips them over the emotional edge into an abyss of negative, hopeless thinking powerful and sustained enough to trigger a full-blown episode of (typically) months-long depression. A setback at work or a romantic rejection escalates to "Nothing will ever go right for me; life is hopeless, and I will always be a complete loser." As described above, cognitive therapy teaches patients to think about these triggering thoughts and feelings so they do not bring on a cascade of depression-triggering thoughts and major depression itself but instead become "short-lived and self-limiting," as John Teasdale of the University of Cambridge, England, suggested.

Here's why cognitive therapy looked as if it might be more efficacious than antidepressants in preventing relapse: the ease with which this type of dysfunctional thinking is triggered by dysphoria reliably predicts the likelihood that a patient will suffer a relapse of depression. If cognitive therapy can break the connection between sadness and aberrant, wildly exaggerated extrapolations, maybe it can vanquish the very mechanism that leads to relapse. It was analogous to how Schwartz taught his OCD patients to think about their obsessions as a fleeting misfire of their brain, one they had the power to keep from exploding into pointless and disruptive compulsions. But first, Segal had to see whether the basic hypothesis was right: that sad thoughts unleash beliefs that make people vulnerable to depressive relapse.

So he made people sad. By then head of the Cognitive Behaviour Therapy Clinic at the Center for Addiction and Mental Health in Toronto, he recruited thirty-four people who had been successfully treated for depression within the previous twenty-four months. To induce sadness, he had two surefire methods: asking the volunteers to think about a time when they felt sad and having them listen to Prokofiev's *Russia under the Mongolian Yoke.* Played at half-speed, Segal says, it induces five to ten minutes of deep sadness as reliably as Beth's death scene in *Little Women.*

Once the volunteers were feeling blue, Segal asked them to indicate how much they agreed or disagreed with statements such as "If I fail at my work, then I am a failure as a person," "If someone disagrees with me, it probably indicates he does not like me," "If I don't set the highest standards for myself, I am likely to end up as a second-rate person"—all known to reveal whether someone holds attitudes that make him vulnerable to depressive relapse.

Segal found that when people had been made melancholic by remembering a sad episode in their lives or listening to the brooding Slavic melody, they were much more likely to hold these attitudes. "The experience of depression can establish strong links in the mind between sad moods and ideas of hopelessness and inadequacy," he says. "Through repeated use, this becomes the default option for the mind: it's like mental kindling. Even among recovered depressed patients, the degree to which sad moods 'switch on' these attitudes is a significant predictor of whether the patient will relapse eighteen months later." In some people, sad thoughts unleash beliefs that put them at risk for depression.

For these unfortunate souls, successful treatment for depression helps with sleeplessness and other symptoms but leaves their gnawing personal doubt intact. As long as things go well, they can sidestep the doubt. But if they suffer a setback or reversal and become sad, this way of thinking creeps back in: "Yeah, things really are hopeless; I was stupid to believe otherwise," or " I really can't hold on to a relationship; I should just accept that." The acute setback makes them feel hopeless, worthless, unloved—exactly the state of mind that characterizes the deep despair and even paralysis of depression. Their memory works in such a way as to activate these concepts more strongly, and with greater probability, once the emotion of sadness arises. This makes it more likely that the brain's whole depression network will switch on. "The experience of depression imprints a tendency to fall back on certain patterns of thinking and to activate certain networks in working memory," Segal says.

What these patients needed, he realized, was a different way to relate to the inevitable sadness everyone experiences at one time or another, a way that would not let a passing sense of unhappiness (from schmaltzy music, no less) send them tumbling down the rabbit hole of depression. And for that, they needed to forge new neuronal connections.

Mindfulness and Depression

In 1992, Segal met with Cambridge's John Teasdale and Mark Williams to turn his theory of depressive relapse—that people who hold despairing attitudes are more vulnerable to falling back into depression as a result of minor setbacks—into a treatment. Teasdale, who had been practicing mindfulness meditation for a number of years, had been learning about a mindfulness program developed by Jon Kabat-Zinn of the University of Massachusetts, a longtime participant in the Mind and Life Institute's meetings with the Dalai Lama. Although Kabat-Zinn used it mostly for stress reduction, Teasdale saw other possibilities: to harness the power of the mind to treat depression. He suspected that patients might escape repeated descents into clinical depression if they learned to regard depressive thoughts "simply as events in the mind," as he put it. The key would be to help patients become aware of their thoughts and relate to them as merely brain events rather than as absolute truths. Instead of letting a bleak experience or thought kindle another episode of depression as predictably as a spark ignites a fire in bone-dry kindling, instead of allowing their feeling to drag them down into the pit of depression, patients would learn to respond with "Thoughts are not facts" or "I can watch this thought come and go without having to respond to it." That, Teasdale suspected, might break the connection the brain made between momentary unhappy thoughts and the memories, associations, and patterns of thinking that inflate sadness into depression. It would be like putting a wall of asbestos between the spark and the kindling. It would be, literally, rewiring the brain.

The program the scientists developed, called mindfulness-based cognitive therapy, consisted of eight weekly individual sessions, each lasting two hours. Using the mindfulness training pioneered by Kabat-Zinn, the patients steered their attention to one region of the body after another, trying to focus intently on the sensations their hand, knee, foot was feeling at that moment. They then learned to focus on their breathing. If their mind wandered, they were to acknowledge it with "friendly awareness"—not frustration or anger—and focus once again on the breath, which served as a magnet pulling them back to mindful awareness of the moment. The patients also practiced at home, trying to notice their thoughts impartially rather than reacting to them, and regarding their feelings and thoughts (especially the bleak, despairing ones) as merely transient mental events that happen to "come and go through the mind" and that are no more significant than a butterfly floating into your field of vision. Most crucially, they kept telling themselves that the thoughts did not reflect reality.

To assess the power of mindfulness to prevent the relapse of depression, Teasdale, Segal, and Williams randomly assigned half of their 145 patients (all of whom had suffered at least one past episode of major depression in the previous five years) to receive mindfulness-based cognitive therapy and half to receive their usual care. After eight weeks of mindfulness-based treatment, the scientists followed the patients for an additional year.

Treatment as usual left 34 percent of the patients free of relapse. With mindfulness-based cognitive therapy, 66 percent remained relapse-free, Teasdale and his colleagues reported in 2000. That translates to a 44 percent reduction in the risk of relapse among those who received mindfulness-based cognitive therapy compared to those receiving usual care. Interestingly, the preventive effect of mindfulness was found only in patients who had suffered three or more past episodes of depression, who made up three-fourths of the sample. These were not easy patients. They had what is called a recurrent form of depression and suffered many, many depressive episodes. Yet mindfulness-based cognitive therapy nearly halved the rate of relapse. This was the first evidence that mental training can reduce the rate of relapse in depression.

In 2004, Teasdale and his colleague Helen Ma replicated the findings, showing again that mindfulness-based cognitive therapy reduced relapse. This time, in a study of fifty-five patients, they found that for patients with three or more episodes of major depression, the rate of relapse fell from 78 percent in the treatment-as-usual group to 36 percent in the mindfulness-based cognitive therapy group. "Mindfulness-based cognitive therapy," they concluded, "is an effective and efficient way to prevent relapse/recurrence in recovered depressed patients with three or more previous episodes." Or as Segal put it, "There are modes of thinking which are more easily triggered the more they're accessed. Mindfulness works to keep you from triggering the depression network." By monitoring their own thoughts, patients who practice mindfulness are able to keep the dysfunctional products of their mind from cascading into full-blown depression.

You don't have to believe in any spooky power of mind over brain to guess what might be happening in these patients. Somehow, mental training was altering brain circuits, in what we might call top-down plasticity, since it originates in the brain's cognitive processes. ("Bottom-up" plasticity is the kind that arises when plain old sensory inputs resculpt the brain, as they do when dyslexic children hear specially crafted sounds or lab monkeys carry out a repetitive finger motion.) Brain-imaging technology would show precisely how mindfulness meditation was training the mind to alter brain circuitry.

Changing the Depressed Brain

Neuroscientist Helen Mayberg had not endeared herself to the pharmaceutical industry by discovering, in 2002, that antidepressants and inert pills—placebos—have identical effects on the brains of depressed people. In patients who recover, whether their treatment consisted of one of the widely prescribed selective serotonin reuptake inhibitors (SSRIs) such as Paxil or a placebo that they *thought* was an antidepressant, brain activity changed in the same way, she and colleagues at the University of Texas Health Science Center, San Antonio, found: according to fMRI scans, activity in the cortex increased and activity in limbic regions fell. Based on that finding, she figured that cognitive-behavior therapy would act via the same mechanism. Soon after the University of Toronto recruited her away from Texas; she therefore asked Zindel Segal to collaborate on a study to see whether there are differences between how cognitive-behavior therapy and antidepressants affect the brain.

"I definitely expected there must be a common pathway," Mayberg said. "I'd thought about doing psychotherapy while I was at Texas, but there was no one qualified to work with me on a study like that. But in Toronto, I met Zindel. It was like a gift."

The Toronto scientists first used PET imaging to measure activity in the brains of depressed patients. Then they had fourteen depressed adults undergo fifteen to twenty sessions of cognitive-behavior therapy. Thirteen other patients received paroxetine (the generic name of the antidepressant sold as Paxil by GlaxoSmithKline). All twenty-seven had depression of approximately equal severity and experienced comparable improvement after treatment. Then the scientists scanned the patients' brains again. "Our hypothesis was, if you do well with treatment for depression, your brain will have changed in the same way no matter which treatment you received," says Segal.

Mayberg's study showing that the brain's response to placebo and to antidepressant has the same pathway had made her expect that there is only one route through brain circuitry from depression to recovery. But no. "We were totally dead wrong," she said. Depressed brains responded differently to the two kinds of treatment. Cognitive-behavior therapy muted overactivity in the frontal cortex, the seat of reasoning, logic, analysis, and higher thought—as well as of endless rumination about that disastrous date. Paroxetine, in contrast, raised activity there. Cognitive-behavior therapy raised activity in the hippocampus of the limbic system, the brain's emotion center. Paroxetine lowered activity there.

The differences were so dramatic that Mayberg "thought we were doing something wrong in how we were analyzing the data," she said. "With cognitive-behavior therapy, activity in the frontal cortex was turned down, activity in the hippocampus was turned up—it was the opposite pattern of antidepressants. Cognitive therapy targets the cortex, the thinking brain, reshaping how you process information and changing your thinking pattern. We finally convinced ourselves that it wasn't a technical error."

Putting it in terms of mind rather than brain, cognitive-behavior therapy "decreases rumination, decreases the personal relevance of triggers that once tipped you into depression, increases reappraisal of thoughts," Mayberg explains. "Does a lousy date really mean that I am a failure as a human being and will never be loved? Cognitive-behavior therapy also increases new patterns of learning, as reflected in the increased activity in the hippocampus, the brain structure associated with the formation of new memories. It trains the brain to adopt different thinking circuits, to switch off ruminative modes of thinking, and to practice relating differently to negative thoughts and feeling. Cognitive-behavior therapy works from the top down, and drugs work from the bottom up," modulating different components of the depression circuit. Mindfulness-based cognitive therapy keeps the depression circuit from being completed.

It may seem surprising that mindfulness-based cognitive therapy should work so well in depression, targeting a system quite different from what a barrage of commercials and friendly media coverage have insisted is the basis for depression—namely, a shortage of the neurochemical serotonin. From the development of the first drug, Prozac, that apparently acted by keeping serotonin from being eliminated from the brain's synapses, it has been drummed into our heads that depression reflects a biochemical imbalance and that Prozac or another SSRI is the avenue to recovery. After the arrival of Prozac was greeted like the second coming of penicillin, however, reality set in. Prozac takes several weeks to work, when it works at all (some one-third of patients with depression do not respond to it). It has a high relapse rate, and many patients seem to need to stay on the drug forever.

"Massive marketing has depicted the challenge in depression as one of correcting a chemical imbalance in the brain," says Zindel Segal. "This may be true at the neural level, but we now know that there are multiple pathways to recovery, and a chemical imbalance itself can be restored in different ways."

Thinking Makes It So

The discovery that mindfulness practice quiets the OCD circuit as effectively as medication, and that mindfulness-based cognitive therapy strengthens emotionally healthy patterns of thinking and short-circuits those that lead back to depression, showed the power of mind over brain in at least one arena: altering patterns of activity in targeted circuits. Both have also benefited patients, of course. But a much more modest study, one conducted almost as a lark, came even closer to addressing the Dalai Lama's question to the neurosurgeon: can the mind physically alter the brain?

In the mid-1990s, Pascual-Leone conducted an experiment that, in retrospect, seems like a bridge between the discovery that outside stimuli can alter the brain and the more recent work showing that self-generated stimuli—thoughts and meditation—can, too. What he did was teach a group of volunteers a five-finger exercise on a piano keyboard. They were instructed to play as fluidly as they could, without pausing, trying hard to keep to the metronome's sixty beats per minute. Every day for five days, the volunteers practiced for two hours. Then they took a test, in which they played the exercise twenty times while a computer counted their errors. Over the five days, the players made fewer and fewer errors while improving their beat so that the intervals between notes came closer and closer to what the metronome called for.

The volunteers underwent one further test. For a few minutes once a day, they sat beneath a coil of wire that sent a brief magnetic pulse into the motor cortex of their brain. This transcranial magnetic stimulation briefly disables the neurons just beneath the coil, allowing scientists to infer what function they control. In the piano players, the pulse was directed at their motor cortex—specifically, the stretch that controls the flexion and extension of the fingers. In this way, the scientists could map the boundaries of that stretch, discerning the area of motor cortex devoted to finger movements needed for the piano exercise. What the scientists found was that, after a week of practice, the stretch of motor cortex devoted to these finger movements took over surrounding areas like dandelions on a suburban lawn.

That finding was completely in line with the ever-growing pile of discoveries, including those discussed in chapter 2, that greater use of a particular muscle causes the brain to devote more cortical real estate to it. But Pascual-Leone did not stop there. He had another group of volunteers merely *think* about practicing the piano exercise. They played the simple piece in their heads, imagining how they would move their fingers to generate the notes on the score. Result: The region of the motor cortex that controls the piano-playing fingers expanded in the brains of volunteers who merely imagined playing the piece just as it did in the brains of those who actually played it. Mental rehearsal activated the same motor circuits as actual rehearsal, with the same result: the increased activation caused an expansion of that bit of the motor cortex.

"Mental practice resulted in a similar reorganization" of the brain, Pascual-Leone and colleagues later wrote. "Mental practice alone may be sufficient to promote the plastic modulation of neural circuits." That, by the way, should let people master a skill more quickly. If his results hold for other forms of movement (and there is reason to think they do), then mentally practicing a golf swing or a forward pass or a swimming turn would lead to mastery with less physical practice. More profoundly, however, the discovery was one more bit of evidence supporting the power of mental training to physically change the brain.

The Buddhist Brain

Through the many tragedies that have befallen the Tibetan people, the Dalai Lama has seen firsthand what he believes is the power of mind to transform the brain. He tells the story of Lopon-la, a monk he knew in Lhasa before the Chinese invasion. Imprisoned by the Chinese for eighteen years, Lopon-la fled to India after he was finally freed. Twenty years after that, the Dalai Lama saw him again. "He seemed the same," the Dalai Lama told his friend Victor Chan. "His mind still sharp after so many years in prison. He was still the same gentle monk. . . . They tortured him many times in prison. I asked him whether he was ever afraid. Lopon-la then told me, 'Yes, there was one thing I was afraid of. I was afraid I may lose compassion for the Chinese.' I was very moved by this, and also very inspired. . . . Forgiveness helped him in prison. Because of forgiveness, his bad experience with Chinese not get worse. Mentally and emotionally, he didn't suffer too much."

The Mind and Life meetings typically include a philosopher in addition to scientists and Buddhist scholars, and in 2004, that role was filled by Evan Thompson. After earning an undergraduate degree in Asian studies at

Amherst College, Thompson studied in Paris with neuroscientist Francisco Varela, a founder of the Mind and Life Institute, and coauthored a book, *The Embodied Mind,* with him. Now at Canada's University of York, Thompson works in the areas of cognitive science and philosophy of mind, trying to "deepen our understanding of human experience by integrating" the two.

As the five scientists sat with the Dalai Lama, Thompson zeroed in on the Buddhist view of mind and brain, one of the deepest schisms between the Buddhist and science sides of the room. Buddhism distinguishes between the familiar world of matter or physical things, on the one hand, and mind and subjective experiences such as thoughts, sensory perceptions, and emotions, on the other. Mind "enjoys a status separate from the material world," argues the Dalai Lama. "From the Buddhist perspective, the mental realm cannot be reduced to the world of matter, though it may depend upon that world to function." As far as the scientists were concerned, however, the proposition that the mind is some ethereal, incorporeal, even spooky entity that can act back on the brain to alter its physical or chemical structure is at best quaint. They were no more sympathetic to it than was the neurosurgeon with whom the Dalai Lama raised the possibility of the mind's acting back on the brain. As Thompson politely noted, "In Western science, there is a reaction against that kind of dualistic view. The stumbling block from science's perspective has been how to understand, conceptually, how there could be any kind of interaction between an autonomous consciousness, assuming this is what mind is, and the brain. So what I would like to ask is, from the Buddhist point of view, how is the relationship accounted for? How does something with no corporeality act on something plainly physical?"

After a whispered conversation with the Dalai Lama, Thupten Jinpa gave it a try. "There are really two questions here from the Buddhist point of view," he said. "One is, there is a category of mental states, such as sensory experiences, which in the Buddhist point of view are completely dependent and contingent upon the physical body. Each of these sensory experiences has its own physical basis, its own sense organ. But these sense organs are not the external physical organs that we see. In the Buddhist texts, they are referred to as the refined sense organs. They are said to be beyond the scope of human visibility. You can't see them with the naked eye. So His Holiness was speculating that brain neurons could be understood as these refined sense organs, which serve as the basis for the arising of the sensory experience. What is very evident, however, is that sensory experiences are contingent upon the sense organs. So when a sensory experience such as a visual perception arises, there is an understanding that it is an outcome of a multiplicity of factors and conditions, including the sense organs."

The more interesting mental states, however, include those such as attention and compassion, both of which Buddhism believes can be cultivated through mental training. If Western science insists that all mental states are actually brain states, then the question becomes, how can mental training act back on the brain so the brain is more likely to generate attention and compassion? Or as Thompson put it, "How can sustained, voluntary mental activity affect the brain? How can it be causally efficacious at the neural level? How do we conceptualize mental-to-physical causation—downward causation—in which activity at a higher level can bring about effects at a lower level?"

The Dalai Lama earnestly asked Jinpa in Tibetan, "How can a mental state act upon matter?"

Buddhism not only has no trouble with this possibility, it positively embraces it. "There's a particular form of meditation in which you focus on the quintessences of different elements, the very essence of earth or water or fire, and you kind of capture that essence with your mind," said Alan Wallace. Wallace was, with Jinpa, serving as the Dalai Lama's English interpreter, a role he has played at most of the Mind and Life meetings. In 1980, Wallace had spent five months meditating in the hills above Dharamsala after studying Tibetan Buddhism for ten years in India and Switzerland. Wallace became a student of the Dalai Lama in the early 1970s and received monastic ordination from him in 1975. Four years later, the Dalai Lama asked Wallace to serve as his interpreter.

"You capture the essence of water element, or fluidity, and then you may actually transform something—something earthen, perhaps—into the water by the power of your mind," Wallace continued. "This is a widely accepted fact of meditative experience in multiple Buddhist schools. But His Holiness was asking, well, in that kind of projected water, what is it that actually transforms into water? What may actually happen here is that by the power of *samadhi*—meditative concentration—you manipulate earth element, for example, so it takes on the guise of water element. And the reason is that in the Buddhist atomic theory, you have molecules that are composed of eight particles, earth, water, fire and air, and the derivative elements. So each molecule has each of the four elements, which confer solidity, fluidity, heat, and motility. Each one is there. The meditator will then, by projecting, by manipulating these molecules, draw the water element out of something that was previously manifesting dominantly as earth. He suppresses that and draws out from it the water element.

"His Holiness heard this explanation and said that's pretty nifty."

What the Dalai Lama was interested in, he told Jinpa in Tibetan, "is the intersection of the mental processes and the physical processes that serve as the basis for the mental experiences. What seems to be very obvious is that, at the gross level of mind, the relationship between mental and physical is very tight. But at a subtle level, from the Buddhist point of view, there will be a state of consciousness which will be autonomous"—not dependent on brain function.

"The most explicit one is called the Clear Light of Death," Alan Wallace offered. "It's a dimension of consciousness that manifests in normal people only at the time of death, at the very concluding stages of the dying process. And that level is said to be not contingent upon the human organism. It is autonomous from the embodied brain. This is where Buddhism just differs from modern neuroscience's view that all mental processes are functions of the brain. In Buddhism, anger, joy, fear, and so forth are said to emerge not from the brain but from more and more subtle levels of consciousness."

Even under circumstances significantly less extreme than death, Buddhist adepts testify to the power of mind to transform brain. One of the most accomplished Buddhist meditators at the 2004 meeting was Matthieu Ricard. He was born into a family of French intellectuals: his father is one of France's leading philosophers and political theorists and one of the forty "immortals" of the Académie Française, his mother is an artist, and his godfather was the Russian mystic G. I. Gurdjieff. As a young man, Ricard was entranced by a 1966 documentary film made by one of his mother's friends, *The Message of the Tibetans.* Soon after seeing it, he decamped to India, intent on meeting some of the meditation masters whose stories the film recounted. In 1967, he met one of those masters, Kangyur Rinpoche, and lived with him for three weeks before returning to university in France. Ricard earned a doctorate in biology from the Institut Pasteur in Paris, going on to work with some of the greatest geneticists of the time. But his mind kept returning to the Tibetan masters. In 1981, he became a Buddhist monk and ever since has devoted his life to meditation practice, scholarship, and his "day job," working at the Shechen Monastery in Nepal and bringing health and education services to the impoverished villagers of that beleaguered nation. He serves as the Dalai Lama's French interpreter.

"If you take the example of a practitioner during retreat, nothing changes in the environment except, perhaps, more or less clouds through the window," Ricard said. "From morning till evening, the person will go through a series of exercises. It could be visualization. It could be training the mind to react in different ways to emotional arisings. There is not any reaction [visible to an observer]. Nothing. It is very blank. Yet, for hours and hours, there will be a constant transformation, enrichment, dealing with momentary emotions and thoughts that will transform into moods and perhaps, after months and years, into traits. This is a very rich experience, and with time, this leads to more permanent changes."

As adamantly as they reject dualism, scientists are nevertheless beginning to appreciate the causal power of purely internal mental processes to give rise to a biological effect. That intrigued the Buddhists, with Alan Wallace suggesting that the discovery of the power of thought to alter the brain—for that is what Schwartz found with his OCD patients, Segal and Mayberg with their depressed patients, and Pascual-Leone with his virtual piano players—"calls for scientific research into these different strata of consciousness that does not just assume they're all dependent upon the brain."

"From the scientific perspective," said Richie Davidson, "the honest answer is that we don't know" how mental processes influence the physical brain. "The same is true from the Buddhist perspective," Jinpa said to laughter.

Attention Must Be Paid

Even without knowing exactly how mind influences brain, neuroscientists have evidence that it somehow involves paying attention. Pascual-Leone's mental pianists, Schwartz's OCD patients, and Segal and Mayberg's depressed patients all focused intently. Because a conscious, awake mind is bombarded by countless bits of sensory information every second, billions of neurons are tickled all the time. In your visual cortex, for instance, millions of neurons are registering the images of the letters on this page, as well as the white space between letters. Presumably, you are not really seeing the white spaces, because you are not paying attention to them as you are the black lines and curves. Without attention, information that our senses take in—what we see and hear, feel, smell, and taste—literally does not register in the mind. It may not be stored even briefly in memory. What you see is determined by what you pay attention to.

How the brain manages this became clear only in the first years of the twenty-first century. Basically, neurons compete. Imagine that you are standing on the edge of a beach where sunbathers are jammed towel-to-towel. You scan the sand for friends you are supposed to meet. Images enter your retina and zip back to your visual cortex in the form of electrical signals. Which ones register is determined by the strength of the signal (perhaps your friends are all wearing fuchsia bathing suits), by its novelty (we tend to pick out, say, the group flying a big balloon over their towel), by its strong associations (in a crowd scene, you can generally pick out someone you know), or—and this is what matters for our purposes—by attention. If your brain is carrying out the job of "looking for friends," it enhances neuronal responses to the target images. The electrical signal associated with the target is stronger than the signal corresponding to nontarget images. Paying attention physically damps down activity in neurons other than those involved in focusing on the target of your attention.

Everything we see has a multitude of attributes, of course, from motion to shape to color. Different bits of the visual cortex, it turns out, specialize in each trait. Neurons that process shape have nothing to do with color, and vice versa, and neurons that process motion are an entirely different bunch. Attention can strengthen the activity of one bunch compared to another. If monkeys are trained to look for the color of an object on a screen, neurons in the visual cortex that respond to color become more active. When monkeys are trained to notice the direction an object is moving, neurons that process directional movement become more active. In people, paying attention to faces increases activity in the neurons that specialize in scanning and analyzing faces. Paying attention to color turns up the activity of neurons that process and register color. Paying attention to motion turns up the activity of neurons that process and register motion. The intensity of activity in a circuit that specializes in a particular visual task is amplified by the mental act of paying attention to what that circuit specializes in. Remember, the visual information reaching the brain hasn't changed. What has changed is what the monkey, or the person, is paying attention to. Attention, then, pumps up neuronal activity. Attention is real, in the sense that it takes a physical form capable of affecting the physical activity of the brain.

Attention is also, as it happens, indispensable for neuroplasticity. Nowhere was that shown more dramatically than in one of Mike Merzenich's experiments with monkeys. The scientists rigged up a device that tapped the animals' fingers one hundred minutes a day every day for six weeks. At the same time as this bizarre dance was playing on their fingers, the monkeys listened to sounds over headphones. Some of the monkeys were taught, pay attention to what you feel on your fingers, such as when the rhythm changes, because if you indicate when it changes, we'll reward you with a sip of juice; don't pay attention to the sounds. Other monkeys were taught, pay attention to the sound, and if you indicate when it changes, you'll get juice. At the end of six weeks, the scientists compared the monkeys' brains. Let me underline that every monkey, whether trained to pay attention to what it was hearing or what it was feeling on its fingers, had the exact same physical experience—sounds coming in through headphones plus taps on its fingers. The only thing that made one monkey different from another was what it paid attention to.

Usually, when a particular spot on the skin suddenly begins receiving unusual amounts of stimulation, its representation in the somatosensory cortex expands. That was what Mike Merzenich discovered in his monkeys. But when the monkeys paid attention to what they heard rather than to what they felt, there was no change in their somatosensory cortex—no expansion of the region that handles input from the finger feeling the flutter. Yet the only difference between the monkeys whose brain had changed after tactile stimulation and monkeys whose brain remained the same after identical stimulation is that the former paid attention to the taps. Attention had taken the exact same physical input, the feeling of taps on a finger, and transformed it from something that had no more power to alter the brain than a mote of dust has to alter a bronze statue into something that took the material stuff of the brain and treated it like modeling clay, stretching it out in one place and smooshing it together somewhere else.

"If you look at neurons in the part of the brain that represents the fingers, in those monkeys that paid attention to the sounds, even though their fingers were stimulated, this finger region didn't change at all," Helen Neville told the Dalai Lama. "All that stimulation made no difference because they weren't paying attention to it." But in monkeys that did pay attention to the fluttering on their fingers, their state of mind made a huge difference: the amount of cortical area devoted to the fingers increased two- to threefold.

The same thing held true for listening. In the monkeys who paid attention to the sounds, the region of their auditory cortex that processes the frequency they heard increased. But in monkeys who heard the exact same sounds but who paid attention to the finger flutters, their auditory cortex showed no change. "It's a beautiful experiment because it's showing the pure effect of attention," Neville said. "The stimulation was the same. The only thing that was different was what the monkeys were paying attention to. It's showing that attention is very necessary for neuroplasticity."

Looking back on the discovery of the importance of attention in neuroplasticity, Merzenich and a colleague wrote in 1996, "The pattern of activity of neurons in sensory areas can be altered by patterns of attention. . . . Experience coupled with attention leads to physical changes in the structure and future functioning of the nervous system. This leaves us with a clear physiological fact . . . moment by moment we choose and sculpt how our ever-changing minds will work, we choose who we will be the next moment in a very real sense, and these choices are left embossed in physical form on our material selves." Buddhism had long taught that mental training, in which focused attention is key, can alter the mind. Merzenich's monkeys showed there was something to this.

Neville, too, has demonstrated the physical reality of attention. "If I tell you to sit here and read this book, and pay attention to it, and at the same time, I play sounds over a speaker, then the brain has a very tiny neural response to the sound," she told the Dalai Lama. "But then if I say, put the book away and listen to the sounds and detect every time the frequency changes, then you get a much more powerful signal in the auditory cortex.

This suggests that attention works like a gate, to open and let more neural information in. People think attention is some kind of a psychological construct, but you can touch it. It has an anatomy, a physiology, and a chemistry."

"In the Buddhist epistemological texts, specific distinctions are made between attentive hearing—when you are paying attention—and inattentive hearing," said Jinpa.

"Attentional training is so important in Buddhism, and it also is recognized to be very important by scientists," Richie Davidson added. "In many ways, attentional training can be thought of as the gateway to plasticity."

Attention seems to develop over the course of many years, Neville added. Drawn-out development is the mark of a brain system that displays high levels of neuroplasticity. Attention should therefore be trainable, just as the long course of development of the auditory cortex makes it trainable with inputs such as Fast ForWord for dyslexic children. "The ability to pay attention selectively, ignoring distractions, develops throughout childhood at least until adolescence," Neville said. "So does the ability to shift attention quickly and efficiently." Indeed, the strength of brain signals associated with the perception of something to which you are *not* paying attention decreases with age, reflecting greater ability to suppress unattended inputs.

As the afternoon session with the Dalai Lama drew to a close, the scientists and Buddhists agreed to leave unresolved whether or not volition, effort, attention, and other mental states qua mental states can physically affect the brain or whether only the brain events—electrical activity, neurochemicals being released from this neuron and taken up by that one—that correspond to the mental states do. In practical terms, whether the mind acts directly on the brain to change it, or whether the electrical signals jumping from neuron to neuron do so, doesn't really matter. With or without a physical intermediary, it is becoming clear that thought, meditation, and other manifestations of mind can alter the brain, sometimes in an enduring way.

Chapter 7

Nature through Nurture

Turning On Genes in the Brain

T he fall of the totalitarian regimes in the former Soviet empire in the late 1980s revealed seemingly unending horrors that had been hidden from the outside world by the Iron Curtain. But few were as heartrending as the plight of Romanian orphans. Victims of dictator Nicolae Ceausescu's decree that every woman bear at least five children, under penalty of steep fines, the children had been abandoned by impoverished or overwhelmed parents to the care of state institutions, which, the government assured the public, would take good care of Romania's future. But when Western scientists, government officials, and humanitarians toured some of the orphanages in 1990, just after Ceausescu was toppled from power and executed, they saw conditions that they thought had been left behind in Dickens's era.

Babies spent eighteen to twenty hours a day lying in their cribs with little to engage their eyes and not even much to hear, for the children hardly even cried and the (misnamed) caretakers almost never talked to them, let alone played with them. They picked up the children only to move them. Children who should have been toddlers had rarely set foot outside their cribs and could hardly walk. Older children had never learned to play. An outpouring of sympathy led hundreds of parents in North America and elsewhere to adopt Romanian orphans. And with that, an experiment on the effects of early deprivation, and its reversibility, was under way.

Psychologists and other experts in child development studied the children in their new homes. Some expected the neglect the children suffered in infancy to vanish under the love and caring of their adoptive families, at least for those children adopted at a young enough age. Others wondered whether the years of deprivation would leave a lasting mark.

Almost all the orphanage children were developmentally delayed, as measured by tests of cognition. Many made rapid progress, with those adopted at the youngest ages indeed doing the best. Later adoptees tended to remain slow learners. It was their social and emotional development, however, that marked the children most deeply. They were, for the most part, withdrawn and anxious, engaging in repetitive movements such as rocking back and forth or staring mutely and expressionlessly at their hands. They avoided other children. Even three years after adoption, some orphanage children had not shaken their past. They had trouble getting along with others, and the more years they had spent in an orphanage, the more behavior problems they had. Although about one-third of the children had no serious problems, another 30 percent had an IQ below 85, serious behavior problems, emotional attachments weaker than 95 percent of children in the general population, and persistent stereotyped behaviors such as rocking. Another 35 percent had one or two of the four problems. One thing almost all the adoptive parents noticed was that these children did not form close, secure emotional attachments to their mothers. By the time the children were six, a 2004 study of Romanian children adopted by British families concluded, there were "major persistent deficits in a substantial minority" of them. The scientists attributed that to "some form of early biological programming or neural damage stemming from institutional deprivation."

It may seem a long way from Romania's abandoned children to the rats in cages at McGill University in Montreal. But neuroscientist Michael Meaney begs to differ.

A Mother's Experience

On this morning of the Mind and Life meeting, Meaney settled into the armchair beside the Dalai Lama and reached for something beside him on the floor. "To a religious icon around the world, I bring a small icon that is somewhat religious from my own country," he began, unfolding the gift. "This is a Team Canada hockey jersey."

As the laughter settled down, Meaney launched into his story. Since the 1980s, he and his colleagues at McGill University have been documenting how the behavior of mother rats affects their offspring. That may seem fairly pedestrian, but the work targets one of the most vexing questions in human development: how much of what we become reflects the genes we inherited from our parents and how much reflects the environment in which we grew up. The nature/nurture debate has a long and politically tinged history, since asserting that genes are the strongest influence on how people turn out—their intelligence, their personality, their character, their kindness—is tantamount to minimizing the power of parents or schools or the cultural surround to shape these traits. But the 1990s brought evidence that nurture in the form of the experiences we have and the environment in which we live acts back on nature in the form of an organism's genes.

Consider the water flea, Meaney invited the Dalai Lama. In this tiny aquatic species, some individuals have a long and spiny tail as well as a helmet; others lack this impressive armamentarium. That may seem no more surprising than the statement that some people have type A blood and others do not, due to different genes for blood type. But the odd thing about water fleas is that two individuals with identical genetic material can be opposites when it comes to tails and helmets. And that is something you do not see with blood types. If two people have identical blood-type *genes,* they darn well have identical blood types.

If you put a young water flea in an aquarium in which there are no predators, Meaney explained, it will remain unarmed, as it were, with neither helmet nor spiny tail. But if you put its genetically identical clone into an aquarium to which you have added the chemical odor of a fish that regards water fleas as a nice hors d'oeuvre, the flea grows a helmet and a long and spiny tail. "That has all occurred because of exposure of the animal to an environmental signal, the perception of a threat," said Meaney. But nurture is not finished with the water flea. If you move the armored flea into an aquarium free of the odor of predators, its defensive accoutrements recede.

So far, the story is not too surprising. Growing a helmet and scary tail doesn't seem all that different from, say, a yak's growing a shaggier coat in response to a frigid spell. "But what is fascinating about this, and what makes it relevant for our discussion, is that if these are female water fleas, and if you move them to an aquarium in which there is no predator and allow them to lay their eggs, what you find is that offspring born to mothers who earlier in life had seen or smelled a predator have a larger helmet, even though the offspring had never seen or smelled a predator," Meaney explained. "The experience of the mother is passed on to the offspring."

It is a process that nature has used more than once. Skink lizards, which snakes find quite appetizing, have a higher likelihood of winding up as lunch if they are small, have short tails, and react too slowly to the smell of the snake. If a mother lizard is exposed to the smell of a snake, even if she lays her eggs in a snake-free environment, her offspring grow up to be large, with long tails, and to react more strongly to snake odors than those whose mothers had never smelled a snake. For both the water flea and the skink lizard, "the mother's environment influences the activation of defensive responses in the offspring," said Meaney. "I would suggest that these same processes may occur in mammals and in humans."

Rat: Handle with Care

To figure out how maternal behavior affects rat pups, Meaney dug up some old studies. In the late 1950s and early 1960s, psychologists noticed that if newborn laboratory rats are removed from their cage every day for the first twenty-one days of their lives, the result is a remarkable lifelong change in their behavior and disposition. In a typical experiment, scientists would remove newborn pups from their mothers and place them in a small container. After fifteen minutes or so, the newborns would be returned to their mothers—and the whole thing reprised the following morning.

Although the change in the rats' routine lasted just a few minutes, scientists began noticing that it had effects that lasted a lifetime. When the "handled" rats grew up, their stress response was under much greater control than that of rats that had not been handled. When the frequently handled rats were stressed, such as by an electrical shock, they released the expected burst of stress hormones called glucocorticoids, which prime the body for flight or fight. But the release amounted to no more than a trickle. In contrast, rats that scientists had not handled as newborns released a veritable flood of stress hormones when subjected to an identical stress. The differences lasted until the rats were two years old, which for this creature is downright geriatric. Even though the only difference between the rats was whether they had been handled for a mere fifteen minutes daily in infancy, the "handling effect" had resulted in lifelong mellowness: the rats did not jump out of their skins when they experienced a stressor. "Rats that have been handled more as newborns are more exploratory, less fearful, and less reactive to stress when they are adults," says Stanford University biologist Robert Sapolsky, who studies the neurobiology of the stress response.

Over the years, scientists doggedly worked out the biochemistry behind the handling effect. In 1989, Meaney and his colleagues found that handled rats are much more sensitive to the effects of those stress hormones, glucocorticoids, than not-handled rats are. Glucocorticoids have what is called a negative-feedback loop, in which a lot of something causes less of it to be produced and a little of something results in more of it being produced. Heat and furnaces constitute a simple negative-feedback loop. When heat fills a house, then (assuming the thermostat is working) production of more heat tapers off. So it is with glucocorticoids. When the body is awash in them, it produces fewer of them. In handled rats, Meaney found, the negative-feedback loop is way more sensitive than it is in not-handled rats. Just a drip of glucocorticoid in the former, and production of more glucocorticoid plummets. It was as if the rats' stress thermostat were set on fifty-five degrees. As soon as the first wave of heat emanates from the radiator, the furnace clicks off. Thanks to this negative-feedback loop, the stress response dies down.

Meaney even figured out how the "stress thermostat" gets set so low. In the handled rats, there is a profusion of "receptors" for glucocorticoid in the little guys' brains, in the region called the hippocampus. Receptors do as their name says, acting as molecular docking stations for glucocorticoid.

When a glucocorticoid molecule wanders by, the receptor embraces it and takes it inside. There, the glucocorticoid triggers a cascade of biochemical reactions, which add up to the fight-or-flight response. "Receptors interpret signals from outside the cell," Meaney explained to the Dalai Lama. "It is, if you will, the way the cell hears what's going on around it. And so the more receptors you have, the more sensitive is the detection of that signal."

"It's like how many antennae you have," said Jinpa.

In the heat-and-thermostat analogy, it would be like having a dozen thermostats in every room of your house. As soon as one catches the slightest hint of warmth, it signals the furnace to shut down. The more thermostats you have, the more likely it is that one will sense a burst of heat, if only from proximity to a radiator. So it is in the rats' brains. With a blooming profusion of glucocorticoid receptors, just a few stray molecules of glucocorticoid flowing through the hippocampus are sufficient to shut down production of this hormone. With numerous receptors the message filters down to the hypothalamus, which sends out orders to release more glucocorticoid: we're getting inside these cells just fine, no need to keep releasing more. The reverse also holds. If the hippocampus has a paucity of glucocorticoid receptors, a very different message filters down: very few of us are getting inside these cells, so you better send up reinforcements. The "Make stress hormones!" signal remains at a high level.

This feedback loop is a clever adaptation, in evolutionary terms. As long as sufficient glucocorticoids are getting into cells of the hippocampus, thanks to an abundance of glucocorticoid receptors, there is no need to flood the brain with stress hormones; the mission of getting enough glucocorticoids into cells of the hippocampus has been accomplished. Conversely, if there is a dearth of glucocorticoid receptors, then in order to respond to a stressor in a lifesaving way, it's a good idea to flood the hippocampus with glucocorticoids. That way, at least some of them will get into the cells.

Licking and Grooming

If lifelong differences in rats' stress response, and permanent differences in their brains, seem like an awfully extensive consequence of being handled for just a few minutes every day, well, Meaney thought so, too. After all, the only thing different about the handled and the not-handled rats was being plopped into a container and back to their natal cage. That seemed too inconsequential and fleeting to have such strong and enduring effects. But a number of scientists, going back to the 1960s, had speculated that mother rats treat handled pups differently than not-handled pups. That is, although the pups were handled for mere seconds, and were away from mom for just fifteen minutes, when she got them back, she treated them differently than pups that never left the cage.

And that is what, in the mid-1990s, Meaney set out to investigate. Every day for newborn rats' first twelve days of life, he or a colleague would scoop up babies from their natal cage, park them in a container for fifteen minutes, and then return them to mom . . . and wait to see what she did. "The way we study individual differences in mother/pup interaction is, we watch," Meaney told the Dalai Lama. "We do this eight hours every day for the first twelve days after they're born. It's a perfect activity for long Canadian winters."

But not an activity that offered much opportunity for daydreaming. The scientists "scored" the behavior of each mother once every four minutes, fifteen times an hour for each of the eight hours for each of the twelve days, noting whether she was nursing the pups or licking them or grooming them or ignoring them. (Twelve days is the so-called critical period when handling had been shown to affect a rat's stress system and all the complicated balances of glucocorticoid receptors and other hormones that go into it.) Some rat mothers conscientiously licked and groomed their newborns. Other mothers took a paws-off approach to maternal responsibility, nursing the pups but doing little else.

"What you see when you look at this behavior for a long time is that while all mothers lick and groom their pups, some mothers do it much less than others," Meaney said. A pattern emerged. The mothers of handled pups, he reported in 1997, frequently gather up their squirming brood and tuck them under them, licking and grooming the pups. And that was the solution to the mystery. It was not just that infant rats had been handled by scientists. This handling caused the rats' mothers to treat them differently when they returned to the cage, licking and grooming them madly as if to make up for lost time. (If you were wondering what it is about the handled pups that makes mom lick and groom them so much, it's this: when a baby rat is plucked from its nice warm nest and dropped into a container, it emits ultrasonic vocalizations. Humans can't hear them. Mother rat can. And she responds the way a human mother does to a wailing baby.) This, then, is what Meaney focused on: how maternal behavior affects what a rat becomes.

It is a natural fact of the rat world that some mothers are inclined to lick and groom their pups assiduously, and others are, shall we say, more stand-offish. This difference in maternal behavior is independent of whether her pups have been handled and scooped up by meddling scientists. In a labful of litters, none of whose pups have been handled, some rat mothers lick and groom their pups a great deal, others, less so. "The variability is sub-stantial," Meaney explained to the Dalai Lama. "So we took mothers who lick at very low rates and mothers who lick at very high rates, and studied their pups as adults. At this stage, we simply correlated individual differ-ences in maternal care in the first week of life to the pups' response to stress in adulthood. What we found is that this response is altered by the level of licking and grooming the pup received."

Mellow Rats

Rat pups that had been attentively licked and groomed as newborns by their mothers had a muted response to stress, Meaney reported in 1997. They were curious, mellow little bundles of well-adjusted rodenthood. They explored new environments and withstood stress. In contrast, pups reared by neglectful mothers grew up into fearful, stressed-out, neurotic wrecks. They jumped out of their skins at the slightest stress, startled easily, were fearful in unfamiliar surroundings, reacted to strange environments by freezing in fright, showed precious little inclination to explore, and had more stress hormones coursing through their veins than a drunk does gin. "The greater the frequency of maternal licking and grooming during infancy, the lower the response to stress in adulthood," Meaney and his colleagues reported.

The differences extended to the rats' behavior when they became moth-ers themselves. Those raised by inattentive mothers were just as neglectful of their own pups, perpetuating the cycle of maternal neglect and childhood angst. The offspring of attentive mothers dutifully licked and groomed their own pups. When these grandchild pups became adults, the results reprised what a long line of studies had found about the effects of maternal behavior: fearful mothers beget fearful, easily stressed offspring. (Father rats have nothing to do with raising pups.) "You do become your mother," said Meaney to the Dalai Lama, adding with a smile that this statement always "makes shudders go through the room."

This is a "naturally occurring plasticity," Meaney said. It seems to be nature's way of sculpting animals best equipped for the world in which they will live. Since most animals spend their adult lives in an environment very similar to the one they were born into, "programming" the response to stress makes sense. A jumpy, quick-to-startle mother living in a dangerous environment is inattentive to her pups, setting in motion the cascade that reduces the number of glucocorticoid receptors in the brain and results in a jumpy, quick-to-startle offspring—which is just right in a threatening, dangerous, resource-poor world. A mellow, laid-back mother living a sheltered existence is all over her pups, licking and grooming them, setting in motion the cascade that leads to a profusion of glucocorticoid receptors in the brain and results in a mellow, laid-back offspring—a reasonable way to be in a safe, resource-rich world.

You might say, so what? Everyone knows how powerful genetic inheritance is. Surely it is no surprise that rat mothers that are high-strung and standoffish themselves, neglecting their newborns, have offspring that grow up to be the same way. In an age smitten with genetic determinism, it would be only natural to presume that what Meaney was seeing was the result of inherited genes. That is, some rats carry genes that cause them to be high-strung and fearful, as well as (in the case of females) neglectful mothers. They pass those genes to their offspring, which grow up to be high-strung and fearful and neglectful mothers themselves.

The way to test that possibility was obvious: take pups born to less-responsive, less-attentive mothers and give them to conscientious foster mothers to raise, and take pups born to attentive mothers and give them to neglectful mothers to raise. This sort of adoption study neatly separates the effects of genes from the effects of environment, of nature from nurture. When Meaney did just this, he found that genes are not destiny. Once the rats grew up, those born to inattentive, low-licking mothers but adopted and reared by dutiful, high-licking mothers were indistinguishable from the biological offspring of high-licking, attentive mothers. They were significantly less fearful when put in unfamiliar surroundings and were as able to withstand stress as the rats born to and reared by attentive mothers. The reverse also held: rats born to attentive, conscientious mothers but reared by neglectful, low-licking adoptive mothers grew into neurotic, stressed-out adults.

The reason, as his rodent adoption agency showed, was once again the number of glucocorticoid receptors in the rats' brains. The brains of rats born to neglectful mothers but raised by high-licking, attentive ones had as many glucocorticoid receptors as rats both born to and raised by high-licking mothers. Similarly, rats born to attentive, high-licking mothers but raised by neglectful, low-licking mothers had glucocorticoid receptors typical of rats both born to and raised by low-licking, inattentive mothers, Meaney and his colleagues reported in 1999. Whatever mellow tendency the rats born to attentive, well-adjusted mothers might have inherited was swamped by the effect of rearing: the lack of maternal attention translated into fewer glucocorticoid receptors in the hippocampus and a souped-up physiological reaction to stressful events. Birth mother had no effect on the offspring's glucocorticoid receptors. What mattered was who raised them, and how. Attentive mom, lots of receptors and muted stress response; inattentive mom, few receptors and hair-trigger stress response.

The mother rats literally groom their offspring to have the adult temperaments and mothering styles they do. Young rats inherit maternal *behavior*. No matter what kind of mother a pup is born to, if it is reared— adopted—by a high-licking mother, it grows up to behave that way with its own pups. Even rats born to low-licking mothers become high-licking mothers if they are reared by one.

"So that means it's not fixed," the Dalai Lama interjected.

"It is definitely not fixed," Meaney said emphatically. It is maternal behavior toward the offspring over the course of weeks, not maternal genes transmitted to the offspring through the random process of conception, that permanently alters the offspring's response to stress.

Since one of the goals of this experiment was to investigate the transmission of maternal behavior across generations, the scientists let some of the female adoptees mate and give birth, to see what kind of mothers they made. The new mothers who had themselves been born to inattentive mothers but reared by high-licking and high-grooming mothers resembled their adoptive mother in maternal behavior more than their biological mother. In fact, they were indistinguishable from female rats born to and reared by high-licking and high-grooming mothers. In contrast, females born to attentive mothers but reared by inattentive ones were as neglectful and inattentive as their own (adoptive) mothers had been. And thus, the cycle was perpetuated, with the next generation reared by inattentive mothers growing into fearful, stressed-out adults who neglected their offspring, and the next generation reared by attentive mothers growing into well-adjusted, mellow adults who cared attentively for their own litters.

The Dalai Lama wondered just what it is about licking and grooming that has such an effect on the pups. Is it purely a physical process of the contact of the mother's tongue with the body of the infant pup? Something chemical, perhaps due to the saliva touching the skin? Is affection necessary?

"If you look at areas of the brain that are activated by licking in the pup, they include areas that are activated when, for example, a normal animal experiences a pleasurable event," said Meaney. "It's reasonable to suspect that the pup's experience of licking goes beyond simply a touch."

"So it's not just a function of a transfer of molecules in the saliva," Jinpa translated.

"No," said Meaney. "The evidence would suggest that the touch and the interpretation of that sensory experience is what's critical."

"It would be interesting to see whether the mental component from the mother is really crucial or whether you can have some kind of robotic device that would give a licking stimulation, a grooming stimulation, and get the same results," said Alan Wallace. "This is the essence of what His Holiness is getting at."

Inheriting Behavior

"The critical question was, how are these nongenetic maternal effects not only sustained over the lifetime of the offspring but passed down through generations?" Meaney continued. To find out, he and his colleagues began meticulously measuring the activity of the gene that produces the gluco-corticoid receptor in the hippocampus. "What you find is that in the hip-pocampus of adult rats, the gene is about twice as active in pups reared by a high-licking mother as in those reared by a low-licking mother," he ex-plained. "So the gene produces more receptors." The more receptors, of course, the mellower the rats. "What these studies suggest is that the quality of maternal care alters the activity of a specific gene in a particular brain region, which then influences the way the offspring, once they reach adulthood, respond to stress," Meaney told the Dalai Lama.

Just a few months before he sat in Dharamsala, Meaney had discovered precisely how maternal care influences the activity of the gene that pro-duces the glucocorticoid receptor. A mother's licking causes an increase in a molecule, called a transcription factor, that turns up production of the glucocorticoid receptors in the hippocampus. "It actually seems to be a fairly decent explanation of how mother's licking can increase the produc-tion of glucocorticoid receptors," he told the Dalai Lama. "Offspring that are reared by high-licking mothers produce more transcription factor. The transcription factor causes the pup's brain to produce more glucocorticoid receptors."

Score another point for nurture over nature. The genes of the mellow rats are identical to the genes of the neurotic rats, at least in terms of how genetics traditionally defines "identical"—the sequence of molecules that were the holy grail of the Human Genome Project. But this sequence does not represent nature's orders. It's more like a suggestion. Depending on what sort of world a creature finds itself in, that sequence might be silenced or amplified, its music played or muted, with diametrically different effects on behavior and temperament.

"Genes can be silent, or they can be very active," Meaney explained to the Dalai Lama. "What determines the activity of the gene is the environ-ment. And that's what is modified by parental care: the chemical environ-ment in which the gene functions. In the nature/nurture debate, people have long suspected that the environment somehow regulates the activity of genes. The question has always been, how? It took four years, but we've now shown that maternal care alters the activity of the gene in the brains of their offspring. And that influences the way their children respond to stress." As a result of alterations in gene expression, he continued, "the influence of parents can persist over the life span of the child. This plasticity doesn't involve connections between neurons. The modifications occur at the level of the gene itself. If you were reared by a low-licking mother, the glucocorticoid-receptor gene is always silenced. If you were reared by a high-licking mother, it is rarely silenced. That means we can talk about creating an environment that will affect the DNA and thus the way the animal responds to stress."

Mothers and fathers pass traits to their children in two ways. The first, of course, is through genes in the sperm and egg from which the child develops, the "nature" part of the nurture/nature dichotomy. The second way is through behavior. For as long as scientists have been studying this social transmission of traits, they have assumed that it occurs by children's consciously or unconsciously modeling themselves after their parents, adopting (or rejecting) the parent's love of baseball or adherence to a particular faith, his generosity or patience, her values or personality. Now it is clear that how parents behave can shape their offspring by altering the chemistry of genes. Meaney had discovered that a mother rat's behavior can alter gene expression in her offspring, with a long-term effect on behavior and temperament. Early experience can have consequences that last a lifetime. "That's an optimistic message, I think," Meaney said. "One can only imagine what type of events may give rise to alterations in the chemistry of the DNA. Maybe one day we'll speak of such changes in much the same terms as we speak of the changes that occur between the connections of neurons."

By now, it should be clear that little is forever, even the state of a gene that leads rats to be mellow and curious or neurotic and fearful. In fact, Meaney was able to reverse the on-off status of the gene for the glucocorticoid receptor by injecting rats with a chemical that silences it. Artificial though it is, that intervention is a crucial proof that the system that acts like a thermostat for rats' temperament is plastic, not set in stone (or DNA). But are there events in the real world of a rat—or of a child—that might lead to the same outcome, reversing the detrimental effects of early maternal neglect or the beneficial effects of maternal care?

Not surprisingly, the answer is yes. As mentioned above, female rats whose mother licked and groomed them attentively grow up to treat their own offspring the same way, as do female rats whose mother acted more in the lick-and-a-promise vein. You can think of it as the grandmother effect, in that the behavior of the grandmother rat affects her offspring in a way that causes them to treat their own pups in a way that elicits the very same behavior grandma showed. But when Meaney took adult female rats who had been raised by attentive mothers and who treated their own pups with the same attention and care, and exposed them to stress, it was as if he had given them a personality transplant. Mothers who were highly attentive to their first litter, licking and grooming them all the time, became the Joan Crawfords of rats. And their pups felt it: they produced few glucocorticoid receptors, becoming neurotic messes.

"The quality of the environment directly influences the quality of parental care," said Meaney. "Maternal care then influences the development of the brain, and in particular, it alters the development of particular genes. That lays the basis for differences in the way individuals respond to stress and care for their offspring. The message that emerges from our studies is that when you expose the parent to stress or to adversity, the offspring show increased responses to stress in adulthood."

Ironically, that may be the right way to go in the game of survival. Mother rats reduce their attentiveness to their pups under stressful conditions, such as when food is scarce. This laissez-faire behavior—minimal licking and grooming of their pups—results in jumpy, neurotic offspring. But is that necessarily a bad thing? In an era obsessed with stress reduction, it may seem so. But there are conditions in which a brain, and a body, awash in stress hormones has advantages over a mellower brain and body. Stress hormones increase fear and vigilance and make an animal better and quicker at learning what is dangerous or what signs precede a lethal threat (known as avoidance learning and fear conditioning, respectively). Rats born into a high-stress environment have a better chance of surviving if they are hypervigilant, jumping at the slightest sign of danger, and if they get an adrenaline rush when another rat looks at them cross-eyed. A high-stress environment also shapes mothers—to be low-licking. It's a perfect match: mothers worn down by stress neglect their pups, which, as a result, grow up to be hypervigilant and fearful, and therefore well suited to a tough world.

Nature has also arranged it so that the major stress hormones, gluco-corticoids and noradrenalin, protect animals against famine (food short-ages are a hallmark of high-stress environments). In animals deprived of food for long periods of time, stress hormones increase the availability of energy produced by the metabolism of fat and sugars, allowing them to survive longer—ideally, until food shows up again. True, chronically high levels of stress hormones also increase blood sugars and fats, and disrupt sleep and normal cognitive and emotional function, predisposing a rat, as well as a person, to chronic illnesses such as diabetes and cardiovascular disease. Bad as those are, however, they are arguably better than being chomped by a cat because you were not vigilant enough, or starving to death because your body could not switch to a thrifty, energy-conserving metabolism in the face of food shortages. Those tend to kill you before your time. A little diabetes or heart disease may or may not do you in, whether you are a man or a mouse. In a world of privation and scarcity, of dangers and threats, perhaps mellowness is a luxury neither a rat pup nor a child can afford. "Under conditions of poverty, animals that are most likely to survive are those who have an exaggerated stress response," Meaney said. "It then becomes important to reinterpret the behavior of the mother. Her low level of licking may be an adaptation, if you will, to prepare her off-spring for what she anticipates will be a very stressful environment. We think that natural selection has resulted in offspring that interpret mater-nal behavior—interpret it physiologically, not consciously—as an indica-tion of what environmental conditions they are likely to face after they leave the nest and are on their own."

Poverty Gets under Your Skin

What goes for rats also applies to people. Among boys growing up in poverty and in crime-ridden neighborhoods, those who do the best—who do not die young, who finish school, who avoid crime—are more fearful and more reactive to stress, just like rats reared by neglectful mothers. According to one interpretation, these boys are too timid and shy to become involved in gangs and criminal activity. And they have an acutely sensitive internal radar tipping them off to danger, whether from an abusive stepfather or a stranger.

Such findings suggest that, as Meaney puts it, poverty can get under your skin and inside your brain. It is well known that people from more advantaged social classes enjoy better mental and physical health than do those living in poverty and broken homes, where creditors are always at the door and homelessness lurks behind every overdue rent payment. Researchers have proposed various mechanisms to explain the association between socioeconomic status and health. A plausible one is stress. It has been shown that individuals lower in socioeconomic status report greater exposure to stressful events than better-off individuals. Poor children have higher levels of stress hormones than do better-off children, which may shape their brains in undesirable ways, leading to poorer cognition and emotional control.

"Specific forms of early family experience lead to alterations in the way children respond to stress," Meaney told the Dalai Lama. "Children who are exposed to abuse or neglect are more reactive to stressors. Pretty subtle variations within the normal range of parental care can alter development very dramatically. In rats, how the mother cares for her offspring can program their responses to stress for the rest of their lives, by affecting the expression of genes in brain regions that mediate responses to stress. We think that this provides a plausible explanation for how parental care influences how vulnerable or resistant to stress and the illnesses associated with stress the rats are over a whole lifetime."

This might explain the effects of lousy social and economic conditions. We have been talking about rats, but Meaney is interested in rats because he is interested in people. It has been well documented that adversity ratchets up parents' levels of anxiety. Worries about being unemployed, about losing housing, about where the next meal is coming from do nothing good for parental care. To the contrary. The anxiety and depression that trying conditions induce tend to make parents harsh and inconsistent disciplinarians, even neglectful and abusive. (This is not to say that all parents who live in poverty, in illness, or in dangerous conditions react this way.) This is precisely the kind of parenting that can enhance a child's stress reactivity, explains Meaney: "The anxiety of the parents is transmitted to the children." Being poor, jobless, or homeless induces a physiological stress response in adults, which is somehow transmitted to the children. Although that "somehow" remains to be worked out in detail, Meaney's two decades of studies on how maternal behavior in rats influences the temperament of their offspring points in one direction: parental behavior may alter the expression of genes in their children. In this way, says Meaney, "The effects of poverty on emotional and intellectual development in children are mediated by the parent."

To be sure, people are more complicated than rats. For lab animals that spend all their lives in a cage, the opportunities to be shaped by something other than the mother that rears them, and to a lesser extent by the siblings they grow up with, are pretty limited. Even children in the worst family situations, however, often have an escape hatch—a trusted teacher or clergyman, a youth counselor who takes them under his wing, a grandparent or other relative who at least partly makes up for the neglect they suffer from their mother and father.

The Dalai Lama wondered whether the effects of poverty and neglect are mediated at all by the context in which they occur. "For example, one could imagine a difference between the condition of poverty in a poor country where the sense of being poor is not so dramatic, as opposed to more affluent countries where people are generally quite affluent, giving poor families a much greater self-consciousness of being poor," Jinpa translated.

"The worst outcomes occur when you are very poor in a very rich country," Meaney agreed. "In countries where there is a great difference between the lowest wages and the highest wages, the poor have the worst health. People in countries where there isn't such a discrepancy have much better health, and live longer."

"His Holiness is wondering," Jinpa said, "whether, on this biochemical and brain level, there would be a difference between a child who is conceived willingly on the part of the mother and one who is conceived unwillingly or accidentally?"

"Absolutely," said Meaney. "The mother's emotional well-being determines her hormonal state. Mothers who are depressed and anxious produce more stress hormones, which affect growth in the fetus. The single best predictor of the growth of the baby is to ask the mother, Did you want this child?"

A Dickensian Legacy

In the autumn of 2005, scientists at the University of Wisconsin–Madison unveiled a study showing what can happen to children whose parents answer "no" to that question. The researchers studied children who were, they said, "reared in extremely aberrant social environments where they were deprived of the kind of care-giving typical for our species." In more human terms, that meant that for seven to forty-two months after their birth, the twelve girls and six boys had lived in Russian or Romanian orphanages that the World Health Organization described as poor to appalling. In many of them, the de facto orphans—many were actually abandoned by their parents—spent whole days in toyless cribs packed into colorless rooms. Their caregivers interacted with them so infrequently, the University of Wisconsin's Seth Pollak told the 2003 annual meeting of the American Association for the Advancement of Science, "that the environments were generally void of stimulation and human interaction." In particular, the children seldom experienced the love and caring of adults who recognized and responded to their needs.

The children were adopted by American families. Within a year, most of their medical problems—ear infections and stomach problems, malnutrition and delayed growth—vanished. But the legacy of neglect did not. Many of the children were diagnosed with attachment disorders, an inability to form emotional bonds to those closest to them.

In laboratory animals, years of studies had identified two brain hormones as crucial to establishing social bonds and regulating emotional behavior. The two, oxytocin and vasopressin, are associated with the emergence of social bonding and parental care. As levels of these hormones rise, animals form social bonds more readily; infants become more strongly attached to their parents and parents more strongly attached to their offspring. Oxytocin in particular seems to be the brain's social hormone. Levels rise when you have warm, physical contact with someone you are close to, generating a sense of security and safety that lays the foundation for you (or the lab animal) to go out and have social interactions. In people, we call that making friends and forming close emotional attachments. As for vasopressin, it seems to be the "Oh, it's you!" hormone, rising when an animal recognizes someone familiar. What more obvious systems to investigate in the orphanage children, Pollak figured, than oxytocin and vasopressin?

Meaney's work had suggested that experiences in early life—meaning, for most animals, including the human kind, how much care and attention they receive from their mother or other primary caregiver—can alter the level of stress hormones in a brain. The level of stress hormones, some studies had hinted, affects how well receptors bind oxytocin and vasopressin. If receptors bind these sociability hormones poorly, the hormones cannot have their effects. What might be happening to oxytocin and vasopressin in the orphanage children, Pollak wondered, even three years after they had been adopted by loving families?

He and his colleagues tracked down eighteen of the children, all living in Wisconsin. The scientists collected two urine samples from each child, a week or two apart, soon after the children had played a computer game while sitting on the lap of their mother or a stranger (one of the female scientists). Throughout the thirty-minute game, the mother or the scientist would whisper to the child, pat him on the head, tickle him, or count his fingers and let him count hers, turning the otherwise impersonal game into a bit of a cuddle session. In lab animals, such sensory stimulation and social interactions increase levels of oxytocin and vasopressin. The scientists also collected urine samples on four mornings, to assess the children's baseline levels of oxytocin and vasopressin, the better to gauge whether human contact raised the levels.

The orphanage children had lower baseline levels of vasopressin, suggesting that "social deprivation may inhibit the development of the [vasopressin] system," Pollak and his colleagues reported in 2005. The children's levels of oxytocin after playing a game with their mother or a stranger told an even more sobering story. Levels of this social-bonding hormone were not expected to rise after the interaction with the stranger, and indeed they did not, in either the orphanage children or the control children. After the children born to loving families sat on their mother's lap and cuddled, however, their levels of oxytocin rose. In the orphanage children, they did not. Oxytocin is the system that cements the bonds between children and those who love them, producing a sense of calm and comfort that provides a base from which children go out and embrace the world, form childhood friendships and, eventually, deep adult relationships. In the orphanage children, this system was not what it should have been.

Meaney's discoveries suggest that the lives we lead and the behavior of those who care for us can alter the very chemistry of DNA. Genes are not destiny. Our genes, and thus their effects on the brain, are more plastic than we ever dreamed.

"An important issue underscored by Michael's work is that parental influence has a dramatic effect on offspring," said Richie Davidson. "His work beautifully illustrates the mechanisms by which maternal influence can occur, and that it can occur in ways that affect gene expression. This is powerful evidence for the impact of parenting on the capacity to change the brain and raises the issue of how we can promote better parenting."

"This point, of course, since many years I have keen interest," said the Dalai Lama in English, which he uses when he can't wait for translations. "Sometimes, like myself, something fixed in our brain, sometimes maybe too difficult to transform now," he said with a chuckle. "But this coming generation, we have to show them to become a peaceful individual. That eventually will create peaceful family, peaceful community, and through that, a peaceful world.

"So the key thing is the peaceful mind. Naturally and obviously, anger, hatred, jealously, fear, these are not helpful to develop peace of mind. Love, compassion, affection—these are the foundations of peaceful mind. But then the question, how to promote that? My approach, not through Buddhist tradition, I call secular ethics. Not talking about heaven, not of nirvana or Buddhahood, but a happy life for this world. Irrespective of whether there is next life or not. Doesn't matter. That's individual business."

After an exchange in Tibetan with the Dalai Lama, Jinpa said, "His Holiness was saying that his own approach in these matters, particularly on the question of how to promote the appreciation of basic human goodness and values such as compassion in society, it's not so much to present these ideas as spiritual or religious ideas, but as universal human values which transcend the divisions of different religious traditions."

Meaney agreed. "Our challenge is not simply to prevent disease. It's to help people move beyond the absence of pathology and to increase human capacity for social good, to increase the happiness of the individual. That's an area where we could use some help."

Charming as rats are, most scientists study them not because of any passionate interest in the rodent world but because of what rats can tell us about people. And while there are all too many cases of a discovery in lab rats failing to translate into humans (think of the many paralyzed rats that have walked again and the rats with the rodent version of Alzheimer's that have had their memory restored), the discovery of how variations in maternal care affect babies' reactivity to stress is, happily, not one of them.

In 2006, scientists at the University of Maryland reported a human version of Meaney's rat studies. Observing 185 pairs of mothers and infants, they catagorized them by how caring the mother was when she fed her baby, changed the baby's clothes or applied lotion, or was simply busy in the kitchen with her baby nearby. The interactions were captured by the scientists on videotape, and analyzed for how often the mother hugged or kissed the baby, smiled or laughed with the baby, or frowned or ignored the baby.

Examining the two extremes of maternal behavior—extremely caring mothers and extremely standoffish mothers, comparable to Meaney's high- and low-licking and grooming mothers—the Maryland scientists found that "infants receiving low-quality" maternal caring behavior showed greater fearfulness (especially when presented with sights, sounds, objects, and people they had never seen before), reacted more to stress, spent less time focusing on the same thing that Mom did (such as a toy), and displayed greater asymmetry in the electrical activity of the brain's frontal regions (a mark of shyness, distress, low sociability, and unhappiness) than infants receiving high-quality maternal caring behavior. Ordinary variations in the level of caring a mother shows her baby, they concluded, "may influence the expression of neural systems involved in stress reactivity in human infants." Just as in rats. Their work, the scientists concluded, "support the work of Meaney and his colleagues who have demonstrated that naturally occurring variations in maternal caring behavior in the rat are of substantial consequence. . . . [T]emperament and maternal behavior act in concert to shape development."

How we are treated as babies by the people who care for us the most really does mold at least some aspects of our temperament. Traits as basic as fearfulness, curiosity, openness to new experiences, and neuroticism are not, despite the drumbeat of "gene of the week" discoveries, woven immutably into our DNA. Nor, as another of the Dalai Lama's guests that October week would show, are they stamped irrevocably into our brain circuits.

Chapter 8

Blaming Mom?

Rewired for Compassion

I f you were to curl up with almost any issue of a journal that publishes studies in social psychology, you would not get a very pretty picture of humanity. Racism. Aggression. Mindless conformity. Failure to come to the aid of someone in distress. An inflated sense of self-worth. Prejudice against anyone who doesn't belong to your ethnic, religious, or socio-economic group. Reflexively seeing members of your group through rose-colored glasses. Making only the rarest appearance are qualities such as compassion, sympathy, tolerance, kindness, and accurate perceptions of yourself and of others.

Darkening this picture even further is that social psychologists, who study how people behave and interact with one another, are remarkably adept at spinning explanations of why these less-than-noble traits are natural to the point of near inevitability and universality. According to their theory, people have such a strong innate need to feel superior that they seek the flimsiest pretexts to justify this delusion. Most notably, people imagine that there are important differences in character, integrity, kindness, and the like between "people like me" and "people different from me." Imagining what are in fact illusory differences helps people maintain their sense that their group is better than others, paving the way for prejudice, aggression, unrealistic self-esteem, and a paucity of empathy and com-passion.

Phillip Shaver wasn't buying it. In the early 1990s, he began to wonder, what if the depressing portrait of humanity that social psychology had long painted—of people as insecure, closed-minded, deluded, biased, defensive, and selfish—does not describe human nature at all? What if it is true of only some people?

He began to wonder whether social psychology had unwittingly fo-cused too much of its attention on the behaviors and attitudes of people who have a troubled history—specifically, a history of not being able to count on the important people in their lives for love and support. If so, then the portrait painted by social psychology fails to describe people who have a very different history, those who have been able to count on those to whom they are closest for comfort, support, and love. And if this were true—if the experience of deep disappointment when those closest to you let you down leaves such lasting traces in the mind that it forever colors how you interact with other people and how you view the world—then the question was obvious: can new experiences or mental training rewire that neuronal legacy and give those who carry the mental scars of past dis-appointments new mental circuitry, enabling them to overcome what so-cial psychology has deemed an inevitable aspect of the human condition?

This is what drew Shaver to Dharamsala, the idea that neuroplasticity might provide a means for changing the brain circuitry of those whose pasts have wired them for selfishness, bias, defensiveness, and other ills of humankind. Unique among the scientists who were making their maiden voyages to the Dalai Lama's home, Shaver had immersed himself in Bud-dhist history and philosophy. He had read the Dalai Lama's autobiography, *Freedom in Exile,* and his *Ethics for a New Millennium,* as well as a pile of volumes on Buddhism, including Pankaj Mishra's *An End to Suffering: The Buddha in the World,* Chögyam Trungpa's *Cutting Through Spiritual Materialism,* and Alan Wal-lace's *The Four Immeasurables: Cultivating a Boundless Heart.* Spirituality was not completely foreign to Shaver, however. As a high school student, he had flirted with the possibility of becoming a Trappist monk.

At nearly every turn, the consonances between Buddhism and his own work jumped off the pages he read. Compassion is a key virtue in all major religions, but in none more so than Buddhism. In Buddhism, the greatest wish is "May the suffering of all sentient beings be relieved"—the very definition of compassion. One of the primary forms of mental training for monks, yogis, and other practitioners is compassion meditation, in which one trains the mind to feel deep and abiding empathy for all sentient beings. But whether one calls it compassion, empathy, altruism, or (as social psychologists do) prosocial behavior, it clicked with the question that had come to dominate Shaver's research. In study after study, he was finding that whether a person acts with compassion or not reflects the person's sense of emotional security. People who feel emotionally secure, who feel that there is someone to whom they can turn in times of need, are more sensitive to the suffering of others, Shaver found—not only better able to perceive when someone is in distress but also more willing to respond to that suffering. In contrast, people who lack that sense of a safe harbor, of having someone to whom they can turn, are less inclined to feel empathy and compassion.

But here is where Shaver saw a ray of hope. Yes, people's sense of emotional security is strongly shaped by the experiences they have in childhood with the person who is closest to them. But when we say "strongly shaped," that is more than metaphor. If people tend to feel and behave in a certain way, it is because their brain's circuits are organized a certain way. And if some brain circuits can be tweaked, as Mike Merzenich's monkeys and Ed Taub's stroke patients and Helen Neville's blind or deaf children had shown over and over again, then maybe the circuits that reflect or underlie emotional security can also be tweaked.

What he has been searching for, says Shaver, is a way to enhance compassion and altruism in the real world. "In a world burdened by international, interethnic, and interpersonal conflict, all people of goodwill wish it were possible to foster compassion and willingness to help others rather than ignore others' needs and exacerbate their suffering," he says. "Many people have thought, if only people could feel safer and less threatened, they would have more psychological resources to devote to noticing other people's suffering and doing something to alleviate it. I thought, if you enhance attachment security, even temporarily, can you foster compassion and altruism?"

Attachment Theory

Attachment theory was created by British psychiatrist John Bowlby in the mid-twentieth century to explore the childhood roots of unhappiness, anxiety, anger, and delinquency. It focuses on the sense of emotional security or insecurity a child develops in the first years of life. Simply put, some children come to feel that the person who takes care of them is a reliable source of safety and comfort; other children find that this person is either an unpredictable harbor who is sometimes there to comfort them and sometimes missing in action, or is outright rejecting. Attachment theory was initially an attempt to explain the behavior of very young children—in particular, how babies become emotionally attached to their mother, in the sense of being dependent on her for protection and comfort. Although "attachment" is a problematic concept in Buddhism—it has overtones of grasping, of being dependent in an emotionally unhealthy way—in attachment theory, it is considered a sign of emotional health. It connotes viewing another person as an emotional "safe haven" or, as the Dalai Lama put it, "that in which you entrust your hope."

As advanced by American psychologist Mary Ainsworth, attachment theory explains why different children react differently to, for instance, being left alone with a stranger. In what she called "the strange situation," Ainsworth had a mother and her twelve- to eighteen-month-old baby enter a room filled with unfamiliar toys, a situation that has been duplicated in psychology labs many times since. At first, the child begins to play with the toys, looking back at the mother from time to time to make sure she is still there and approving. Then the mother leaves. A stranger enters. Now two of the child's natural tendencies, to seek security and to follow his curiosity, are at loggerheads. When the child is frightened, the need for security dominates, with the result that the child is no longer curious or playful. "The child doesn't have mental space for caring about anything else," Shaver told the Dalai Lama. "If you're threatened, you're looking first for protection, and all other drives are inhibited." When Mom comes back after a few minutes, the typical child greets her, holds on to her, and relaxes. If the child then returns to playing with the toys, his stress at bay and his curiosity in full bloom again, he is deemed secure. "By reconnecting with his mother, he has come to feel that 'it's okay, everything is safe. Now I'm curious again,' " Shaver explained. "As soon as you feel secure and protected, you don't keep hanging on to the attachment figure but are curious, caring, humorous, playful."

What Ainsworth and her students found over the years is that children who seem secure in the "strange situation"—who are confident that someone will always be there for them and that the person on whom they depend is sensitive, interested, and appropriately responsive—are easier to comfort. If they become upset, once they see that someone is going to take care of them, they relax. Here is what most intrigued Shaver: "These children, by age three, already are more empathic and play more creatively," he said. "The way their mind is structured over time shows in a whole range of behaviors. We believe that the experience of sensitive, empathic parents and others makes the child more confident, less stress-prone, and all of those good things."

Three Attachment Styles

As refined over the decades, attachment theory holds that attachment "styles" are formed early in life, as a result of how a child interacts with her primary caregivers. (Lest you get the idea that everything is set in stone by the end of childhood, be assured that interactions throughout life, with people who are important to you, shape your attachment style. What you experience of your significant others' sensitivity, responsiveness, and goodwill shapes your view of whether you can count on them.) If the child's primary caregiver—we'll say it's the mother, for simplicity's sake, and because mothers assume the lion's share of child care in most societies—is available and responsive, comforting her when she is upset, then the child develops a foundation of faith that key people in her life will be available and supportive when she needs them. In all likelihood, she develops what is called a "secure" attachment style.

A child who has regularly and reliably found those closest to her to be a source of comfort develops a sense that the world is a pretty okay place, populated by people of goodwill. She is able to recall, even decades later, not only positive but also painful memories, which Shaver illustrated with a passage from the Dalai Lama's autobiography. In it, the Dalai Lama re-called as a young child knocking over a scripture book from which one of his uncles, a monk, was reading prayers. "He picked me up and slapped me hard," the Dalai Lama recalled some fifty years later. "Thereafter, whenever I caught sight of him, I became very frightened."

"To be able to recall that feeling freely is extremely important," Shaver said. "It implies not having defensively walled off negative experiences."

Those early experiences, as well as experiences throughout life that re-inforce them, leave a deep imprint on the personality, attitudes, and behav-ior of a child as well as the adult he becomes. People who are emotionally secure are comfortable with closeness and interdependence, trusting that they will find solace in those to whom they are closest. From this founda-tion, they are able to form rewarding relationships. But the sense of emo-tional security reverberates beyond personal relationships. People who are securely attached tend to view life's problems as manageable and, as a re-sult, maintain their sense of optimism. They believe that the obstacles the world throws in their way can be overcome. They tend to size up stressful events in less-threatening terms than insecure people. Because, as children, they were loved and valued, they view themselves not only as strong and competent—the facet of character from which their optimism springs—but also as valuable, worthy of love, and special. They believe that their own actions can often reduce their distress and solve their problems but that, when that fails, they can turn to others. They feel generally safe and pro-tected, both by their own strength and competence and by the reliability and availability of those closest to them.

In people who are securely attached, self-esteem is reasonably high and not subject to every little change in fortune; they can maintain it without defensively running down other people. Their relationships, personal as well as professional, tend to be mature, rewarding, mutually supportive, and confident rather than defensive or suspicious. Securely attached people have a relatively positive view of human nature, seeing partners as support-ive (unless faced with unmistakable evidence to the contrary) and expecting that their partner will behave in a loving and honest way. They believe in the existence of romantic love and in the possibility of maintaining deep and in-tense love for a long, long time—even until "death do us part." They believe in the goodwill of others, with the result that their default position in a relationship is trust, gratitude, and affection, as well as tolerance for and forgiveness of behavior on the part of the partner that occasionally falls short of the ideal. Having had the approval of those who matter most, they can easily revise erroneous beliefs without feeling belittled or rejected. The inner reserves on which a securely attached person can draw in times of stress make it less necessary to rely on neurotic means of coping, such as irrationally lashing out at others or succumbing to self-delusion or defensiveness.

Some children have very different experiences. When they feel frightened, they fail to find comfort in those who are supposed to care for them. Those closest to a child, and those on whom he needs to rely, are not reliably available or sensitive to his needs. The child feels uneasy and alone rather than safe and secure in the love and attention of the person who takes care of him. He is repeatedly left to suffer the hurts and disappointments of early life alone and comes to learn that he cannot count on those closest to him. This, repeated over and over in the first years of life, raises profound doubts that there are any reliable, safe harbors in the world or that others can be trusted. "The resulting sense of vulnerability and uncertainty can interfere drastically with a whole range of life activities," Shaver said. The most direct effect is that, if the individual learns through painful experience that those closest to him are not reliable sources of emotional comfort, he must go to plan B, what Shaver calls "the best a person can do under dreadful circumstances." The "best" is either of two compensatory mechanisms, according to years of studies that have linked the behaviors of older children, teens, and adults to their history of interactions with those who were, or should have been, the loving adults in their lives as children.

Especially if a child's experience is inconsistent, with caregivers sometimes comforting her and sometimes abandoning her to her own devices, she is likely to develop what is called an anxious attachment style. "That kind of parenting makes the child anxious, partly because it isn't possible to relax if you don't know whether your safe haven will be there for you or not," said Shaver.

A child such as this typically tries desperately to become close to people, anxiously trying to attract their attention and gain their protection. Rather than giving up on finding emotional comfort, the emotionally anxious person intensifies her efforts, trying to coerce love and support. As an adult, she has an almost palpable need for closeness and frets constantly that she will never have it or is about to lose it. She is in a perpetual state of anxiety that her partner will not be available in times of need, that he will let her down, or—the ultimate unavailability—leave her. She is therefore hypervigilant for any sign that people in her life are about to withdraw and hypersensitive to the slightest hint of rejection or abandonment. She sees signs of distance, rejection, and unavailability in the most innocuous words and behaviors, such as her significant other's not being immediately and totally available whenever she calls. She is clingy. Overdependent on her partner as a source of comfort, she typically has little confidence in her own abilities and skills to overcome problems or pain, makes incessant demands for attention and care, and is prone to manipulative behavior designed to hold his affection and support. She makes showy displays of distress. People who are emotionally anxious describe their romantic relationships "in terms of obsession and passion, strong physical attraction, desire for union with the partner, and proneness to fall in love quickly and perhaps indiscriminately," said Shaver. "At the same time, they characterize their lovers as untrustworthy and nonsupportive and report intense bouts of jealousy and anger toward romantic partners as well as worries about rejection and abandonment."

An anxiously attached person prefers to work with others but feels unloved at work. Her acute sensitivity to the possibility of rejection makes her wallow in thoughts about personal weaknesses and memories of personal failures, with the inevitable result that she has chronic doubts about her self-worth. She is hyperdefensive, regarding new ideas as threatening and potentially destabilizing. She loathes confusion and ambiguity and, as a result, blocks out anything that challenges her worldview. Unlike someone who is securely attached, she has no faith that if she encounters a problem or becomes distressed, she can find help from a significant other. She has no faith that other people can be counted on to provide relief and comfort.

There is another way that people react to, and cope with, the failure to feel secure in the love and caring of other people. In some ways, it is the polar opposite of anxious, grasping attachment: they give up on others, emotionally and psychologically. Their instincts for seeking love and companionship wither. People who cope this way have a style called, oxymoronically, avoidant attachment. In the "strange situation," an emotionally avoidant child cries infrequently despite the mother's absence. When the mother leaves the room, he acts as if he doesn't care, neither crying nor trying to follow her (even though objective measures, such as heart rate, show that he is experiencing intense stress). "It's sort of 'I'm not going to reach out and show that I need things,' " Shaver explained to the Dalai Lama. "In such cases, the parent typically doesn't like physical contact with the child or dealing with the child's dependency, and so she has a whole set of mostly nonverbal methods of keeping the child away."

An emotionally avoidant person believes that trying to get close to people is unlikely to alleviate his distress. Not illogically, then, he tends to keep a big emotional distance from others and becomes so good at not needing people that he often feels uncomfortable with closeness. He strives for emotional independence and self-reliance—"I don't need anyone." To make this work, he also has to turn a blind eye to his own personal faults or weaknesses, for recognizing them threatens to reveal a need for the very others on whom he has decided he cannot count. These feelings lead him to be emotionally detached and to form superficial, cool relationships devoid of real affection and intimacy. Because an emotionally avoidant person tends to—no, more: needs to—avoid confronting problems in a relationship, he leaves conflicts unresolved. And because he repeatedly rejects his partner's bids for intimacy and affection, his intimate relationships are typically rocky. Compulsively self-reliant, he prefers to work alone and uses work to avoid meaningful relationships. He distrusts the goodwill of those closest to him—parents and siblings at first, significant others and friends later. Having turned off his need for others, he can be oblivious to genuine signs of caring or emotional availability.

A person's attachment style can be measured reliably with questions that probe beliefs and expectations, as well as relationship history. In what is called the Adult Attachment Interview, people spend about one hour answering open-ended questions about their childhood relationships with parents. People's recollection of their childhood is a strong tip-off to their current state of emotional security and all it brings. If the person describes positive relationships with her parents clearly, convincingly, and coherently, for instance, she probably has a secure attachment style, Shaver explained to the Dalai Lama. One man recalled, "My mother was undoubtedly one of the kindest people I've ever known. She was truly wonderful and was loved, I'm quite certain, by all who knew her. She was very compassionate."

The Dalai Lama interjected, in Tibetan, "That's my mother!"

Shaver continued reading from the Dalai Lama's autobiography: "There were two consolations to life at the monastery. First, my immediate brother was already there. He took good care of me."

Although the young Dalai Lama was dropped into an alien and even frightening environment, the presence of another good person gave him a sense of a safe haven, a secure base, Shaver explained: "Once you begin life this way, you tend to agree that people are generally well intentioned and kindhearted."

In the attachment questionnaire, an emotionally secure person tends to agree that "I find it relatively easy to get close to others," "I'm comfortable depending on others," and "I don't often worry about being abandoned or about somebody being too close." Secure attachment characterizes a bare majority of young adult Americans.

If, on the other hand, the person answers the questions in a way that seems dismissive of the importance of close relationships or else idealizes them, he likely has an avoidant style. He agrees with statements such as these: "I try to avoid getting too close to my partner," "I prefer not to show a partner how I feel deep down," and "I seldom turn to my partner for many things, including comfort and reassurance." He agrees that "I'm uncomfortable being close to others," "I find it difficult to trust them completely, difficult to allow myself to depend on them," "I'm nervous when anyone gets too close and relationship partners often want me to be more intimate than I feel comfortable being." He describes romantic relationships as cool, and low in emotional involvement. He believes that love fades with time. This avoidant style characterizes about 25 percent of American college students and adults, Shaver said.

If someone is entangled in conflicted feelings about her parents and has trouble keeping anger and anxiety out of her recollections of childhood and—especially—the times she sought comfort from her parents, she is likely emotionally anxious. She agrees with statements such as these: "I need a lot of reassurance that I am loved by my partner," "I often worry about being abandoned," and "I get frustrated if romantic partners are not available when I need them." She agrees that "relationship partners are reluctant to get as close as I would like," "I often worry that my partner doesn't really love me or won't want to stay with me," and "I want to get very close to my partner and this sometimes scares people away." About 20 percent of young adult Americans have an anxious style of attachment.

This breakdown—just over half showing secure attachment, about one-quarter showing avoidant attachment, and one-fifth showing anxious attachment—matches the breakdown of babies in the strange-situation assessment devised by Mary Ainsworth.

The Child Is Father to the Man

The attachment system is active over the entire life span, shaping how we interact with others, the kinds of relationships we form, and how we react to threats and danger. It strongly shapes emotional stability, self-image, attitudes toward others, and—most obviously—how we respond to stress or trauma: if you can turn to someone close to you and find support and comfort there, you are much more likely to cope and recover than if you are emotionally alone. In childhood, threats and stress cause the child to seek out her primary attachment figure physically, turning to her, holding up her arms in a mute (or bawling) plea for help and soothing. When adults feel threatened or uneasy, however, they do not necessarily physically seek out the person to whom they are closest. Instead, they are more likely to find comfort in just the thought of that person, calling up memories of someone who once offered love, care, and protection or still does. This can create the same sense of safety and security that a child finds in his mother's arms, with the result that the adult can better deal with stress or threat. As Shaver puts it, "Mental representations of attachment figures can become symbolic sources of protection."

This ability is important for the obvious reason that it lets us deal with stress and threat. But it matters for another reason. When we encounter a threat, we tend to be so focused on our own anxiety that we're not good for much else. Everything except our own needs goes out the window, mentally speaking: someone in emotional distress is not likely to care about, or even notice, the needs of anyone else. Only when he finds comfort and has his sense of security restored can he turn his attention and energy to others.

The implication is clear. A person who can quickly find comfort in the mere thought of someone—one of Shaver's "symbolic sources of protection"—is going to snap back and engage with humanity more quickly than someone who flounders around, desperately seeking some idea or memory that will ease his distress or fear. The power of the mind to call up the image of an attachment figure would prove crucial in Shaver's quest to see whether someone who is initially unable to find this comfort can, through mental training or intervention, rewire the circuits of his mind to do so. That would make a world of difference in how that person interacted with others.

For instance, people who are emotionally avoidant suppress negative thoughts about themselves, feelings of personal weakness and imperfection, and memories of personal failures. The result is a defensive (and, inevitably, delusional) inflation of self-esteem. Hand in hand with this strategy go attempts to convince others that you don't need them (the better to avoid disappointment when they fail to come through for you). These efforts blind people to others' positive traits, intentions, and behaviors, since none of those matter. Such information therefore plays no part in the social judgments that emotionally avoidant people make. They simply maintain an inflexibly negative image of humankind.

A New Portrait of Humanity

Now you can see why Shaver had begun to suspect that the dreary portrait of humanity—selfish, deluded, defensive—that social psychology painted might well be an overgeneralization. With the researcher's penchant for studying what is wrong with something, social psychologists had made a beeline for the dark side of human nature. But there were other kinds of people in the world. Shaver began to think that the generalizations of social psychology applied more accurately to insecure than to secure people.

If the dark portrait of humanity in fact portrays only those who are emotionally anxious or avoidant, an obvious question arises. A person's sense of attachment security or insecurity is rooted in childhood experiences and in a mental representation of past experiences, such as how a caregiver responded to her long-ago fears and emotional needs. Indeed, the sense of attachment is so reflexive that it must be tightly wired in the brain. Can anything alter those representations, which, like every other representation in the brain, take the physical form of neuronal circuits? Does even this system retain neuroplasticity? Are we stuck with the way we were, or might it be possible, through either mental training or experimental context, to change?

If so, there would be "important consequences for mental health and prosocial behavior," Shaver said. For instance, individuals who are anxious or avoidant tend to maintain a sense of their own worth by emphasizing real or imagined ways in which their demographic group—"white male American," "female Latina urbanite," "black male teenager"—is superior. Social psychology has long pegged this as a human universal. But there is evidence that while it is characteristic of insecure people, both the anxious and the avoidant kind, it is not true of those who have a secure sense of attachment. A person who can maintain a sense of his own value by tapping into deep memories of being loved and valued should have less need to fear and disparage members of other groups or to maintain a sense of self-worth by tearing down others. The result should be greater tolerance. If this is so, then the stronger a person's sense of emotional security, the less his hostility to members of groups other than his own. Is there any way to reshape the brain circuits so that someone who was once anxious or avoidant can become secure instead, with the result that he has less need to tear down others in order to maintain his sense of self-worth and, in practical terms, is less prejudiced and hostile toward other ethnic groups?

Take another example. A related tendency, and another one that social psychology holds to be a human universal, is to reject anything that challenges the validity of your beliefs—and instead to protect and defend what you believe even when confronted with evidence that it is wrong. The result is cognitive rigidity and a deep need to deny that one holds erroneous beliefs or has done something stupid or wrong.

Feeling secure in your emotional attachments makes it easier to explore new ideas and makes you more open to new information. Securely attached people are more intellectually curious than insecurely attached people (avoidant ones shy away from new ideas for fear the ideas will bring their carefully constructed self-image tumbling down, while anxious people wall themselves off from new ideas for fear of being unable to cope with challenges). Secure people have a higher tolerance for ambiguity and tend to be less dogmatic in their thinking—a manifestation of intellectual openness. They are less likely than the insecure to judge people hastily and superficially, and more likely to keep an open mind. Insecure people reject information that does not fit their initial impression. Secure people are less likely to make judgments based on stereotypes. Surely any training that brought this result, by reshaping the mental circuits that encode a person's sense of attachment, would be a great benefit to humankind.

Tweaking the attachment system might also affect how altruistic people are. For decades, psychologists have thought of attachment style as describing, and explaining, only close relationships, primarily to parents and other caregivers, to lovers and potential lovers, to spouses and potential spouses. "But there are good reasons for believing that attachment style influences all sorts of attachment-related thoughts and relationships, not only those involving a romantic partner," says Shaver. Both forms of insecure attachment—anxiety and avoidance—are associated with low levels of altruistic empathy for strangers and acquaintances, for instance. Those with an avoidant style are so deft at maintaining emotional detachment and so unwilling to become involved with other people's problems and feelings that when they witness suffering or need, they are unable to muster empathy. They distance themselves from others' suffering and, as a result, are disinclined to engage in altruistic helping. In contrast, people who feel attachment anxiety feel such intense personal distress when they see suffering that they become emotionally overwhelmed, leaving them good for almost nothing in the way of comfort or assistance.

Buddhism distinguishes between acting because you truly wish to relieve the suffering of another being, for that being's sake, and acting because his suffering causes you distress that you want to stop. "There is helping because you really want to help, and there is helping because you feel so distressed by the sight of suffering that you act to alleviate your own suffering," said Matthieu Ricard, the French-born monk who contributed insights from Buddhism at the 2004 meeting. "So when we speak of unbearable distress, it's not that we want to do something about our own. It's that we feel it is unacceptable, it is intolerable, to let the suffering be. It is not because I feel personally uncomfortable." The Dalai Lama added, "Those who feel distressed and want to be removed from the object of suffering might not do anything to relieve the other person's burden of suffering if they can simply escape. But in true compassion, you don't want to escape. You say there's no way I can allow that suffering to continue."

By causing a person to feel more securely attached, might it be possible to increase altruistic empathy, to help people see others as what Buddhists call "suffering sentient beings," equal to oneself in value? Can making people feel emotionally secure foster compassion and altruistic behavior? For if attachment insecurities keep people from feeling both the compassion and the competence to help a suffering being (because emotionally anxious individuals tend to focus on and be overwhelmed by their own distress, while emotionally avoidant individuals are so uncomfortable with closeness that they just don't give a damn), then replacing those insecurities with security might lift the emotional burdens that interfere with compassion and altruism.

Attachment in the Lab

In the 1980s, Shaver had seen hints that attachment security affects compassion and selfless caregiving. On the standard attachment questionnaire, secure people were more likely to say they were sensitive to their spouse's or lover's needs and provided that partner emotional support. People who scored high in avoidance or anxiety were less compassionate. In one experiment, for instance, when told that a friend of the experimenter had been diagnosed with cancer, those who were avoidant or anxious hardly cared. Those who felt secure in their own relationships expressed greater compassion and sympathy, even for this stranger.

In two studies conducted in Israel, the Netherlands, and the United States, Shaver and a colleague, Mario Mikulincer of Bar Ilan University in Israel, looked for connections between people's attachment styles and their likelihood of engaging in volunteer activities. Each study began by having the volunteers fill out questionnaires probing two things: their attachment style—secure, avoidant, or anxious—and how much they volunteer to help others, such as by giving blood or delivering food to the sick.

People who scored high on attachment avoidance engaged in relatively few volunteer activities, spent less time doing so, and showed little indication that their reasons for doing so had anything to do with altruism. "The more avoidant they are, the less they volunteer to help others," said Shaver. "If avoidant people are involved in some helping activity, their reasons tend to be less altruistic and more selfish, such as getting school credit."

Anxious people don't volunteer more or less than secure people. But when they do so, it is for self-centered reasons and, occasionally, career enhancement. The higher people scored on attachment anxiety, the more weight they gave self-enhancement or socializing as a reason for volunteering. That is, they volunteer in order to feel included and to be less lonely. "Again, 'It's all about me,' " said Shaver. "It's sort of, 'I'll help you because you'll thank me.' "

While studies like these are suggestive, all they do is show an association between attachment security and compassion. They do not show what causes what. Indeed, this problem had beset almost every study that linked different attachment styles to various behaviors and beliefs. The connections are what statisticians call correlational. Sure, a particular attachment style is more likely to be associated with, say, well-grounded self-esteem. But correlations tell you nothing about causation. Does the snow cause the cold, or does cold bring snow? Does being open to challenging ideas cause a person to feel securely attached, or does being securely attached lead to such openness? None of the studies could tell for sure whether attachment security was the cause of how people responded to another person's suffering. Maybe the arrow of causality pointed the other way, with people's compassion for others leading them to feel securely attached in their own relationships.

Likes, Dislikes, and Unlikes

To probe for cause and effect, Shaver embarked on what would be a years-long collaboration with Mikulincer. They wanted to tease out whether particular attachment styles *cause* the attitudes and behaviors that had repeatedly been associated with them or whether living and thinking a certain way leads people to exhibit a particular emotional style. They had a hunch that the former was true. If it was—if, in fact, attachment style matters in a deep way—then they wanted to answer the ultimate question: how malleable is the sense of attachment?

Mikulincer had the perfect population for the kind of studies he and Shaver had in mind: the roiling ethnic stew that makes up Israeli society. There, narrowly defined groups harbor intense biases, and even hostility, toward anyone who does not belong to their own group: secular

Israeli Jews, Israeli Arabs, ultra-Orthodox Jews, Russian immigrants, homo-sexuals . . . the list goes on.

The scientists suspected, however, that negative reactions to strangers and intolerance toward out-group members might not be set in stone. If emotional security *causes* people to be more accepting toward those who are different from themselves, what would happen if the experimenters in-duced, even temporarily, a feeling of secure attachment? One of the ele-ments of social psychology's dark portrait of humanity is that people tend to perceive and recall members of their own social or ethnic group as hav-ing more positive qualities than members of other groups. According to the conventional wisdom, this bias serves a self-protective function: group membership is an important source of self-esteem, and the "my-people-are-better" reflex helps individuals maintain self-esteem. "Once the concept of 'us' is formed," said Shaver, "people may maintain self-esteem by search-ing for intergroup differences that favor their group." But recall that secure attachment is correlated with tolerance and the lack of such bias, and an ability to maintain high self-esteem without defensively tearing down oth-ers. Perhaps activating a sense of attachment security would soften negative attitudes to members of out-groups, at least temporarily.

To find out, Shaver and Mikulincer recruited Jewish university students in Israel. For such students, Israeli Jews are the in-group and Israeli Arabs are the out-group. Israeli Jews tend to view Israeli Arabs with hostility and prejudice. The participants first completed the usual attachment-style questionnaire, indicating how strongly they agreed or disagreed with state-ments such as "I often worry that my partner does not love me" or "I find that other persons are reluctant to get as close as I would like," indicative of emotional anxiety, and "I'm somewhat uncomfortable being close to oth-ers" or "I find it difficult to trust others in close relationships," indicative of attachment avoidance.

The scientists had shown in earlier studies that they could induce at-tachment security temporarily, even in people who were, by disposition, anxious or avoidant. The latter almost always have some memories of emo-tional security and of someone who cared for them, assuming they did not have a truly Dickensian childhood, and these memories can be activated. In particular, they can be activated by a technique called priming, in which the person is induced consciously or subliminally to access mental circuits associated with security. In the case of subliminal priming, the person is briefly exposed to words associated with emotional security, such as *closeness, love, hug,* and *support.*

Some of the Jewish students received this kind of security priming. Others, serving as a control group, were subliminally exposed to neutral words (the Hebrew words for *office, table, boat,* or *picture,* for instance) or to words that were also unrelated to attachment but that had a positive connotation (*happiness, honesty, luck,* or *success*). The 148 participants were then given information about 2 other supposed participants (sex, age, marital status, the religion of the students' parents) and asked to evaluate them. In fact, the scientists had put together the information, to make it seem as if one of the students was an Israeli Jew, like the study participants, and the other an Israeli Arab. The information also described the pseudoparticipants' academic careers, expectations, and lifestyle, which were virtually identical for the pseudo-Arab and the pseudo-Jew. With all this information in hand, the participants evaluated the two students on fifteen traits: nine positive (honest, cheerful, reliable, trustworthy, intelligent, warm, patient, kind, stable) and six negative (argumentative, sleazy, spineless, impulsive, manipulative, lazy).

In a result that does not exactly restore your faith in humanity, participants who thought they were evaluating another Israeli Jew ascribed more positive traits, on average, than when they thought they were evaluating an Israeli Arab—but only when they had been subliminally exposed to the neutral priming or non-attachment-related positive priming. The higher the person's attachment anxiety, the more negative the evaluation of the Israeli Arab, just as attachment theory predicts. Securely attached participants had less-negative reactions to the Israeli Arab. And here's where Shaver saw a ray of hope: participants who had received the attachment-security priming evaluated Jew and Arab the same. Most important, they gave a more-positive evaluation of the Israeli Arab than did students who received a positive or neutral prime. Perhaps people's attachment security could be changed, with beneficial results.

Cultural conflict between secular and ultra-Orthodox Jews in Israel has not produced anything like the horrific body count of the Israeli-Palestinian conflict, but it is a major source of social tension, with each group feeling hostility and prejudice toward the other. In a follow-up study, Mikulincer and Shaver had 120 student volunteers rate their willingness to interact with an ultra-Orthodox religious Jew or with a secular Jew. This time, rather than seeing a subliminal word, some of the volunteers were asked to visualize themselves "in a problematic situation that you cannot solve on your own, and to imagine that you are surrounded by people who are sensitive and responsive to your distress, want to help you only because they love you, and set aside other activities in order to assist you." In other words, in this study, the security prime was conscious, not subliminal. Another group imagined something more neutral: "Imagine yourself going to a grocery store and buying products you need for your house, and imagine other persons who are also buying products, talking among themselves about daily issues, examining new brands, and comparing different products." A third group imagined something happy but unrelated to emotional attachment or security: "Imagine yourself receiving a notice that you win a large amount of money in the national lottery, and imagine other students in your class hearing about this notice, approaching you, congratulating you, and telling others about your good fortune." As in the Jew-Arab study, the participants filled out the questionnaire that assessed their attachment style.

All of the participants then received questionnaires like those in the Jew-Arab study, with demographic and other information. But this time, it was supposedly filled out by either a secular Jew like themselves or an ultra-Orthodox Jew. Everything except the information that identified the person as secular or ultra-Orthodox was identical, even answers to political questions. The participants were then asked about their willingness to interact with the person, such as, "Would you like to invite him to your home?" and "Would you like him to join you when you go out with your friends?"

People's natural dispositions had the effects predicted by attachment theory: those who were characterized as having attachment anxiety were less willing to interact with the ultra-Orthodox Jew. That didn't change when participants imagined the neutral scenario or the win-the-lottery scenario. But among participants who imagined receiving emotional comfort and support, there was an equal willingness to interact with secular Jews like themselves and with ultra-Orthodox Jews unlike themselves.

Once again, activating mental circuits for secure attachment "led to greater willingness to interact with an out-group," said Shaver. By giving people a feeling of attachment security, the researchers were able to reduce negative reactions to members of an out-group. Activating mental circuits that encode a feeling of emotional security, Shaver concluded, "attenuated derogating reactions to out-group members or to targets that threatened the participants' worldview. . . . Having a sense of being loved and surrounded by supporting others seems to allow people to open themselves to alternative worldviews and be more accepting of people who do not belong to their own group."

Activating this sense of security, through priming, achieved this beneficent result even in people who are dispositionally anxious or avoidant. That suggests that merely a temporary activation of attachment security leads even chronically insecure people to be more accepting and tolerant. Thinking about, say, a time when you felt that you could count on someone for comfort and support may remind you of similar memories at the expense of memories of times when you were rejected or ignored. As a result, you respond to members of an out-group in ways consistent with the activated memory, even if this memory is at odds with your innate attachment style. As Shaver told the Dalai Lama, "It has something to do with love. Attachment words trigger a kind of comfort that makes tolerance for others more available mentally, even in insecure people, whose natural inclination is intolerance and lack of compassion."

Experimental manipulation—subliminal presentation of security-related words such as *love* or the name of an attachment figure, visualizing the faces of those to whom you turn for comfort, recalling times when someone cared for you—heightens the sense of attachment, albeit momentarily. But in that moment, hostile responses to out-groups vanish. Enhancing people's sense of emotional security can eliminate differences in how they view members of out-groups, something that is supposedly a core aspect of the human psyche. "These are issues that are so close to those in Buddhist psychology that I think it would be great to try to figure out how it works," Shaver said. The greater a person's sense of emotional security, the less his or her hostility toward and bias against members of out-groups and the more willing the person is to interact with members of out-groups. What if "momentarily" could become "forever"?

The Power of Primes

Of course, expressing your willingness to meet with or bring to your home a member of an out-group, while definitely a step in the right direction for social harmony and kindness toward strangers, still falls short of what Buddhism teaches: acting so as to decrease the suffering of sentient beings. Mikulincer and some of his students therefore explored whether attachment security correlates with willingness to take action to reduce other people's suffering.

The scientists again used a standard assessment to gauge whether volunteers generally felt anxious, avoidant, or secure in their relationships. They then had the volunteers (depending on which version of the experiment they were running) read a story about a student who was in trouble, sought help from his or her parents, and received support, comfort, and reassurance from them; recall memories of when someone cared for them; or subliminally encounter words such as *love* and *hug*. The story, the memory, and the words were each meant to trigger a sense of attachment security. For comparison, volunteers also read a funny story (to see if their willingness to help a suffering being arose from just being in a jolly mood) or a neutral story. Finally, the volunteers read a short story about a student whose parents had been killed in a car crash and rated how much they felt compassion or sympathy for the student as well as how personally distressed they felt.

You can probably anticipate the result. Volunteers who scored high on attachment anxiety or avoidance, and who were not primed with the story about a loving and secure relationship or the memory or the words associated with caring, felt minimal compassion for the student whose parents died in a car crash. Those who were anxious in their own relationships felt distress, but that did not translate into compassion: they felt so personally uncomfortable that their whole focus was on alleviating their own distress, with nothing left over for the real sufferer. Those marked by avoidant attachment, in contrast, tended to ignore the orphan's suffering, downplay it, move away from it, or be cynical about it. "This attachment style seems to foster a lack of concern for other people and their needs and suffering," Shaver said.

But once again, psychology was not destiny. Regardless of whether they were innately secure or anxious or avoidant, volunteers primed with an attachment-security story, memory, or words reported higher levels of compassion toward the orphaned student than did participants who read the funny story or the neutral story. They also felt less distress, suggesting that their compassion arose from a higher, selfless, altruistic plane.

Buddhism has practices analogous to this priming. Serious meditators, for example, keep pictures of their teachers, which remind them to adopt certain behavior throughout the day. "In Buddhism, it is obviously a voluntary, self-induced priming or preparation of the mind in order to develop positive qualities such as loving-kindness or benevolence or concern," said Matthieu Ricard. "And it is combined with mindfulness in the sense that you remind yourself at all times that this is how I should treat a sentient being or begin a project or start the day. You constantly, whenever you're going to act or make a decision, remind yourself what is your motivation. So the mindfulness is there to at all times rekindle and revive that kind of attitude. You might begin the day by saying, 'Whatever I might do today, may it be for the benefit of all sentient beings.' "

The subliminal priming that Shaver used was effective in eliciting a particular mental attitude from people, regardless of whether they were anxiously attached, securely attached, or avoidant, the Dalai Lama said through Jinpa: "But as to a method of radical transformation of the individual, His Holiness is wondering to what extent this is going to be effective."

"Buddhist practices are conscious, deliberate," said Shaver. "They're part of a program, a long-term effort. To transform your mind, to be mindful and remember all these goals, obviously takes a lot of training." As he learned from one of the monks attending the meeting with the Dalai Lama, thinking vividly of how your mother loved you is a traditional Buddhist meditation technique to enhance compassion. "That seems exactly like the primes we use in our studies," Shaver said. "The common Buddhist prayer that begins 'I take refuge in the Buddha' also has the flavor of attachment theory." In contrast, the "primed environment" in the West includes a large serving of media violence and materialism. "It's conducive to having ready images of striking back," he said. "I wouldn't be surprised if just changing that environment would have a subtle effect, conducive towards a different mental state."

Take My Tarantula . . . Please

Expressing compassion in the abstract is all well and good, but the acid test would come when people moved beyond characterizing their feelings to acting on them. It's one thing to feel sympathy for a child pinned under a car but infinitely better to grab other passersby and lift it off him.

In experiments carried out in Israel and the United States, Shaver and Mikulincer examined whether enhancing attachment security would change not only how people said they felt and thought—about, say, people different from themselves—but how they acted. University students completed the standard questionnaire assessing their attachment style. ("I worry about being abandoned" and the like.) Three or four weeks later, they returned to the lab. Each volunteer was told that a young woman, also a volunteer and a student, had been randomly assigned to perform some unpleasant tasks, while the volunteer receiving the instructions had been randomly chosen to watch and evaluate her performance. Although none of the tasks was actually dangerous, they were told, people sometimes did not want to carry out all of them: looking at gory photographs of people who had been severely injured or killed, petting a laboratory rat, immersing a hand in ice water, petting a live tarantula, touching a preserved sheep's eye, petting a live snake, letting cockroaches crawl on one's hand and arm. The woman, they were told, was in the next room being filmed by a video camera connected to a monitor the volunteer could watch. In reality, she was one of the researchers and was on a previously recorded videotape.

Each volunteer was subliminally exposed to the name of someone they regarded as an attachment figure, the name of someone close to them but not an attachment figure, or the name of a casual acquaintance.

At first, the volunteer saw "Liat," on the monitor, listen to a male experimenter explain that she would be asked to perform several unpleasant and even painful tasks and that she was free to stop whenever she chose. She agreed. (Again, this was all on videotape, but the volunteers thought they were seeing a live, closed-camera feed.) Liat began the first task, looking at gory pictures—a burned man, an injured face. She acted moderately horrified. After a short break, the experimenter on the tape put a large lab rat in Liat's hands. She seemed dismayed but held it for a few seconds. For the third task, the experimenter took a bucket from under the table and filled it with ice. Liat put her hand in it but, stung by the pain, immediately pulled back. She tried again. Although she kept grumbling, "Ooh, it's painful and cold," she managed—but said, "I'm not sure I can go on with it." The experimenter on the tape asked Liat if she wanted to quit, but she said, "No, I had better finish the experiment."

The experimenter took a large, hairy tarantula from a box and placed it in the middle of the table. He asked Liat to touch it. She made one valiant attempt but stopped before her fingers touched the thing, saying plaintively that it was just too much for her. Asked to try again, she did, but again broke off and almost screamed, "I can't go on. Maybe the other person can do it." "OK," the experimenter responded, "I'll stop the camera, and we'll try again later."

The monitor went dark. At this point, the volunteer rated his emotional reactions to watching Liat, indicating how much compassion, personal distress, sympathy, tenderness, discomfort he felt. The experimenter sitting with the volunteer then said, "I'll go over and see if she can go on."

When the experimenter returned to the room, he told the volunteer, "We have a difficult situation here. Liat is very uncomfortable with these tasks. I wonder if you would agree to help her by replacing her in the tarantula task and the four remaining tasks? The study can't go on unless somebody actually pets the tarantula while another person watches, and the next task is just as bad or worse, having cockroaches run up your arm."

"We wanted them to feel that if they were going to replace Liat so that she could stop suffering, it was going to be at some cost to themselves," said Shaver. "They were going to have to do something they really didn't like."

The scientists saw firsthand the power of attachment insecurity. Participants who scored high on attachment avoidance reported lower levels of compassion toward Liat and were less willing to help her. Those who scored high on attachment anxiety reported personal distress while watching the suffering woman but were no more willing to help her. They seemed to feel that "it's alarming and distressing to me to see this going on"—but they did not care to trade places. Presumably, that would have distressed them even more.

"Attachment avoidance was consistently associated with less compassion and less willingness to help," Shaver said. In contrast, "attachment anxiety was consistently associated with higher levels of personal distress that did not translate into helpful behavior. . . . In other words, personal distress appears to be mostly a self-oriented reaction, not an instigator of care for another person."

Hearing this, the Dalai Lama recalled an eleventh-century Tibetan who was a great master of compassion but was known as the master with the gloomy expression. Whenever he meditated on compassion, tears would stream down his face. When you have a strong feeling of compassion, you experience a form of distress, he explained. But the distress experienced as a result of cultivating compassion is very different from the distress experienced during one's own suffering. In the latter case, there is no real choice; suffering grips you and overwhelms you. When you experience distress as a result of deliberate cultivation of compassion, however, there is a real strength and resilience, and therefore less likelihood of discomfort or distress leading to discouragement or depression. "Here we can see the clear effect of insight and understanding," the Dalai Lama said, "which greatly help compassion and, ideally, cause one to attempt to relieve the suffering of another."

Although personal distress did not translate into helping Liat, something else did. When volunteers were subliminally primed with the name of someone they had said they could rely on for emotional support, or thought about how such a person had once actually supported them, the results were striking. They not only reported feeling higher levels of compassion and more willingness to help Liat; compared to participants who were subliminally exposed to attachment-neutral names or asked to think about a neutral scenario, they were more likely to agree to actually relieve her distress by taking her place with the tarantula and roaches. The sense of security seems to trigger altruistic compassion at a subconscious, automatic level or at least allow it to emerge without interference. Moreover, the subconscious reminder of attachment security induced greater compassion and altruism regardless of the person's innate attachment style—that is, it worked on the emotionally avoidant as well as the emotionally anxious.

"Those who got the security prime were significantly more compassionate," said Shaver. "They felt more inclined to help the suffering woman. This makes it seem that if you can make a person feel more secure, he will have a greater capacity to feel for someone who is suffering and will be moved to do something about it. They're saying, 'Okay. I'll go to the room with the tarantula, and it will be me instead of her.' Making a person feel more secure had this beneficial effect independent of their inherent avoidance or anxiety. It worked on everyone."

People who are inherently more secure, or who are made to feel more secure through subliminal priming, consistently express greater compassion and willingness to relieve the suffering of another sentient being. Feeling emotionally secure allows you to forget your own needs and act as a selfless caregiver, showing compassion toward others even when it does not produce any other personal benefit and can actually cause personal distress (assuming you don't like petting tarantulas).

Like most science, the discovery about the power of primes has the potential for good as well as ill. Shaver hopes that by understanding the attachment system and learning what triggers people to feel emotionally secure enough to help others, to engage in volunteer work, to refrain from prejudice against people different from themselves, the world will be a better place. This is in line with what the Dalai Lama calls "secular ethics." Independent of Buddhism as well as other religions, secular ethics embraces tolerance, compassion, and peace.

In the wrong hands, however, one can imagine how primes quite different from what Shaver used to induce compassion for Liat might be used to make people less tolerant, more belligerent, more selfish. Perhaps reminding them of someone from their past who failed to comfort them when they needed emotional support would awaken a dormant sense of attachment anxiety or avoidance. As decades of studies have shown, both are associated with some of the worst attributes of humanity. But it might be just the ticket for rousing a population to war.

Teach Your Children Well

If we want children to grow into compassionate, altruistic adults, helping them become emotionally secure would be a big step in the right direction. More than a dozen studies have confirmed that if you assess an adult's attachment style with the Adult Attachment Interview, "you can predict with 70 percent accuracy how the person's child will be classified in the 'strange situation,' " said Shaver. That is, an avoidant mother usually has an avoidant child; an anxious mother, an anxious child; a secure mother, a secure child. But just as Michael Meaney discovered in his lab rats, there is no evidence that the cross-generational consistency is attributable to genes. "It seems to be a consequence of one generation's treatment of the next," Shaver said. Indeed, studies of twins in which behavior geneticists teased apart how much of attachment style is due to genes and how much to the environment produced no evidence for a strong genetic component.

This offers hope in a way that a strong genetic influence would not. Although the persistence of attachment style might lead you to believe that attachment style is fixed, determined irrevocably by one's experiences as a very young child, in fact, "it's very clear that it can change," said Shaver. That optimism is borne out by the growing number of discoveries that the brain can change. For attachment style, like every other aspect of behavior and personality, is rooted in the brain. With numerous studies showing that brain circuitry can be altered by experience, there is every reason to think that the circuitry underlying attachment can change, too. If you can teach parents how to give a child a sense of emotional security, for instance, then you have a good chance of sculpting a child who is emotionally secure, with all the attendant attitudes and behaviors that brings.

"Intervention works," Shaver explained to the Dalai Lama. "The interventions are fairly simple, such as explaining to parents that every child is wired so that if you comfort them and pay attention to them sensitively, they will go out to explore. For anxious parents, you explain that when the child goes out, it's important to let him go; don't interfere. Then, once the child is playing, it's natural for them to look back once in a while to see if you care, and even come over and show you a toy. It's important to let the child come in for refueling. In secure relationships, the parent gently explains, 'I love it when you're curious about the world. You want to explore, and that's fine. But I also don't want you to be hurt. I want you to understand this.' Over time, if that's done sensitively, the child understands that the parent is both supporting exploration and also protecting the child. A two- or three-year-old can sense that. The parent is essentially saying, 'I recognize your feelings, and those feelings are okay, but we want to make sure that your feelings don't lead you to fall off a cliff.' In fact, by the time children who have been treated like this reach the ripe old age of three or four, they are already more sophisticated in talking about their feelings, and in recognizing other people's feelings, than children who have not been treated so considerately. They show increased empathy because someone has been telling them we all have feelings and has been modeling compassionate behavior."

"Secure attachment plays an important role in promoting positive emotions, in cultivating compassion, in increasing altruistic behavior," Richie Davidson added. What is the Buddhist perspective, he asked the Dalai Lama, on enhancing a child's sense of security and of knowing that he can find a safe refuge?

"Our natural instinct when we are faced with a threat is to seek a safe haven, to seek protection," the Dalai Lama said through Thupten Jinpa. "At least among Tibetans, a universal tendency is, when you are faced with a real danger and a threatening situation, regardless of whether or not your mother is there or is capable of protecting you, you shout, 'Mother.' This is universal. In religious practice, when we consciously seek refuge, we imagine the source of refuge to be someone or something that has the capacity to protect, whether this is realistic or not."

Jinpa continued, "One thing that is very explicit, if not unique to the Buddhist approach of seeking refuge, is that it's not so much seeking refuge in an external force but is more of an internal state. When we list the three objects of refuge—the Buddha, the dharma, and sangha—we say, 'I go for refuge to the Buddha. I seek refuge in the dharma. I seek refuge in the spiritual community, the sangha.' Of these three, seeking refuge in the dharma is considered to be the true act of seeking refuge. Dharma is defined as the process that leads to freedom from the particular fear you are trying to escape as well as the achievement of that state of freedom. So that is the true refuge, because—at that moment, at least—the individual is free from that threat or fear. That's why in Buddhist texts you find lines like 'Oneself is one's own master. Oneself is one's own enemy, and savior.' The emphasis is on bringing about that state of freedom within oneself."

Recalling his own childhood, the Dalai Lama described his natal village in rural Tibet as very simple, with almost no secular education and only a little religious education. His mother, he said, was full of affection. There was a genuine atmosphere of loving-kindness and true compassion. He often wonders, he said, whether in childhood we have a keener appreciation of such noble qualities but let them languish in ourselves as we grow older.

"At that time, childhood, these human affections are very necessary to survive," he continued in English. "When we are grown up, not so obviously crucial, no immediate need. So sometimes we neglect about that."

Shaver jumped in. "Can I ask one thing about your autobiography? You say that your mother let you sit at the head of the table even though neighbors didn't approve of this. They thought she was being too lenient. And you also recalled going to the chicken house with your mother, and staying in a nest and clucking, and pretending to be a chicken. Was she unusual, or was this way of caring for children fairly typical?"

Fairly typical, the Dalai Lama answered, except that, in his village, there was a widespread recognition that his mother was an especially kind-hearted person. It affected how he interacted with others, he believes: "In my book, I mentioned, quite often there was a fight with my elder brother. No traces of ill feeling. . . . Fight . . . one moment, separate . . . crying sometimes . . . then few minutes, forget. Play together."

Short of turning back the calendar and giving every child the love, reliable attention, and comfort that provides the foundation of attachment security, the discovery that exposing people to subliminal reminders of that security leads to greater compassion and willingness to help—whatever someone's inherent sense of attachment—suggests that compassion can be enhanced. "Temporary activation of the sense of attachment security allows even chronically insecure people to react to others' needs in ways similar to those of people with a more secure attachment style," causing them to become more compassionate and helpful, Shaver says. "Because attachment patterns can change, there must be considerable plasticity in the brain circuits that underlie them. Attachment security can be increased, decreasing selfishness and ethnocentrism."

The discoveries left him more convinced than ever that the "human nature" described by traditional social psychology was little more than a picture of Dorian Gray, obscuring the reality of what people have the potential to become.

Chapter 9

Transforming the Emotional Mind

Challenging the Happiness "Set Point"

Into the Hills

It was a glorious morning in late September, the most beautiful time of the year in Dharamsala, when the monsoons have blown by and the hills are carpeted in emerald green. The Westerners, three neuroscientists and a Buddhist scholar, had lumbered down from their rooms at Kashmir Cottage, a guest house owned by the Dalai Lama's youngest brother, with hundreds of pounds of scientific equipment—laptop computers and battery packs, electroencephalographs and lead-acid batteries, a gas generator and two hundred feet of extension cords—that they planned to take into the hills where some of Tibetan Buddhism's most adept meditators sit in retreat for months and even years at a time. The researchers' hope was to launch the first comprehensive study of how the intensive, long-term practice of meditation—"long-term" being something north of ten thousand hours—changes the brain. And for that, they would have to persuade some of the hermit monks and lamas living in stone huts to donate their minds to science.

What we'd like to do, the scientists had written to the Dalai Lama in the spring of 1992, is measure whether, and how, thousands of hours of meditation alter the pattern of activity in the brain. The idea was not to document brain changes that occur during the real-time practice of meditation. Since meditation is an activity of the mind, it goes without saying that it is marked by particular patterns of brain activity. After all, whatever the brain does—meditate, send "move!" signals to the body, or think of pink elephants—produces a characteristic and potentially discernible pattern of activity. Meditation would of course have a neural correlate. No, the scientists were interested instead in whether the form of mental training that constitutes Tibetan Buddhist meditation produces enduring changes in the brain. Their quarry was not mental *states,* the brain activity that goes along with meditation, but mental *traits,* habits of thinking and feeling that are manifest when the brain is not meditating and that would presumably reflect an enduring physical or functional change in the circuitry of the brain rather than a fleeting burst of activity.

The Dalai Lama was intrigued by the proposal. Not only did it tap into his growing interest in science, but it also made sense from the standpoint of Buddhist philosophy, which holds that mental training is intended to change the mind in ways that spill over into everyday life. "I felt very strongly (and still do feel) that application of science to understanding the consciousness of meditators is most important, and I made a great effort to persuade the hermits to allow the experiments to take place," he recalled more than a decade later. "I argued that they should undergo the experiments out of altruism; if the good effects of quieting the mind and cultivating wholesome mental states can be demonstrated scientifically, this may have beneficial results for others. I only hope I was not too heavy-handed."

Of the sixty-seven hermits, yogis, lamas, and monks then living in the hills above Dharamsala, a number volunteered to cooperate with the strange men and their stranger machines, even though they had dedicated themselves to a life of solitude and, for the most part, didn't see the point. They believed that the best instrument for investigating the mind *is* the mind, not the blinking boxes and other contraptions the scientists had in tow. From these volunteers, the Dalai Lama chose ten senior meditators. For comparison, the scientists would also study ordinary Tibetans in Dharamsala, many of whom had fled Tibet soon after the Dalai Lama's own escape in 1959.

In the West, meditation is typically viewed as a means of stress reduction. Some forms of it are. But in Buddhism, meditation is a rigorous regimen of mental training, in which the mind observes itself. Through introspection and other techniques, the mind tries to free itself of afflictive tendencies such as hatred and jealousy and develop wholesome tendencies such as the power of attention or the capacity for compassion.

Some of the adepts recommended by the Dalai Lama practiced *shamatha,* a Sanskrit word best translated as "meditative quiescence." The goals of *shamatha* practice are to quiet the noise that bedevils the untrained mind, in which one's focus darts from one sight or sound or thought to another like a hyperactive dragonfly, and replace it with attentional stability and clarity. Those two qualities of attention, according to Buddhist philosophy, allow the practitioner to gain insight into the nature of mind and human experience. To do this, yogis cultivate a sense of mental and physical relaxation, from which attentional *stability* follows. That enables the mind to focus either on an object in the outside world or on a thought or feeling generated within the mind, something that in a person less practiced in attentional training tends to vanish like surf on the sand. A mind trained in *shamatha* is better able to resist distraction and feels a sense of peace and calm. Attentional *clarity,* which follows from attentional stability, is the ability to focus on a chosen object with vividness and in sharp detail, no longer dulled by the boredom or mental fidgets typical of the untrained mind.

Accomplished meditators claim they can focus on a single object for hours at a time and hold an intricate mental image—of a highly detailed wall hanging, for instance—with such clarity that they can see with their mind's eye the curlicue in the lower right corner or the baby monkey in the left center or any other element. That, according to Western science, is biologically impossible. According to the textbooks, the human brain is incapable of sustaining attention like this for more than a few seconds before it dissolves in a haze of distraction. And the mental clarity required to see any of the thousands of details in an intricate image is thought to be beyond the ability of most brains. The exceptions, such as musicians able to mentally zoom in on a few bars anywhere in a symphony or electrical engineers capable of holding a mental image of the thousands of connections and transistors in a microprocessor, reflect expertise and, presumably, mental training. It was the potential of mental training in the form of meditation in which the Western scientists fanning out over the hills of Dharamsala were interested.

Curiously, the effects of mental training are largely unknown. Although there have been no fewer than twelve hundred studies of meditation, according to a pair of scientists who surveyed the research literature back to 1931, no consistent pattern has emerged. However, most of those studies treated a kaleidoscope of meditation practices as if they were simply variations on a theme, when in fact they are radically distinct. Looking for effects on the brain of some hodgepodge called "meditation" had approximately the same likelihood of paying off as looking for the effects of "thinking." Yet there was reason to hope that by focusing on the specific meditation practices of Tibetan Buddhism, in the adepts the Dalai Lama recommended, the scientists might uncover clear effects of meditation (or, more generally, mental training) on brain function.

The scientists included Cliff Saron, who is now a neuroscientist at the University of California–Davis, Center for Mind and Brain. Francisco Varela, cofounder of the Mind and Life Institute, hoped that the annual dialogues it sponsored between scientists and the Dalai Lama would bloom into actual collaborative research. Richard J. Davidson, who would join the Mind and Life dialogues in 1994, was on the verge of seminal discoveries about patterns of brain activity that correspond to happiness and depression. Alan Wallace would be the scientists' ticket into the lamas' huts, for in 1980, he had spent five months meditating in these same hills after studying Tibetan Buddhism for ten years in India and Switzerland. Wallace became a student of the Dalai Lama in the early 1970s and received monastic ordination from him in 1975. Four years later, the Dalai Lama asked Wallace to serve as his interpreter during his European lecture tour, a role Wallace has also played at most of the Mind and Life meetings.

On this first foray, the scientists set their sights low. All they aimed to do was make contact with the yogis, describe the goals of the research, and familiarize them with the experiments' methodology and technology. Wallace, whom many of the yogis remembered from the months he had spent in retreat among them, translated the scientists' English into Tibetan, and the yogis' questions and responses back into English.

"We spoke to each of them for two to three hours," Cliff Saron recalled.

"We introduced ourselves, told them the history of our project, and explained that on this trip, all we wanted to do was establish a relationship with them, become familiar with their practices, and show them the kind of experiments we hoped to do." Those included such psychology classics such as the Stroop test, in which the word for a color is written in ink of a different color. *Red* is printed in green ink, for instance, and you have to read the word without being distracted by the ink color. It is a test of concentration, of the ability to screen out distraction. The experiments also included the Posner test, in which you look at a screen and see an arrow pointing, say, left. When a little box, the target, pops onto the screen, you are supposed to press a button, something that the arrow is supposed to help you do more quickly if it points to where the target appears but that slows you down if the target appears elsewhere. The Posner test, too, gauges attention—specifically, the ability to stay focused on the boring little arrow.

It was good the scientists kept their expectations in check. On the first morning, the quartet presented themselves at the hut of Monk A (the scientists promised the monks anonymity). In his sixties and in failing health, this monk was one of the most experienced hermits on the scientists' list of ten. But when they asked if they could record their conversation, he demurred. "He thought he had reached only very minimal attainment in this life, primarily due to problems with his gallbladder," Saron says. "He did not want any misinformation he might give us to be disseminated. He thought we should meditate if we wanted to understand the effects of meditation." The scientists had failed to take into account the humility that is central to Tibetan Buddhism: giving a candid account of one's meditative experiences and insights runs counter to twenty-five hundred years of Buddhist tradition, which discourages practitioners from discussing their spiritual or mental accomplishments.

The scientists didn't have much more luck with Monk B, one of Alan Wallace's *shamatha* teachers, who was in his fifties. It was with him that they first encountered the specter that would haunt their study. Cordial but skeptical, Monk B recounted how, several years before, a scientist at Harvard Medical School who pioneered studies of mind-body medicine had recruited an eminent yogi, Lobzang Tenzin, from these very hills. Assuring the yogi that nothing invasive would be done and, in particular, that no drugs or other substances would enter his body, the Harvard researchers got the yogi to agree to travel to Boston to be tested. But the scientists had, among other transgressions, drawn his blood. Three months after his return to Dharamsala, Lobzang Tenzin died. Needless to say, the tragedy affected the remaining yogis deeply. Lobzang Tenzin "had suffered greatly from the experimentation," Monk B told these new scientists.

Their visit turned into a three-hour debate about the validity of applying science to the study of the mind. How can the mind, which is formless and nonphysical, be physically measured? Monk B asked. Given that, of what importance is any physical correlate of mind such as that measured by the fancy EEG machines and other gizmos the scientists had lugged along? And since there are great differences in the attainments of individual yogis, might not unimpressive results from one or two diminish the standing of Tibetan Buddhism in the West? He had had bad dreams about being a subject, Monk B continued; he didn't even want to glance at the experiments, displayed on a scientist's laptop. "We left discouraged, with the thought, 'If a would-be ally had these many qualms, would we ever find enough participants for the study?' " Saron recalled.

And so it went. A fifty-nine-year-old monk, though delighted to learn that Alan Wallace had trained as a monk, wanted nothing to do with the study, explaining that he just wished to be left to practice his meditation (which he encouraged the scientists to do, too, advising them to say a mantra several hundred thousand times—which would have the advantageous side effect of causing them to grow new teeth—and to pray to the Dalai Lama for success in their research). A fifty-one-year-old thought he might be able to attain *shamatha*—the ability to place the mind, with minimal effort, on an object with clarity and stability—in two years or so. The scientists, he said, should come back then.

With each rejection, it was becoming clear that the yogis had deep concerns. Submitting to the odd tests, they worried, might impair their meditation practice. But that was the least of it. It was the mismatch of assumptions that probably doomed the project. The scientists were working on the premise that what the yogis' brains were doing during meditation, and how thousands of hours of meditation affected the brain, would be discernible with standard scientific techniques—that is, physical measurements. "That was a problem for many of them, our materialistic, reductionist perspective," says Alan Wallace. "We seemed like primitive Nean-derthals to them."

When the scientists showed a few yogis the Stroop test—in which a word for a color is printed in ink of a different color—they were singularly unimpressed. "It seemed like such a no-brainer to them," recalls Wallace. "Why would anyone be surprised that it takes longer to read the word *red* written in green ink than it does to read *red* in red ink? 'This is your best shot?' they wanted to know." One monk seeing the Stroop test suspected it measured only mental cleverness, a far cry from the august goals of Tibetan mental training with its emphasis on cultivating compassion for the bene-fit of all living beings. The yogis were no more impressed with the idea of measuring brain waves, Wallace recalled: "They thought, 'What are you people measuring, anyway, since you don't know the EEG correlate of compassion or loving-kindness or anything else?' "

The Posner test of visual attention fared no better in the yogis' eyes. Usually, if a target appears on-screen in a place to which the arrow pointed, you see it and react faster than if it appears elsewhere, but only if the target pops up less than half a second after the arrow. If the interval is longer, it seems, people's attention wanders, and they derive no benefit from seeing which way the arrow points. The scientists wondered if the lamas' mental training would have so improved their visual attention that the arrow would cue them to the location of the target even if more time elapsed. Trouble was, when the target appeared somewhere other than where the arrow pointed—which is supposed to cause someone with good powers of attention to take even longer to notice the target than if there had been no cue, since his attention is directed to where the arrow points—the yogis be-came confused. *Why did you lie to us? You said the cue would show where the target would be,* they asked the scientists.

No, studying the effects of mental training on the mind and brain was not going to be easy.

Culture clashes also loomed large. For instance, the scientists had cho-sen an expansive landscape of purple dunes and sun for an image meant to evoke contentment, whose neural correlate they would measure. But the image made the yogi who agreed to sit for this test sad, not content: he imagined the suffering of someone who had to cross such a place under a broiling sun. The image of a cute bunny also backfired. Rather than filling the yogi with a sense of contentment, it made him wonder anxiously who would protect such a weak animal from predators.

In the end, the scientists got no usable data during their time in Dharamsala. But they did manage to persuade one yogi to travel to the University of Wisconsin–Madison to spend a week in Richie Davidson's lab. There, he was tested in visual attention. One task was to stare at an image of a Buddha on a computer monitor. The image flickered very briefly at different intervals over the thirty to sixty minutes of the test. The yogi was to press a button each time he detected a flicker. Control subjects, typically bored out of their minds, are usually unable to sustain sharp attention, and as the minutes drag on, they take longer and longer to register a flicker. The yogi's reaction time, however, hardly slowed, so intent was his visual attention. The scientists had established that devoting years and years to training one's power of attention improves one's power of attention.

Well, it was a start.

Flash forward to the spring of 2001. One at a time, they made the trek to the University of Wisconsin–Madison medical center, maroon-robed monks and lamas and teachers, all meditation "adepts." A decade had made a huge difference in the willingness of accomplished Tibetan meditators to participate in studies of how mental training affects the brain, thanks in large part to a chance exchange. At the 2000 Mind and Life meeting in Dharamsala, where the subject was destructive emotions, the Dalai Lama peppered Davidson with questions about how he conducts his research— how the fMRI works, what EEGs measure. Why don't you come and see for yourself? Davidson asked.

In May 2001, the Dalai Lama was standing in Davidson's basement lab. He peered into the tank-size fMRI tube that detects areas of heightened brain activity and pinpoints these hot spots to within a millimeter. He examined an electroencephalograph that measures brain waves down to changes that occur in one-thousandth of a second. After silently taking in the technical information, he had a question for the scientists: can the machines tell if a thought appears before changes arise in the brain? That is, can mind or consciousness precede electrical and chemical activity? If so, then an inescapable conclusion would be that it is mind that is acting on brain and not only that brain gives rise to mind.

It was an echo of the question the Dalai Lama had asked the neurosurgeon after witnessing the brain operation, as described at the beginning of chapter 6. Unlike the neurosurgeon, however, the Madison scientists did not shut him down. Instead, they thought seriously about the possibility of a two-way causal arrow, with mind being both the expression and the cause of physical changes in the brain.

In addition to providing inspiration for this line of research, the Dalai Lama offered practical help. He asked accomplished practitioners who had undergone training in the Tibetan tradition over fifteen to forty years to participate in Davidson's experiments. They would lie in the cacophonous fMRI, sit still with electrodes plastered all over their scalp, turn their meditative state on and off like a lightbulb. Davidson also put out word that he was in the market for Buddhist contemplatives, the people he calls "the Olympic athletes" of meditation practice. Matthieu Ricard, the French Buddhist monk at Shechen Monastery in Kathmandu, Nepal, who holds a Ph.D. in genetics, was both investigator and subject in these experiments, helping plan them as well as being tested himself.

All the Buddhist adepts who would eventually lend their brains to neuroscience had practiced meditation for at least ten thousand hours. One had racked up fifty-five thousand hours. All had gone on at least one three-year retreat, during which he lived apart from society and passed almost all his waking hours in meditation. For the most part, the adepts made a detour to Madison when they happened to be in the United States, usually for a speaking tour. That made for slow going. Weeks would pass before the next monk came through. But as time went by, Davidson methodically built up a unique database: recordings of the brain waves and brain-activation patterns of long-term practitioners of Buddhist meditation. "I don't believe any of this work would have been initiated without your direct encouragement," Davidson told the Dalai Lama as he began his progress report at the 2004 meeting in Dharamsala. "For this, we are all very, very grateful."

Especially because of what the research has shown.

The Emotional Brain

Davidson had been on a quest that much of modern neuroscience suggested was, to put it politely, quixotic: to discover whether states such as happiness, compassion, enthusiasm, joy, and other positive emotions are trainable. That is, do there exist techniques of mental training that can alter the brain in a way that raises the intensity of these emotions, makes them last longer, or makes them easier to trigger?

Take two data points. In the research that sealed his reputation for rigorous neuroscience, Davidson and colleagues discovered, in the 1970s, striking differences in the patterns of brain activity that characterize people at opposite ends of the "eudaemonic scale"—that is, along the spectrum of baseline happiness. That's fact one: there are specific brain states that correlate with happiness, as I'll discuss in greater detail below.

Second, brain-activation patterns can change as a result of therapy—specifically, as a result of cognitive-behavior therapy and mindfulness meditation, in which people learn to think differently about their thoughts. Jeffrey Schwartz showed that to be the case with patients beset by obsessive-compulsive disorder; Zindel Segal and Helen Mayberg showed it with patients suffering from depression. Thus, we have fact two: mental training, practice, and effort can bring about changes in the function of the brain.

From those facts, Davidson built his hypothesis: that meditation or other forms of mental training can, by exploiting the brain's neuroplasticity, produce changes—most likely in patterns of neuronal activation, but perhaps even in the structure of neural circuitry in the sense of what's connected to what and how strong those connections are—that underlie enduring happiness and other positive emotions. If that is so, then by exploiting the brain's potential to change its wiring, therapists or even individuals might restore the brain and hence the mind to emotional health.

Just to be clear, the goal is not merely the absence of mental illness, which seems to be all that psychiatric and psychological therapies strive for these days, but the enduring presence of robust mental and emotional health.

"That's the hypothesis: that we can think of emotions, moods, and states such as compassion as trainable mental skills," Davidson told the Dalai Lama. "For this to happen, the emotion circuits of the brain must be plastic. But there have been remarkable experiments showing that: we know that experience can induce changes in the structure and function of brain regions involved in regulating emotions. I don't think we have given this a fair shake, the possibility that there might be salubrious effects of mental training on the emotions."

Western psychology has never seriously considered such a possibility. The only research into whether enduring traits can be changed has focused on psychopathology, such as chronic depression, extreme introversion, phobias, and other mental illnesses. In contrast, "no effort has been invested in cultivating positive attributes of mind in individuals who do not have mental disorders," Alan Wallace, Davidson, and colleagues wrote in 2005. "Western approaches to changing enduring emotional states or traits do not involve the long-term persistent effort that is involved in all complex skill learning—for example, in becoming a chess master or learning to play a musical instrument." And why should they? One's baseline level of happiness, after all, is supposed to be as fixed as one's blood type.

Buddhists have a particular interest in whether people's baseline emotions are malleable. People experience a number of afflictive emotions, as Buddhists call them, including jealousy, anger, greed, envy, and hatred. Whatever help they may offer in terms of survival, these emotions are not exactly conductive to collective well-being. Buddhism teaches that, through mental training, one may be able to mute such negative, even destructive, feelings. The question is whether there is any neuroscience to back that up.

As someone who made his reputation with discoveries that reinforce the idea that everything the mind is and does and feels can be traced back— can be *reduced,* to use that loaded term—to the brain, Davidson is not the first scientist you would think of to pioneer the study of the power of mental training to change the brain. He attended a yeshiva for seven years in Brooklyn and became interested in Eastern philosophy as an undergraduate at New York University in the late 1960s and early 1970s, a time when psychology was still in the grip of behaviorism. This school of thought holds that only observable behavior is fair game for science, while the interior life of the mind is a black box whose study is at best quixotic and at worst an unscientific folly. But Davidson was fascinated by internal mental processes— things such as mental imagery, conjuring a picture in the mind's eye.

When he arrived at Harvard as a graduate student in psychology, he took the first tentative steps toward bringing together his academic and philosophical interests. In 1974, he made his first trip to India as well as his first meditative retreat. The remarkable meditative skills of the adepts he encountered made him wonder what distinguishes those contemplatives— men who meditate hour after hour, year after year, making retreats during which they may spend as many as fifteen hours a day in meditation—from those who struggle and struggle to make it through even a daily hour of meditative practice. The former struck Davidson as "attentional athletes," he said years later. He decided to see what psychological testing would reveal about the difference in the attentional powers of meditation adepts and meditation novices. "Harvard let you do what you wanted," he said with a shrug.

What he wanted was to combine his two interests: the interior life of the mind—and, specifically, meditation—with neuroscience. With Daniel Goleman, a fellow grad student who was working on a dissertation on using meditation to improve the ability to handle stress, he published a theoretical paper arguing that regular meditation might yield what they called "trait effects"—enduring changes in the brain. That 1977 paper, "The Role of Attention in Meditation and Hypnosis: A Psychobiological Perspective on Transformations of Consciousness," was the first shot in what would become a decades-long campaign to discover whether mental training, of which Buddhist meditation is one form, can produce lasting physiological changes in the brain.

But even then, Davidson was doing more than theorizing. Among his many simultaneous research projects at Harvard was one investigating the ability to focus attention on a particular target despite distractions. As he and senior colleagues reported in 1976, attentional ability shows up as a distinctive electrical pattern in the brain, as captured by EEG. People differ in their attentional ability, of course. Davidson found that being better able to keep one's attention focused and resist distraction correlated with this EEG pattern.

In a sense, that is not surprising, since, as I've noted before, everything the mind does—such as pay attention—presumably has a counterpart in the brain, a physical correlate that gave rise to the mental activity in the first place. But finding that EEG patterns track attentional ability planted an idea in Davidson's head: that people might train their brains to pay attention just as they train their fingers to fly along the keys of a piano or their feet to switch in the middle of a soccer dribble. As part of that series of experiments, Davidson, Dan Goleman, and their mentor, psychophysiology professor Gary Schwartz, found that the more hours someone had spent practicing meditation, the greater his attentional ability. They had no idea what the basis for the correlation might be. In fact, they had not even done enough research to rule out the more humdrum conclusion—namely, not that meditation trains the brain in a way that improves its ability to focus but that people with an innate ability to focus tend to stick with meditation practice while those who find their attention constantly wandering drop it.

Despite (or perhaps because of) his productivity, which would have been remarkable for a professor let alone a graduate student, "I was getting criticism for doing too many things and specifically for doing this," Davidson recalls—"this" being the meditation research. So he dropped it. But finding a link between meditation and attention was tantalizing enough that he kept it in the back of his mind even as he made his mark in a seemingly different realm of science.

While still at Harvard, Davidson began to study emotions and their neurological underpinnings. At the time, neuroscience dogma held that the limbic system deep within the brain is the seat of emotions. But a course in neuroanatomy that Davidson happened to take down the street at the Massachusetts Institute of Technology planted in him a different idea: that the brain's frontal lobes, usually regarded as the seat of high-order cognitive functions such as reasoning and forethought, forge connections to the limbic system. If this still-nascent, and even heretical, idea were true, then activity in the frontal lobes might affect activity in the limbic system. If you state it as, "Thinking can affect emotions," it sounds like one of those things that everyone knows but that science comes around to late. After all, one can think, remember, or imagine oneself into a variety of emotional states. But in the 1970s, psychology and neuroscience still did not regard emotions, much less their cognitive control, as particularly worthy of study. When he moved to the State University of New York–Purchase in the early 1980s as an assistant professor, Davidson's grant applications and papers on the cognitive control of emotions were frequently rejected.

But other aspects of emotion were ripe for the picking. In the early 1970s, clinical observations of patients who had suffered a lesion in one side of their frontal cortex, usually from a stroke, showed that the consequences for mood are very different depending on whether the injury occurred on the right side or the left. "These studies were the first systematic description of a very different pattern of mood reactions following unilateral brain damage," says Davidson. Damage to the left side of the brain, especially in the prefrontal cortex just behind the forehead, left people unable to feel joy and caused them to experience an increase in sadness that sometimes brought on uncontrollable crying. In contrast, lesions on the right side of the prefrontal cortex left people indifferent to their neurological injury and sometimes prone to laugh at inappropriate moments. Cautious about interpreting the meaning of the differences, scientists concluded that these opposite emotional reactions "pertain only to injury," as one put it.

Davidson, however, had a hunch that the injured brains were telling scientists something about healthy brains. He had joined the faculty at the University of Wisconsin–Madison in 1984 and set out to investigate normal, undamaged human brains to see whether asymmetries such as those studied in brain-damaged patients might have anything to do with happiness and sadness in healthy people. In 1992, he and colleagues reported that activity in the brain's prefrontal cortex, as detected by EEG, is a reflection of a person's emotional state. Asymmetric activation in this region corresponds to different "affective styles," as Davidson called them: when activity in the left prefrontal cortex is markedly and chronically higher than in the right, people report feeling alert, energized, enthusiastic, and joyous, enjoying life more and having a greater sense of well-being. Put simply, they tend to be happier. When there is greater activity in the right prefrontal cortex, people report feeling negative emotions, including worry, anxiety, and sadness. They express discontent with life and rarely feel elation or joy. If the asymmetry is so extreme that activity in the right prefrontal cortex swamps that in the left, the person runs a high risk of falling into clinical depression.

Davidson and a revolving cast of colleagues would, by 2006, publish more than fifty papers on the asymmetry in prefrontal activity that underlies differences in mood and well-being. Along the way, it became increasingly clear that drawing a direct causal line from high left prefrontal activation to happiness was too simplistic. Yes, greater activation in the left prefrontal region is indeed associated with positive emotions such as happiness. But the causal strand takes a long and winding path. People with this pattern of brain activation feel they have their life under control. They experience personal growth and feel they have a purpose in life and good personal relationships; they accept themselves for who they are. People with greater activation in the right prefrontal cortex are, in contrast, discontent, unhappy, glummer. They often feel as if their life is out of control and are disappointed with how it has turned out. They tend to be dissatisfied with personal relationships and with work, and rarely feel emotional highs.

This thing called "happiness," then, just might be the effect of these other characteristics—satisfaction with life, a sense of control, and all the rest—rather than a direct result of high activation of the left prefrontal region. What seems to contribute to greater levels of well-being is the sense of "purpose, mastery, strong relationships, and self-acceptance," as Davidson put it, plus "the subjective sense that life is satisfying." Taking an active role in life, grabbing life by the lapels and jumping into activities and relationships that are likely to bring satisfaction and happiness is what characterizes people with relatively high left prefrontal activation.

A Happiness Set Point?

Affective style—basically, your emotional disposition; simplistically, whether you have a sunny outlook on life or a bleaker one—is remarkably stable. The extent to which happiness is pervasive throughout every day and each moment, not in the sense of continuous jollies but a broad range of positive emotions, tends to return to the level characteristic for that person like a rubber band snapping back into position. This has given rise to the notion of a happiness "set point," an emotional magnet that, whether you win the lottery or file for bankruptcy, get left at the altar by your one true love or enjoy a contented decades-long relationship, pulls you back to your baseline level of happiness. Entire forests have been felled to publish studies supporting the notion of a happiness set point. For instance, scientists have tracked the level of happiness and general satisfaction with life of about one hundred thousand people in several Western industrialized democracies, following them through marriage and parenthood, loneliness and love, widowhood and the occasional lottery win. No matter what joy or disappointment they experience, the studies find, after a short-lived spike or decline in their level of contentment, people tend to return to their baseline level of happiness.

"The idea of a set point is that there are stable differences between people, and that if there is some perturbation—winning the lottery, losing your spouse—we tend to come back to our baseline level of happiness," Davidson explained to the Dalai Lama. "After reaching a trough, a widow's level of happiness begins to climb back up and, after several years, reaches almost the point where she was before her husband died. A lottery winner's level of happiness reaches a peak, then drops to about the level it was before his windfall. In adults, affective style is very stable."

Davidson was careful to preface that last sentence with "in adults." That's because levels of contentment, and the asymmetric pattern of activation in the prefrontal cortex that goes with them, are not stable from childhood into adulthood. A miserable childhood can be followed by a contented adulthood, just as a happy child can descend into an adulthood of emotional misery. If you find high right prefrontal activation—the neural correlate of depression—in a child of three, that tells you nothing about what brain-activation pattern and disposition that child will have at eleven, much less at thirty-one, Davidson says. That could reflect the many changing circumstances of a person's life. The kid who was bullied unmercifully for being a nerd in junior high is likely to feel a lot better about himself when his mathematical prowess lands him a job trading derivatives for a seven-figure salary and brings him the trophy girlfriends, multiple homes, and luxury cars that go along with it. But whatever the outside forces, the fact that prefrontal activity is not constant from childhood to adulthood "was our first big hint that there is plasticity in this [happiness] circuit," says Davidson. True, it looked as if this plasticity disappeared once the brain reached adulthood, since affective style is so stable throughout the adult years. But then, other forms of plasticity were also thought to end with childhood only to be found, with the right stimuli, to persist well into adulthood.

There are several good reasons to question whether the stability of affective style in adulthood reflects something fundamental, for the constancy of someone's baseline level of happiness in adulthood could reflect any of a number of forces. Those with a taste for genetic explanations invoke the notion of a "happiness gene." That is an oversimplification, of course, since the only thing genes do is make proteins, and no one has any good idea how a protein (presumably in the brain) would raise your happiness set point. (Although, come to think of it, DNA whose protein acted— just to speculate for a moment—to halt the development of facial bones at just the perfect point to produce a visage worthy of *Vogue* might serve as a "happiness gene," since if it made you gorgeous in the eyes of the society in which you live, you would likely have a better chance at a life of contentment than someone whose DNA made proteins that made her look like a twin of the Wicked Witch of the West. Studies have shown that even in elementary school, teachers treat attractive children better, giving them more attention and expecting more from them, than they do homely children. A gene that acted in a way that brought you experiences conducive to happiness would show up as a "happiness gene" even if it had nothing directly to do with your brain's emotional circuitry.) An alternative explanation for a happiness set point is that whatever shaped your disposition in late adolescence—resilience, intelligence, kindness, curiosity, and other attributes of contented people—continues to do so in adulthood.

But there is a third possibility. Davidson pulled out a fact he had tucked away years before, back when he was discovering that differences in activity between the left and right prefrontal cortex underlie differences in people's baseline level of contentment. Experiments with animals in the 1960s had hinted that the prefrontal cortex is particularly susceptible to influences from the outside world. These influences affect its function and possibly its structure. Depending on whether monkeys are reared in nurturing or abusive conditions, for instance, activity in their prefrontal cortex is different. Certain environments can alter, seemingly in a permanent way, prefrontal activity. Add to that the fact Davidson had encountered long ago in that neuroanatomy course at MIT—namely, that there are strong connections between the thinking, prefrontal part of the brain and the feeling part of the brain—and an intriguing possibility arises: that you can voluntarily shift the ratio of right-to-left activation in your prefrontal region, altering not only happiness but a whole suite of emotions.

And that led to the question that found monks and lamas traipsing through Davidson's lab: might there be forms of mental training that, perhaps by altering the kind or amount of signals that the cognitive part of the brain transmits to the emotional part, change the basic pattern of prefrontal activation in a way that elicits more frequent and more positive emotions? The discoveries that mindfulness meditation can alter fundamental patterns of brain activity in people with depression or obsessive-compulsive disorder suggest that even rudimentary forms of mental training, falling far short of the long-term practice of highly accomplished Buddhist meditators, "can induce plastic changes in the brain," Davidson said. He calls the possibility that more sustained mental training can shift the happiness set point "transforming the emotional mind." And a parade of monks and lamas would help him discover whether it was possible.

Moving the Needle

Thanks to the Dalai Lama's encouragement, Tibetan Buddhist monks traveling to the United States put Davidson's lab on their itinerary. In May 2001, the "happy *geshe*," as he was known for the aura of contentment he radiated (and seemed to infect everyone he met with), arrived. The abbot of a Buddhist monastery in India, he had practiced meditation, particularly compassion meditation, for thirty years. After being fitted with the EEG skein of 256 electrodes, he followed Davidson's commands to alternate neutral mental activity with six mental states, including compassion meditation. During the neutral state, his prefrontal cortex showed a slight leftward tilt. But during compassion meditation, the left asymmetry was off the charts—higher than 99.7 percent of everyone ever measured.

The Dalai Lama has noted that the most powerful influences on the mind come from within our own mind. The findings that, in highly experienced meditators, there is greater activity in the left frontal cortex "imply that happiness is something we can cultivate deliberately through mental training that affects the brain."

"Yet in the West, happiness is not typically regarded as something trainable," Davidson responded. "What we are seeing, however, is that happiness can be conceptualized not simply as a state or as a trait but as the product of trainable skills, skills that can be enhanced through mental training."

Of course, it is possible that the monk had an intrinsic left asymmetry—maybe he was born happy—and that his mental activity had nothing to do with boosting it. But the fact that activity in the left prefrontal cortex rose so dramatically during compassion meditation certainly hints that mental training can alter the brain's emotional circuitry. As Davidson assembled the pieces, an intriguing possibility took shape. While the specifics of how meditating on compassion might trigger positive emotions remain to be worked out, the basic finding that cognitive activity can alter activity in one of the brain's emotion regions supports the hope that mental training can shift the happiness set point. If so, then the happiness set point must not be all it's cracked up to be.

Consider an analogy. You are studying whether measures of cardio-vascular health—resting heart rate and blood pressure, for instance—can be improved. You are conducting the experiment in a society that has yet to get the news that there is such a thing as aerobic exercise. You dutifully measure the resting heart rate and blood pressure of your couch potatoes every year for several decades. Except for some change due to aging, their heart rate and blood pressure are, you find, remarkably stable. You win fame and fortune and *Time* cover stories for discovering the "cardiovascular set point."

There is only one problem. You neglected to see whether resting heart rate and blood pressure can be lowered through a regimen of regular, rigorous, pulse-raising exercise.

So it may be with the happiness set point, Davidson suspected. What if the brain circuitry that underlies and regulates emotion is as plastic as the brain circuitry in Mike Merzenich's pellet-tapping monkeys or Ed Taub's recovering stroke patients, as the circuitry in Helen Neville's blind and deaf people and Zindel Segal's depressed patients? And what if we have simply failed to identify the regimen of mental training that has the power to alter it?

"The question we ask ourselves when challenged by the Buddhist view is, are we all stuck at our happiness set point, or is change possible?" says Davidson. "The Buddhists say that radical change is possible but that, in our Western culture, we have not given it a chance. But just as people now see the value of exercising the body consistently and for the rest of their life, it's similar with emotional skills."

That is something people acknowledge for many areas of learning and skills. If you don't practice your high school French, you will soon have no idea of the difference between *lever* and *laver*, and if you fail to practice your golf swing for a few years, you'll have a scorecard full of triple bogeys. "But we don't acknowledge it for our emotional lives," says Davidson. "There is a tremendous lacuna in our worldview, where training is seen as important for strength, for physical agility, for athletic ability, for musical ability—for everything *except* emotions. The Buddhists say these are skills, too, and are trainable like any others." If scientists find time and again that people return to their baseline level of happiness, maybe that's because they are studying people who, like virtually every Westerner, have no clue that one can sculpt the brain's emotional circuitry as powerfully as one can sculpt one's pectoral muscles. "Maybe no one has tried the intervention that would shift affective style in an enduring way," says Davidson. "I suspect the happiness set point is movable and plastic. The question is, what moves it?"

And that is what Davidson set out to explore: what is the effect of mental training on emotion, and which components of emotions and their associated brain circuits can be transformed? In particular, might meditation strengthen the cortical circuitry that modulates the activity of the limbic system, like a thermostat regulating this furnace of emotions? Might mental training rewire the brain's emotion circuits and alter forever the sense of well-being and contentment? With such training, says Davidson, we may very well be able to alter our happiness set point. It had been more than twenty years since he first dabbled in the scientific study of meditation. Now he was, as he put it, finally "out of the closet."

It was a lonely place to be. When it came to searching for the effect of mental training on the brain, Davidson did not have a lot of competition. As he told the Dalai Lama in 2004, "In preparation for this meeting, Your Holiness, I surveyed the Western scientific literature. There are precious few experimental studies on the role of pure mental training on either behavior or the brain. The role of mental training in general has been ignored in the Western biobehavioral sciences. There are a few studies in which athletes imagine going through a particular activity and the researcher evaluates its impact on their performance. There are some studies that use mental imagery in therapy. But in the West, the strategies that scientists and clinicians have developed to promote change have been based more on external factors than on mental training. So there is a very big difference in emphasis."

"This is to some extent understandable," said Thupten Jinpa. "Maybe at some subconscious level, [scientists] regard the mental training aspect as belonging to spirituality or religion" and are suspicious of it.

But science was coming around to Davidson's side. Although it is common to refer to "the brain's emotion center," or to "a region of the brain that processes emotion," by the late 1990s, things were looking much less cut-and-dried. Every area of the brain that had been implicated in some aspect of emotion had also been linked to some aspect of thought: circuitry that crackles with electrical activity when the mind feels an emotion and circuitry that comes alive when the mind undergoes cognitive processing, be it remembering or thinking or planning or calculating, are as intertwined as yarn on a loom. Neurons principally associated with thinking connect to those mostly associated with emotion, and vice versa.

This neuroanatomy is consistent with two thousand years of Buddhist thought, which holds that emotion and cognition cannot be separated. Back when thinkers were first probing for connections between the wisdom of the East and the science of the West, that would have prompted one of those *aha!*'s, often accompanied by a self-satisfied smirk that Buddhism had gotten there first. The current collaboration between Buddhists and Western neuroscientists has left such silliness behind. The realization that neuroanatomy confirms what Buddhism has asserted has instead prompted something more sophisticated: the idea that mental training, which engages many of the brain's cognitive circuits, can modulate its emotional circuitry.

To investigate this possibility, Davidson tested volunteers with no prior meditation experience on their ability to dampen negative, afflictive emotions and cultivate positive ones. He showed them photographs such as a baby with a horrific tumor growing out of its eye, and asked them to have an aspiration that the baby become well, be happy, and be free of suffering.

"I'd like to show you what is going on in the brain when people do this," Davidson explained to the Dalai Lama. "Most people in the West, when they see this picture, the most common emotional response is disgust. But what we are doing is mentally training them to change their emotional response."

Again using fMRI, he measured activity in the brain's amygdala, an area that is active during such afflictive emotions as distress, fear, anger, and anxiety. "Simply by mental rehearsal of the aspiration that a person in a photo be free of suffering, people can change the strength of the signal in the amygdala," Davidson said. "We discovered in this experiment that some people are very good at doing this and other people are not so good, for reasons we don't entirely understand. We asked what areas of the brain may be associated with success or lack of success at this task." It made sense to focus on the prefrontal cortex, which has neuronal connections to the amygdala. When they did, the scientists found that "individuals with greater activation in this area are better able, when they have the aspiration to relieve suffering, to change their brain and reduce the activation in the amygdala," Davidson said. "The signal in the fear-generating amygdala can be modulated with mental training."

The Dalai Lama responded, "What seems to be very clear is that a purely mental process—for example, deliberately cultivating this aspiration—can have an effect that is observable in the brain level."

Wired Monks

More than any other adept, Matthieu Ricard was a regular in Davidson's fMRI tunnel and under his EEG hairnet—and also in his office, for unlike the usual practice in which people who volunteer for experiments are little more than well-cared-for guinea pigs, Ricard was an active player in designing the research.

For this study, Ricard was wired up like a latter-day Medusa, a forest of wires snaking from 256 electrodes glued to his scalp to the electroencephalograph on the lab table. Ricard, like seven other Buddhist adepts and eight nonmeditators serving as controls, would engage in the form of meditation called pure compassion, in which the meditator focuses on unlimited compassion and loving-kindness toward all living beings. Compassion meditation, Ricard explained, produces "a state in which love and compassion permeate the whole mind, with no other consideration, reasoning, or discursive thoughts. This is sometimes also called nonreferential compassion, in the sense that it does not focus on particular objects, or all-pervading compassion."

The instructions began. *Okay, Matthieu, please put your mind in a nonmeditating* state . . . *and now begin the meditation . . . and now stop, into the nonmeditating state.* . . . And so it continued, the electrodes picking up the brain waves of different frequencies that Ricard's brain generated during the resting state and during meditation. All the while, the electroencephalogram built up, squiggle after squiggle. It was these data that Davidson took to the Dalai Lama on that October morning. One brain wave stood out: gamma waves.

Brain waves of this frequency, scientists believe, reflect the activation and recruitment of neural resources and, generally, mental effort. They are also a signature of neuronal activity that knits together far-flung brain circuits—consciousness, in a sense. They appear when the brain brings together different sensory features of an object, such as look, feel, sound, and other attributes that lead the brain to its *aha!* moment of, yup, that's a lilac bush, or that's a troop of rhesus monkeys. Gamma waves also stream across the brain when you scrutinize a Necker cube—that line drawing of a cube which, if you stare at it, switches so one of the front lines becomes the back—and make it flip from one perception ("front" line in front) to another ("front" line in back).

At the moment Ricard switched on compassion meditation, the gamma signal began rising and, over the course of meditation, kept rising. On its own, that is interesting but hardly astounding: the intense gamma-wave activity may just be the mark of compassion meditation. Except for two things. As Ricard segued from the neutral state to the meditative state on the scientists' command, the increase in gamma activity was larger than had ever been reported in neuroscience. And in the resting periods between meditations, the gamma signal never died down.

The month after the 2004 Mind and Life meeting, the prestigious science journal *Proceedings of the National Academy of Sciences* published the report of this study of the effects of mental training on the brains of eight accomplished Tibetan Buddhist meditators, including Ricard. This was the first scientific study of the meditative state of pure compassion. "I think it's safe to say that there's been no study of this kind ever published in this journal before," Davidson said. For controls, they had used ten nonmeditating Wisconsin undergraduates who got a crash course and a week's worth of practice in compassion meditation. "What you can see is that some of the controls, after just a very small amount of meditation training, showed a slight but significant increase in the gamma signal," he explained to the Dalai Lama. "But here are the monks."

At the moment the adepts began their meditation, it was plain for all to see on the PowerPoint slide Davidson displayed on screens at both ends of the room, there was an increase in the gamma signal. It rose gradually over the course of meditation for all the monks, just as it had in Ricard's brain. Usually, the gamma signal lasts for a couple of hundred milliseconds. But in the adepts, it lasted five minutes. "Most of them showed very large increases, and some showed extremely large increases of the sort that have never been reported before in the neuroscience literature," Davidson said. "It's like a continuous *aha!* moment."

The fact that the meditators' gamma waves were off the charts was impressive enough, suggesting as it did the power of mental training to produce a heightened brain state associated with perception, problem solving, and consciousness. But arguably even more intriguing were the gamma signals from the brains of monks and controls when they were *not* meditating—during the baseline state. "At the initial baseline period, before meditation, there is a small difference between the practitioners and the control subjects, with the adepts showing a little bit of a higher gamma signal," Davidson said. "But during the neutral state between compassion meditations, the practitioners show a large increase in this gamma signal." That is, even when the meditators are not meditating, their brains are different from the nonmeditators. It was a hint of something Davidson and others had been seeking since their treks to the yogis' huts in the hills above Dharamsala: evidence of the effect of mental training not on an in-the-moment brain state but on an enduring brain trait.

"It's like the imprint of the meditative state," said Thupten Jinpa.

"Exactly, exactly," said Davidson.

Ricard was not surprised that, even during the resting periods, his brain showed an imprint of a compassionate state. "An analogy is the pure love that a mother has for an innocent child," he explained. "You let that grow in the mind, so there's an all-pervading compassion. At some point, nonreferential compassion becomes a state that you can generate in your mind, that can pervade your mind without being distracted by other thoughts. You focus on the understanding that suffering may happen at any time, that impermanence is always there. Then the feeling of altruism and compassion remains even if you don't see suffering right then. And you think that, as long as beings are enslaved and entangled in destructive emotions, they must be the object of your compassion."

Although it's possible that the difference between the monks and the novices reflected something innate—maybe the monks were just born with these characteristic brain patterns rather than developing them through mental training—Davidson's data suggested otherwise. When he examined whether the number of years the Tibetan monks had practiced meditation predicted the magnitude of their baseline gamma signal, he found a linear relationship. The more hours of meditation training a monk had had, the stronger and more enduring the gamma signal. "We can't rule out the possibility that there was a preexisting difference in brain function between monks and novices," he said. "But the fact that monks with the most hours of meditation showed the greatest brain changes—the more practice, the greater the increase in this gamma signal—gives us confidence that the changes are actually produced by mental training."

After he finished having his brain waves recorded, Ricard had slid into the fMRI tube for a different set of measurements. EEGs are excellent ways to pick up particular brain signals but give only a rough approximation of where in the brain the signal arises. In contrast, fMRI pinpoints that genesis spot. Antoine Lutz, a colleague of Davidson's, tucked a blanket around Ricard to keep out the chill in the room. Returning to the control room, Lutz tested the communications system, making sure his words reached Ricard's headphones and Ricard's voice reached the control room. After going through a checklist, he told Ricard when to switch on compassion meditation and when to slip back into the neutral state—on, off, on, off. Each state, neutral and meditative, would occasionally be interrupted by the sound of a scream, piped in through Ricard's headphones. All the while the fMRI machine picked up telltale signs of activity in his brain. As in the EEG study, eight Tibetan Buddhist adepts with tens of thousands of hours of meditation behind them and eight undergraduates who had been taught compassion meditation for one week before the experiment and had practiced daily eventually had their brains scanned.

Davidson brought these data, too, to show the Dalai Lama. As he projected the fMRI images onto the giant screens, everyone peered at them intently. During the generation of pure compassion, the brains of all the subjects, both adept meditators and novices, showed activity in regions responsible for monitoring one's emotions, planning movements, and positive emotions such as happiness. Regions that keep track of what is "self" and what is "other" became quieter, as if, during compassion meditation, the subjects—adepts as well as novices—opened their minds and hearts to others. Areas that become active during negative emotions such as unhappiness and anxiety also showed less activity during all the volunteers' compassion meditation. But the meditating brains showed greater activity in response to hearing the scream than did brains in the neutral state, suggesting that a brain filled with thoughts of compassion and loving-kindness is more attuned to the suffering of others. So far, these results confirm that generating a feeling of loving-kindness and compassion has neural correlates in the brains of all the meditators, experts and beginners alike.

More interesting were the differences between the adepts and the novices. In the former, there was significantly greater activation in brain regions called the right insula and caudate; this is a network that other studies have linked to empathy and maternal love. Not only did this network show greater activation in monks than in novice meditators, but the activity was also more pronounced in monks with the greatest number of hours of meditation practice—those toward the fifty-five thousand lifetime hours. Connections from the frontal regions, so active during compassion meditation, to the brain's emotion regions seemed to become stronger with more years of meditation practice, a hint of what Davidson first suspected more than a decade before: that mental training that engages concentration and thought can alter connections between the thinking brain and the emotional brain.

The brains of the meditating monks also showed greater activity than the brains of novice meditators in a far-flung cortical network involving the anterior cingulate cortex, the insula, the somatosensory cortex, and the cerebellum. These regions would not seem to have much in common; the somatosensory cortex, of course, registers tactile sensations, for instance, while the anterior cingulate has been linked to such cognitive functions as making decisions as well as to empathy and emotion. Yet the whole network fires during one special circumstance: "It is usually activated when you are in pain or when you see someone else in pain, and during emotional experiences," Davidson explained. "The activation of this network was stronger in the adepts than in the nonmeditators, which supports the idea that our experience of another person's suffering is mediated by the brain regions that are involved in our own experience of pain. The idea of 'suffering with' someone makes sense neurologically."

In a surprising finding, when the monks engaged in compassion meditation, their brains showed increased activity in regions responsible for planned movement, as if the monks' brains were itching to go to the aid of those in distress. "This was a novel and unexpected finding," Davidson told the Dalai Lama. "There's no physical activity; they're sitting still. One interpretation of this is that it may reflect the generation of a disposition to act in the face of suffering. It gives real meaning to the phrase 'moved by compassion.' "

"It feels like a total readiness to act, to help," Ricard agreed. "It's a state of complete benevolence, of complete readiness, with no limitation. You do not think, 'Okay, I'm sort of ready to help one or two persons, but there's a limit to what I could do.' What you cultivate instead is a state of unconditional, no-matter-what compassion: 'Now or in the future, in all my lifetimes, I will be totally ready.' "

One final spot of activity in the brains of the meditating monks jumped out: an area in the left prefrontal cortex, the site of activity associated with happiness. During the monks' generation of compassion, activity in the left prefrontal swamped activity in the right prefrontal (associated with negative moods such as unhappiness as well as with extreme vigilance) to a degree never before seen from purely mental activity. In contrast, the undergraduate controls, who had had only brief instruction in compassion meditation, showed no such differences between the left and right prefrontal cortex.

This pioneering study showed that compassion is mediated by brain regions that generate maternal love, empathy, and a desire to help others. The finding that activity in these areas was markedly higher in the adepts suggests that "this positive state is a skill that can be trained," Davidson said. "Because increased training in compassion meditation results in greater activation of areas linked to love and empathy, it suggests that emotions might be transformed by mental training. Science has long held that emotional regulation and emotional response are static abilities that don't much change once you reach adulthood. But our findings clearly indicate that meditation can change the function of the brain in an enduring way."

Freedom from Suffering

Readiness to respond to and act on the suffering of another seemed to be central to the sense of compassion Ricard felt during his meditation, as shown by the activation of areas of the brain that initiate action. Davidson was curious about whether Buddhism views readiness to act as a crucial aspect of compassion.

From the Buddhist point of view, responded the Dalai Lama through his interpreter, "compassion is normally conceptualized as a state of mind that wishes to see the immediate object of that compassion be free of suffering. There are different degrees of compassion. At one level, compassion primarily remains at the level of wish. But there can be more forceful levels of compassion, where it's no longer just a wish but also a willingness to reach out and do something about the suffering. Buddhist literature makes a distinction between these. One is called the wish to see the sentient being free from suffering. The other is called the wish to relieve the being from suffering. Distinctions are also drawn between the different types of compassion depending upon what the accompanying mental states are. Here the role of the intelligence, or what the Buddhists call insight or wisdom, comes into play. You can have a type of compassion where the prime focus is the suffering of another sentient being and the wish to see that being free from suffering. Or a practitioner may use a deeper understanding of the nature of existence of the sentient being, such as a recognition of the transient nature of existence or a recognition of the nonsubstantiality of the sentient being, and feel compassion for that reason, even though there is no overt suffering. And in the Buddhist context, we also speak of Great Compassion, where the compassion is extended toward all beings."

Alan Wallace picked up: "Great Compassion is in fact an even deeper type of compassion, an undifferentiated compassion toward all beings. But it's not only that it's undifferentiated. There is also a strong sense that 'I wish to protect.' It's engaged, it's taking on responsibility, taking on the burden. It's not just the general wish 'May all sentient beings be free of suffering,' but it's taking it much more personally as 'I wish to help.' "

Buddhist training for cultivating Great Compassion begins with the recognition that you first need to cultivate a sense of empathy with other sentient beings. "The more you are able to extend that empathy to a larger group, the greater your capacity to cultivate compassion toward those beings," explained Jinpa. Once one has cultivated empathy, Great Compassion requires an ability to recognize suffering, so one can recognize when empathy and compassion are called for. Then one cultivates "a deeper insight into the nature of suffering and also some recognition of the possibility of gaining freedom from that suffering," he continued. "Because if you know there's a possibility of freedom from that suffering, then your compassion for the suffering being is going to be all the greater; you know that this is a situation that the sentient being can be relieved from. Without the capacity to empathize and without some recognition of the nature of suffering, one's compassion may simply remain at a level of aspiration, which would not have much effect."

The Dalai Lama spoke of a seventh-century Buddhist thinker who argued that no matter how much training an athlete may engage in, and no matter how great an athlete may be, there will be a finite potential beyond which that person will not be able to jump or sprint. "In contrast," he said, "qualities like compassion and loving-kindness have in principle the potential for limitless enhancement."

"This may indicate that, in certain domains, there's limitless neuroplasticity," said Davidson.

"Yes," said the Dalai Lama emphatically.

"There is nothing in Western psychology about how to cultivate compassion," says Davidson. "It is no more than a mission statement—that compassion is an admirable human value. But this amorphous thing called the cultivation of compassion actually leads to measurable changes in the brain."

The power of neuroplasticity to transform the emotional brain opens up new worlds of possibility. We are not stuck with the brain we were born with but have the capacity to willfully direct which functions will flower and which will wither, which moral capacities emerge and which do not, which emotions flourish and which are stilled. Davidson's research supports an idea that Buddhist meditation adepts have long maintained: that the mental training that lies at the core of meditative practice can alter the brain and thus the mind in an enduring way—strengthening connections from the thoughtful prefrontal lobes to the fear- and anxiety-generating amygdala, shifting activity in the prefrontal cortex from the discontented right side to the eudaemonic left side. Connections among neurons can be physically modified through mental training just as a biceps can be modified by physical training. Much as sustained attention can turn up activity in regions of the motor cortex that control finger movements in the virtual piano players, so might it damp down activity in regions from which negative emotions emanate and at the same time dial up activity in regions devoted to positive emotions. Although research into the power of mental training to change the brain is barely out of the starting blocks, the results so far support the idea that meditation produces enduring changes. "The trained mind or brain is physically different from the untrained one," Davidson says.

The power of mental training resonated with the Buddhist scholars listening to Davidson describe his discoveries. "I think the reason why we emphasize mental training is the realization that outer conditions are important contributive factors to our well-being or suffering. But in the end, the mind can override that," said Matthieu Ricard. "You can retain inner strength and well-being in very difficult situations, and you can be totally a wreck where apparently everything seems perfect. Knowing that, what are the inner conditions for well-being and for suffering? That's what mental training is about, trying to find antidotes to suffering and to afflictive mental states—antidotes that let you deal with the arising of hatred, for example, to dissolve it before it triggers a chain reaction. Mental training is gradually going to change the baseline. It is the most fascinating endeavor we can conceive. Mind training is the process of becoming a better human being for your own sake and for the sake of others."

Buddhist philosophy teaches that a person's allotment of happiness is not fixed and that, through meditation, someone can increase his or her capacity for compassion and happiness, even banishing such negative emotions as jealousy, hatred, anger, greed, and envy. As the Dalai Lama has written, there is an "art" of happiness. He tells friends that, as a child, he was angry as often as any other child and sometimes even a bully. But after sixty years of meditation training, these emotions have faded away, he says. Now, it is not that he has to suppress hatred, for instance; he never even experiences it. The science of neuroplasticity refutes the notion that the mental tendencies that lead to so much human suffering are hardwired into our brains. It also promises a coherent physiological explanation for how something such as the Dalai Lama's personal experience, shared by other adept meditators, can occur: that brain wiring responsible for negative emotions withers and that responsible for compassion and happiness becomes stronger. The plasticity of the brain's emotion circuits is the means by which mental training can bring about enduring physical changes in the brain and hence in one's mental and emotional state.

"I believe that Buddhism has something to teach us as scientists about the possibilities of human transformation and in providing a set of methods and a road map for how to achieve that," said Davidson. "We can have no idea how much plasticity there really is in the human brain until we see what *intense* mental training, not some weekly meditation session, can accomplish. We've gotten this idea, in Western culture, that we can change our mental status by a once-a-week, forty-five-minute intervention, which is completely cockamamy. Athletes and musicians train many hours every day. As a neuroscientist, I have to believe that engaging in compassion meditation every day for an hour each day would change your brain in important ways. To deny that without testing it, to accept the null hypothesis, is simply bad science.

"I believe that neuroplasticity will reshape psychology in the coming years," he continued. "Much of psychology had accepted the idea of a fixed program unfolding in the brain, one that strongly shapes behavior, personality, and emotional states. That view is just shattered by the discoveries of neuroplasticity. Neuroplasticity will be the counterweight to the deterministic view [that genes have behavior on a short leash]. The message I take from my own work is that I have a choice in how I react, that who I am depends on the choices I make, and that who I am is therefore my responsibility."

Chapter 10

Now What?

Back in chapter 1, I promised to show that scientists had met the challenge set out for them by the great Spanish neuroanatomist Santiago Ramón y Cajal. He had described the adult brain as "fixed" and "immutable" but also wrote, "It is for the science of the future to change, if possible, this harsh decree. Inspired with high ideals, it must work to impede or moderate the gradual decay of the neurones, to overcome the almost inevitable rigidity of their connections."

That future has arrived. We are the beneficiaries of a revolution in the understanding of the brain and of human potential.

In discussing the many circumstances under which the adult brain displays neuroplasticity, I hope I have not given the impression that neuroplasticity is an occasional property of the brain, one trotted out in response to trauma such as a stroke or blindness or amputation, or to extraordinary demands placed on it such as mastering a musical instrument or engaging in intense mental training. Those are indeed circumstances when neuroplasticity steps up and shows what it can do. But they are only the ones neuroscientists have looked at. The search for other demands on the brain that call forth its power of neuroplasticity is only beginning. From what they have seen so far, researchers are convinced that neuroplasticity is the normal, default state of the brain from childhood to old age. In response to the signals that the senses carry from the outside world, and to the thoughts or movements that it sends back out, the brain "undergoes continuous change," Harvard's Alvaro Pascual-Leone and colleagues concluded in 2005. "Behavior will lead to changes in brain circuitry, just as changes in brain circuitry will lead to behavioral modifications." Or as his former mentor Mark Hallett said, "We have learned that neuroplasticity is not only possible but that it is constantly in action. That is the way we adapt to changing conditions, the way we learn new facts, and the way we develop new skills. . . . We must therefore understand neuroplasticity and learn how to control it."

That holds true for many reasons, but one of the most important is that there is a dark side to neuroplasticity.

Neuroplasticity Gone Wrong

The fact that the brain is so malleable to the input it receives and the experiences its owner has means that wrong inputs and harmful experiences can reshape it in undesirable ways. The simplest of these are the result of the wrong sensory input. I have already mentioned one of them: in some cases of specific language impairment, or dyslexia, auditory problems cause sounds that arrive in the brain to be degraded. As a result, the brain cannot tell the difference between explosive phonemes such as *d* and *b*. When Mike Merzenich and Paula Tallal figured out that such a brain is unable to process and distinguish these phonemes from each other, they developed the auditory repair kit now known as Fast ForWord, which taps the power of neuroplasticity to alter these auditory circuits and, as a result, improve reading skills. But there is no question that if the brain came hardwired for the sounds of language, rather than being shaped by the sounds that arrive (clearly or indistinctly) from the ears, it would not develop this problem in the first place.

Another condition that arises when the brain receives degraded sensory input is focal dystonia. A usually painless condition, it affects some three hundred thousand Americans. It tends to strike pianists, flutists, and string players and is marked by an inability to control individual fingers, usually the three from the middle finger to the pinkie. When someone with focal hand dystonia tries to raise, say, her right middle finger to play a note on the piano, the right ring finger comes along with it. (Focal hand dystonia has ruined the careers of a number of famous pianists, including Gary Graffman, Leon Fleisher, and possibly Glenn Gould.) The culprit seems to be the many hours of daily practice in which dedicated musicians engage, often beginning when they are very young. When the brain is bombarded over and over again with near-simultaneous signals from two different fingers, and when those signals are rapid and repeated and occur in a learning context—that is, when the person is concentrating hard on the movements, as a musician does when practicing—the brain gets the idea that the signals are actually arriving from the same finger. It therefore decides that it needs only one cluster of neurons for both rather than zoning separate clusters for each finger. The somatosensory cortex loses its ability to differentiate between stimuli received from different fingers.

Merzenich's team showed that this merging of the "representation zones" of adjacent fingers can occur when three of a monkey's fingertips are stimulated simultaneously. After hundreds of repetitions of this intense synchronous input every day for a month, the monkey's brain had gotten the message. *Okay, fine; this tap-tap-tapping must be happening to a single fingertip.* As a result, the monkey's brain no longer dedicated a discrete region of the somatosensory cortex to individual fingers. Instead, the fingers' representations in the brain fused, with just a single region responding to the touch of several fingers. The brain now treated several fingertips as one unit and could no longer control them independently. As in the case of degraded auditory input, neuroplasticity left the brain vulnerable to disabilities.

Since repetitive, simultaneous sensory input to several fingers teaches the brain that separate fingers are a single unit, causing focal hand dystonia, then treating the condition requires teaching the brain that the fingers are indeed individual actors. Early findings suggest that if patients perform exercises that stimulate each affected finger separately, and (by restraining the finger that insists on coming along when another one moves) move them individually, they can redraw the map of their own somatosensory cortex, getting it to devote separate clusters of neurons to each finger. Indeed, in a variation of the constraint-induced movement therapy that Ed Taub developed for stroke, hand-dystonia therapy restrains the movement of one or more healthy, less-dystonic fingers. The subject does piano exercises with two or three fingers for some two hours each day for eight days, followed by home exercises. The brain is retrained, learning that the ring finger, say, really is a separate entity deserving of its own cortical space.

Tinnitus, or ringing in the ears, may also reflect neuroplasticity gone wrong. Although not all cases of tinnitus have the same cause, in some people the problem comes when the brain's representation of a particular tone has taken over the surrounding cortical space, much as the representation of the fingering digits of a violinist's hands takes over space once assigned to the hand. Tinnitus is notoriously hard to treat, but if cortical reorganization such as this lies at the root of at least some cases, then it may be possible to craft particular auditory inputs that reduce the amount of space the cortex gives the "tinnitus frequency," reducing symptoms as well.

Just as there is a downside to neuroplasticity, so researchers will almost certainly discover limits to neuroplasticity—brain conditions that yield to no intervention, that are not affected by even the most intense mental training, that remain as impervious to new input reaching the brain as a slab of concrete to a butterfly alighting on it. But research has already blasted through the most obvious limitation—namely, the myth that the adult brain is unable to produce new neurons and incorporate them into existing circuitry. And there are hints that neuroplasticity may be the key to undoing even something as fundamental as the cognitive declines that come with old age.

Turning Back the Clock

Throughout this book, I have stuck to scientific results that are not only well supported by animal studies, the gold standard for giving a biological discovery plausibility, but that also accord with the basic understanding of brain structure and functioning. But the picture of neuroplasticity would be incomplete without a sense of where the field might be headed and what its potential might be. For even if you are not a musician, not a stroke patient, not dyslexic or blind or deaf, not suffering from obsessive-compulsive disorder or depression, the power of neuroplasticity can make a difference to your brain and your life.

No one has pushed the envelope of neuroplasticity harder than Mike Merzenich. He believes that neurological conditions ranging from schizophrenia and multiple sclerosis to mild cognitive impairment and "normal" age-related declines in memory and other cognitive functions not only reflect changes in the brain that result from its neuroplasticity. They can also, he believes, be treated by the same principle he used to understand the causes of and treat dyslexia: figure out what deleterious input caused the brain to change, determine what those changes are, and find a corrective input that will rewire the brain in a way that treats the condition. If neuroplasticity makes the brain vulnerable to disabilities, he is convinced, then it can be exploited to cure them, too.

In the first decade of the new millennium, he began to develop a neuroplasticity-based intervention for normal age-related cognitive decline. The physiological roots of that decline have become better understood in recent years. They include weaker and less-accurate sensory input; older adults neither see, hear, feel, taste, nor smell as accurately as teenagers do. In addition, the brain doesn't get used or challenged as much as it once did; people retire or pursue only activities they're already good at (and enjoy), with the result that the brain engages in fewer activities that drive new learning. Finally, both neuronal metabolism and the metabolism of neuromodulatory control systems slow down. In the first case, the result is impaired production and function of the neurotransmitters and receptors by which one neuron communicates with another, the physical foundation of thinking and remembering. In the second, systems involving biochemicals that are crucial to attention, to detecting when you have encountered something new (novelty detection underlies learning), and to feeling a sense of reward (without which, people lose the will to do much of anything, since nothing brings them pleasure) all weaken.

Merzenich believes it is possible to target these age-related changes with specific training. Improving the fidelity of sensory signals, particularly hearing, is farthest along. With age, the inner hair cells of the cochlea deteriorate, and you lose the ability to hear high-pitched sounds. The problem is not that you won't hear whistles but that normal human speech sounds muffled and muddied. People seem to mumble or speak too quickly, and you can't make out what they're saying if the environment is noisy. In audiologyspeak, the signal-to-noise ratio declines with age. "The brain's representation of speech becomes noisier and degraded, which is why some elderly adults have trouble understanding muffled speech or the speech of young children," says Merzenich. "If you have trouble processing speech, the information fed into memory is crummy." Indeed, when young adults listened to audiotapes on which a speaker intoned a list of words, but with the soundtrack modified so it sounded the way words do to an elderly person, their verbal memory declined to the level of people decades their senior. As Merzenich puts it, "sensory-processing deficits such as these can cause profound deficits in memory and cognitive function."

But speech that has been modified can turn back the hands of time in the brains of older adults. In a study Merzenich presented in late 2005, he had elderly volunteers, sixty-one to ninety-four years old, undergo eight weeks of computer-based training to improve the brain's ability to discern the sounds of speech. As with Fast ForWord for dyslexia, participants listen carefully for when a sound (intoned by an animated cow) changes, listen and remember sequences of phonemes, discern whether two spoken phonemes are identical, and the like. Similar auditory retraining has been shown to rewire the auditory cortex in dyslexic children. The older brains, too, both processed speech better and remembered things better. "The majority improved ten or more years in neurocognitive status," says Merzenich. "Eighty-year-olds had the memories of seventy-year-olds. With more training, I expect we could reduce neurocognitive age by twenty-five years." He foresees a day when the discoveries of neuroplasticity will usher in "a new brain-fitness culture," reflecting "an understanding that you need to exercise your brain as you exercise your body."

He also thinks it possible to stimulate the production of important brain chemicals, including acetylcholine, dopamine, and norepinephrine. Take dopamine. This brain chemical is most closely, and interestingly, associated with the feeling of pleasure. When dopamine circuits go awry, addiction can result: basically, an addict's dopamine circuits become so inured to the pleasures of alcohol, shopping, or opiates that he requires more and more of the substance or activity to derive the same kick. It is a common observation that some, perhaps many, older adults do not derive the same pleasure from life that they once did. To be sure, many have good reason for their joyless outlook, from declining health and loneliness to the death of a spouse and intimations of mortality. But a sluggish dopamine system may also contribute.

For that reason, Merzenich and his colleagues are embedding in the mental-training programs they have developed for age-related cognitive decline little rewards and amusements. Users get little flickers of happiness, which he believes pumps up their dopamine system. Getting joy out of what you do is critical to keep doing it, whether the "it" is physical exercise or ballroom dancing or learning a second language or any of the other attention-intense activities that preserve mental function.

The neurotransmitter acetylcholine is the brain's attention-getter, dominating the circuits involved in focusing and paying attention. As with the dopamine system, when this system gets less exercise, it becomes flabby. We often assume that the reason elderly people have trouble paying attention, or keeping their attention from wandering, is their declining interest in the world around them and their feeling that they have "seen it all." Instead, their brain may simply not be getting the attentional workout it needs. Older adults are frequently told that, to keep their mind sharp, they need to stimulate it with activities such as crossword puzzles and reading. But activities done repeatedly become second nature, demanding less attention than new skills do. The result is a brain that gets fewer and fewer attentional workouts, fewer and fewer chances to keep its acetylcholine system tuned up. The result of an inability to pay attention, which is not uncommon in many elderly adults, is trouble remembering new information and experiences. And because of the centrality of attention to neuroplasticity, a brain that cannot pay attention is a brain that cannot tap into the power of neuroplasticity.

Given this, rather than engaging in activities you are already good at in order to keep an aging brain in shape, it makes much more sense scientifically to take up new challenges, from ballroom dancing to travel to never-before-visited places. Those will exercise the brain's crucial attentional networks. As Merzenich and colleagues point out, animal studies have shown that "under optimal environmental conditions, almost every physical aspect of the brain can recover from age-related losses." New neurons can bloom; gray matter can become thicker. Neuroplasticity makes it possible.

Above-the-Line Science

The question of whether the brain can change, and whether the mind has the power to change it, is emerging as one of the most compelling of our time. This power ties in to a sea change in biomedicine, neuroscience, and psychology.

If we score mental health on a scale that runs from very negative values (mental illness) through a zero point and then up into very positive values, the absence of mental illness is akin to the zero point. Science has always focused on the zeroth level and below, on people and conditions that are pathological, disturbed, or, at best, "normal." As a result, researchers have amassed quite a record when it comes to studying all the ways the mind and brain can go wrong. In its 943 dense pages, the latest edition of the bible of mental illness, *The Diagnostic and Statistical Manual of Mental Disorders,* covers everything from autism and Tourette's to schizophrenia, depression, masochism, and "feeding disorders of infancy." And no wonder it's so full. In the last thirty years, there have been about forty-six thousand scientific papers just on depression and an underwhelming four hundred on joy. When psychology researcher Martin Seligman became the president of the American Psychological Association, he drew attention to the field's one-sided view of the human mind and urged researchers to investigate positive psychological states—happiness and contentment, curiosity and drive, engagement and compassion. "Social science," he lamented, "finds itself in almost total darkness about the qualities that make life most worth living."

There is a more practical effect, too. Virtually all of biomedical science focuses on getting people up to the zeroth level and nothing more. As long as someone can attain nonsickness, that is deemed sufficient. As Buddhist scholar Alan Wallace put it, "Western scientists have an underlying assumption that normal is absolutely as good as it gets and that the exceptional is only for saints, that it is something that cannot be cultivated. We in the modern West have grown accustomed to the assumption that the 'normal' mind, in the sense of one free from clinical mental illness, is a healthy one. But a 'normal mind' is still subject to many types of mental distress, including anxiety, frustration, restlessness, boredom, and resentment." All are considered normal, part of the vicissitudes of living. We call unhappiness a normal part of life and say "it's normal" to feel frustration when thwarted; "it's normal" to feel bored when the mind feels empty and nothing in our surroundings engages us. As long as the distress is neither chronic nor disabling, the mind gets a clean bill of health. "There are so many people who are sick in the same way that we accept that as being normal," Matthieu Ricard added. "In this case, 'being sick' means having a mixture of positive and destructive emotions. Because it's so common, we sort of feel this is natural, normal. We accept that and say, oh, this is life, this is how things are, we have this mixture of shadows and light, of qualities and defects. It's normalcy."

Tapping into the brain's powers of neuroplasticity offers the hope of changing the understanding of mental health. The growing evidence of the brain's ability to change its structure and function in response to certain inputs, combined with discoveries such as Davidson's on the power of mental training to harness that neuroplasticity to change the brain, suggests that humanity does not have to be content with this strange notion of normalcy, with the zeroth level of mental and emotional health. "Cognitive-behavioral therapy is primarily to get people up to normal, not to bring about exceptional states of compassion, of virtue," Wallace continued. "Buddhism is designed to heal the afflictions of the mind. Meditative practice—mind training—is designed to bring about exceptional states of focused attention, compassion, empathy, and patience."

As researchers probe the power of meditation and other techniques to alter the brain and allow it to function at the highest levels, we are therefore poised at the brink of "above-the-line" science—of studying people whose powers of attention are far above the norm, whose wellsprings of compassion dwarf those of most people, who have successfully set their happiness baseline at a point that most mortals achieve only transiently before tumbling down to something comfortably above depression but far from what may be possible. What we learn from them may provide the key to raising everyone—or at least everyone who chooses to engage in the necessary mental training—to that level. Neuroplasticity will provide the key to realizing positive mental and emotional functioning. The effects of mental training, as shown in the brains of the accomplished Buddhist meditators, suggest what humans can achieve.

Secular Ethics

In speeches around the world, the Dalai Lama has argued that humankind needs a new basis for a modern ethics, one that appeals to the billions of people who adhere to different religions or to no religion, one that supports basic values such as personal responsibility, altruism, and compassion. Yet a scientifically literate person—indeed, anyone who gives even a cursory glance at newspaper science stories—may well react to that message with some skepticism. For modern science seems to be offering a radically different view of human responsibility.

Critics call this view neurogenetic determinism. It is the belief, ascendant from the early 1990s and propelled by the mystique of modern genetics, that ascribes inescapable causal power to the genes one inherits from one's parents. Hardly a month went by in that decade without the announcement of another discovery of a gene "for" this or that behavior or mental illness, from risk taking to loss of appetite control, from violence to neuroticism—as well as discoveries linking a deficit of one neurotransmitter with depression and of imbalances in another with addiction. Each connection that neuroscientists forged between a neurochemical and a behavior, and that geneticists made between a gene and a behavior, dealt another blow to the notion of an efficacious will. The discoveries paint an image of individuals as automatons, slaves to their genes or their neurotransmitters, and with no more free will than a child's radio-controlled car. "My genes (or my neurotransmitters) made me do it" might as well be the current mantra. Invoking "a failure of willpower" to explain overeating or addiction or anger began to seem as outdated and discredited as applying leeches to the sick.

"Neurogenetic determinism argues that there is a direct causal relationship between gene and behavior," neurobiologist Steven Rose of the Open University explains. "A woman is depressed because she has genes 'for' depression. There is violence on the streets because people have 'violent' or 'criminal' genes; people get drunk because they have genes 'for' alcoholism."

The validity of this view is more than an esoteric argument raging within the academy. If the source of our happiness and our despair, of our compassion and our cruelty, lies in the twisting strands of our DNA, then it is "to pharmacology and molecular engineering that we should turn for solutions," Rose concludes. And if will is an illusion, then what is the basis for personal responsibility? If we are truly slaves to our neurotransmitters and to the neural circuits laid down in childhood by our genes, then the concept of personal responsibility becomes specious.

I hope that this book has shown that that *if* is empty. Instead, each step in that causal chain is far from deterministic. Because neuroplasticity and the power of mind and mental training effect changes in the very structure and function of our brain, free will and moral responsibility become meaningful in a way that they have not been for some time in the scientific West. The genes carried by Michael Meaney's baby rats are altered by the behavior of the mother rat who raises them, with the result that the babies develop a strikingly different suite of behaviors and "personalities" (or the rat version thereof). So much for genes determining supposedly inborn traits such as shyness and timidity. The visual cortex in the blind children trooping into Helen Neville's lab does not see but, instead, hears; so much for genes being the driving forces behind the structure and function of the developing brain. Something as slight as a reminder of someone who once loved and cared for them is enough to trigger a circuit, presumably involving both memory and emotion, so that the people Phil Shaver studied do not merely feel compassion but act on it to help a suffering person. Neuroplasticity and the ability of the brain to change as a result of mental training step between genes and behavior like a hero in front of a speeding locomotive. If the brain can change, then genes "for" this or that behavior are much less deterministic. The ability of thought and attention to physically alter the brain echoes one of Buddhism's more remarkable hypotheses: that will is a real, physical force that can change the brain. Perhaps one of the most provocative implications of neuroplasticity and the power of mental training to alter the circuits of the brain is that it undermines neurogenetic determinism.

The Buddhist understanding of volition is quite different from the notion that humans are tethered to their genes or to hardwired neural circuitry. In Buddhist philosophy, one's choice is not determined by anything in the physical, material world, including the state of one's neurotransmitters or genes (not that traditional Buddhism had any inkling that brain chemicals or DNA even existed). Instead, volition arises from such ineffable qualities as the state of one's mind and the quality of one's attention. The last of Buddhism's Four Noble Truths also invokes the power of mind, arguing that although life is suffering, and suffering arises from cravings and desires, there is a way out of suffering: through mental training and, specifically, the sustained practice of meditation.

The conscious act of thinking about one's thoughts in a different way changes the very brain circuits that do that thinking, as studies of how psychotherapy changes the brains of people with depression show. Such willfully induced brain changes require focus, training, and effort, but a growing number of studies using neuroimaging show how real those changes are. They come from within. As the discoveries of neuroplasticity, and this self-directed neuroplasticity, trickle down to clinics and schools and plain old living rooms, the ability to willfully change the brain will become a central part of our lives—and of our understanding of what it means to be human.

About the Mind and Life Institute

R. Adam Engle

The Mind and Life dialogues between His Holiness the Dalai Lama and Western scientists were brought to life through a collaboration between R. Adam Engle, a North American businessman, and Francisco J. Varela, a Chilean-born neuroscientist living and working in Paris. In 1984, Engle and Varela, who at this time did not know each other, each independently had the initiative to create a series of cross-cultural meetings where His Holiness and scientists from the West would engage in extended discussions over a period of days.

In 1983, Engle, a Buddhist practitioner since 1974, became aware of the Dalai Lama's long-standing and keen interest in science and His Holiness's desire to both deepen his understanding of Western science and share his understanding of Eastern contemplative science with Western scientists. Varela, also a Buddhist practitioner since 1974, had met His Holiness at an international meeting in 1983 as a speaker at the Alpbach Symposia on Consciousness, where their communication was immediate. His Holiness was keenly interested in science and welcomed an opportunity for discussion with a brain scientist who had some understanding of Tibetan Buddhism.

In the autumn of 1984, Engle, who had been joined on this adventure by Michael Sautman, met with His Holiness's youngest brother, Tendzin Choegyal (Ngari Rinpoche) in Los Angeles and presented their plan to create a weeklong cross-cultural scientific meeting, provided His Holiness would fully participate in the meeting. Rinpoche graciously offered to take the matter up with His Holiness. Within days, Rinpoche reported that His Holiness would very much like to engage in discussions with scientists and authorized Engle and Sautman to organize a meeting.

Meanwhile, Varela had been thinking of ways to continue his scientific dialogue with His Holiness. In the spring of 1985, a close friend, Joan Halifax, then director at the Ojai Foundation, who had heard about Engle and Sautman's efforts to create a meeting on Buddhism and science, suggested that perhaps Engle, Sautman, and Varela could pool their complementary skills and work together. The four got together at the Ojai Foundation in October of 1985 and agreed to go forward jointly. They decided to focus on the scientific disciplines dealing with mind and life as the most fruitful interface between science and the Buddhist tradition. This became the name of the first meeting and eventually of the Mind and Life Institute.

It took two more years of work among Engle, Sautman, Varela, and the Private Office of His Holiness before the first meeting was held in October of 1987 in Dharamsala. During this time, Engle and Varela collaborated closely to find a useful structure for the meeting. Adam took on the job of general coordinator, with primary responsibility for fund-raising, relations with His Holiness and his office, and all other general aspects of the project, while Francisco, acting as scientific coordinator, took on primary responsibility for the scientific content, invitations to scientists, and editing of a volume covering the meeting.

This division of responsibility between general and scientific coordinators worked so well that it has been continued throughout all subsequent meetings. When the Mind and Life Institute was formally organized in 1990, Adam became its chairman and has been the general coordinator of all the Mind and Life meetings; and while Francisco has not been the scientific coordinator of all of them, until his death in 2001, he remained a guiding force and Engle's closest partner in the Mind and Life series and institute.

A word is in order here concerning the uniqueness of this series of conferences. The bridges that can mutually enrich modern life science and particularly the neurosciences are notoriously difficult to engineer. Francisco had a first taste of this when helping to establish a science program at Naropa Institute (now Naropa University), a liberal arts institution created by Tibetan meditation master Chögyam Trungpa Rinpoche. In 1979, Naropa received a grant from the Sloan Foundation to organize what was probably the very first conference on Comparative Approaches to Cognition: Western and Buddhist. Some twenty-five academics from prominent U.S. institutions gathered from various disciplines: mainstream philosophy, cognitive sciences (neurosciences, experimental psychology, linguistics, artificial intelligence), and, of course, Buddhist studies. The meeting provided

Francisco with a hard lesson on the care and finesse that organizing a cross-cultural dialogue requires.

Thus, in 1987, profiting from the Naropa experience, and wishing to avoid some of the pitfalls encountered in the past, Francisco urged the adoption of several operating principles that have worked extremely well in making the Mind and Life series extraordinarily successful. Perhaps the most important was to decide that scientists would not be chosen solely by their reputations but by their competence in their domain as well as their open-mindedness. Some familiarity with Buddhism is helpful, but not essential, as long as a healthy respect for Eastern contemplative science is present.

Next, the curriculum was adjusted as further conversations with the Dalai Lama clarified how much of the scientific background would need to be presented in order for His Holiness to participate fully in the dialogues. To ensure that the meetings would be fully participatory, they were structured with presentations by Western scientists in the morning session. In this way, His Holiness could be briefed on the basic ground of a field of knowledge. This morning presentation was based upon a broad, mainstream, scientific point of view. The afternoon session was devoted solely to discussion, which naturally flowed from the morning presentation. During this discussion session, the morning presenter could state his or her personal preferences and judgments, if they differed from the generally accepted viewpoints.

The issue of Tibetan-English language translation in a scientific meeting posed a significant challenge, as it was literally impossible to find a Tibetan native fluent in both English and science. This challenge was overcome by choosing two wonderful interpreters, one Tibetan and one Westerner with a scientific background, and placing them next to each other during the meeting. This allowed quick, on-the-spot clarification of terms, which is an absolute essential to move beyond the initial misunderstanding from two vastly different traditions. Thupten Jinpa, a Tibetan monk then studying for his *geshe* degree at Ganden Shartse monastery and now a Ph.D. in philosophy from Cambridge University, and Alan Wallace, a former monk in the Tibetan tradition with a degree in physics from Amherst and a Ph.D. in religious studies from Stanford University, interpreted at Mind and Life I and have continued to interpret in subsequent meetings. During Mind and Life V, while Dr. Wallace was unavailable, the Western interpreter was Dr. José Cabezón.

A final principle that has supported the success of the Mind and Life series has been that, until 2003, the meetings had been entirely private: no press and few invited guests. The Mind and Life Institute records the meetings on video and audio for archival purposes and transcription, but the meetings have become a very protected environment to conduct this exploration.

The curriculum for the first Mind and Life dialogue introduced various broad themes from cognitive science, touching on scientific method, neurobiology, cognitive psychology, artificial intelligence, brain development, and evolution. In attendance were Jeremy Hayward (physics and philosophy of science), Robert Livingston (neuroscience and medicine), Eleanor Rosch (cognitive science), Newcomb Greenleaf (computer science), and Francisco Varela (neuroscience and biology).

The event was an enormously gratifying success in that both His Holiness and the participants felt that there was a true meeting of minds with some substantial advances in bridging the gap. At the conclusion of the meeting, the Dalai Lama encouraged us to continue with further dialogues every two years, a request that we were only too happy to honor. Mind and Life I was transcribed, edited, and published as *Gentle Bridges: Conversations with the Dalai Lama on the Sciences of Mind*, edited by J. Hayward and F. J. Varela (Boston: Shambhala Publications, 1992). This book has been translated into French, Spanish, German, Japanese, and Chinese.

Mind and Life II took place in October 1989 in Newport, California, with Robert Livingston as the scientific coordinator and with the emphasis on brain sciences. It was a two-day event, and the conference's intent was to focus more specifically on neuroscience. Invited were Patricia S. Churchland (philosophy of science), J. Allan Hobson (sleep and dreams), Larry Squire (memory), Antonio Damasio (neuroscience), and Lewis Judd (mental health). The event was especially memorable as His Holiness was awarded the Nobel Peace Prize on the first morning of the meeting.

Mind and Life III returned to Dharamsala in 1990. Having organized and attended both Mind and Life I and II, Adam Engle and Tenzin Geyche Tethong agreed that having the meetings in India produced a much better result than holding them in the West. Dan Goleman (psychology) served as the scientific coordinator for Mind and Life III, which focused on the theme of the relationship between emotions and health. Participants included Daniel Brown (experimental psychology), J. Kabat-Zinn (medicine), Clifford Saron (neuroscience), Lee Yearly (philosophy), and Francisco Varela (immunology and neuroscience). The volume covering Mind and Life III is entitled *Healing Emotions: Conversations with the Dalai Lama on Mindfulness, Emotions, and Health,* edited by Daniel Goleman (Boston: Shambhala Publications, 1997).

During Mind and Life III, a new extension of exploration emerged, which was a natural complement to the dialogues but beyond the format of the conferences. Clifford Saron, Richard Davidson, Francisco Varela, and Gregory Simpson initiated a research project to investigate the effects of meditation on long-term meditators. The idea was to profit from the goodwill and trust that had been built with the Tibetan community in Dharamsala and the willingness of His Holiness for this kind of research. With seed money from the Hershey Family Foundation, the Mind and

Life Institute was formed. It has been chaired by Engle since its inception. The Fetzer Institute funded initial stages of the research project. A progress report was submitted in 1994 to the Fetzer Institute.

The fourth Mind and Life conference occurred in October 1992, with Francisco Varela again acting as scientific coordinator. The topic and title for the dialogue was Sleeping, Dreaming, and Dying. Invited participants were Charles Taylor (philosophy), Jerome Engel (medicine), Joan Halifax (anthropology; death and dying), Jayne Gackenbach (psychology of lucid dreaming), and Joyce McDougal (psychoanalysis). The account of this conference is now available as *Sleeping, Dreaming, and Dying: An Exploration of Consciousness with the Dalai Lama*, edited by Fancisco J. Varela (Boston: Wisdom Publications, 1997).

Mind and Life V was held again in Dharamsala in April 1995. The topic and title was Altruism, Ethics, and Compassion, and the scientific coordinator was Richard Davidson. In addition to Dr. Davidson, participants included Nancy Eisenberg (child development), Robert Frank (altruism in economics), Anne Harrington (history of science), Elliott Sober (philosophy), and Ervin Staub (psychology and group behavior). The volume covering this meeting is entitled *Visions of Compassion: Western Scientists and Tibetan Buddhists Examine Human Nature*, edited by Richard J. Davidson and Anne Harrington (New York: Oxford University Press, 2002).

Mind and Life VI opened a new area of exploration beyond the previous focus on life science. That meeting took place in October 1997 with Arthur Zajonc (physics) as the scientific coordinator The participants, in addition to Dr. Zajonc and His Holiness, were David Finkelstein (physics), George Greenstein (astronomy), Piet Hut (astrophysics), Tu Weiming (philosophy), and Anton Zeilinger (quantum physics). The volume covering this meeting was entitled *The New Physics and Cosmology: Dialogues with the Dalai Lama*, edited by Arthur Zajonc (New York: Oxford University Press, 2003).

The dialogue on quantum physics was continued with Mind and Life VII, held at Anton Zeilinger's laboratory at the Institut fur Experimentalphysik in Innsbruck, Austria, in June 1998. Present were His Holiness, Drs. Zeilinger and Zajonc, and interpreters Drs. Jinpa and Wallace. That meeting was written up for a cover story in the January 1999 issue of the German magazine *Geo*.

Mind and Life VIII was held in March 2000 in Dharamsala, with Daniel Goleman acting again as scientific coordinator. The subject and title of this meeting was Destructive Emotions, and the participants were Ven. Matthieu Ricard (Buddhism), Richard Davidson (neuroscience and psychology), Francisco Varela (neuroscience), Paul Ekman (psychology), Mark Greenberg (psychology), Jeanne Tsai (psychology), Bhikku Kusalacitto (Buddhism), and Owen Flanagan (philosophy).

Mind and Life IX was held in May 2001 at the University of Wisconsin–Madison in cooperation with the HealthEmotions Research Institute and the Center for Research on Mind-Body Interactions. Participants were His Holiness, Richard David-son, Antoine Lutz, sitting in for an ill Francisco Varela, Matthieu Ricard, Paul Ekman, and Michael Merzenich (neuroscience). This two-day meeting inaugu-rated collaborative research between neuroscientists and Buddhist adepts and fo-cused on how to most effectively use the technologies of fMRI and EEG/MEG in the research on meditation, perception, emotion, and on the relations between human neural plasticity and meditation practices.

Mind and Life X was held in Dharamsala in October 2002. The topic and title was What Is Matter? What Is Life? The scientific coordinator and moderator was Arthur Zajonc, and the participants were His Holiness, Steven Chu (physics), Arthur Zajonc (complexity), Luigi Luisi (cellular biology and chemistry), Ursula Goodenough (evolutionary biology), Eric Lander (genomic research), Michel Bitbol (philosophy), and Matthieu Ricard (Buddhist philosophy).

In September 2003, the Mind and Life Institute launched a new series of meet-ings. Mind and Life XI was the first public Mind and Life meeting. It was cosponsored by the McGovern Institute at MIT and was held in Kresge Auditorium on the MIT campus. Twelve hundred people attended this meeting, entitled Investigat-ing the Mind: Exchanges between Buddhism and the Biobehavioral Sciences on How the Mind Works. In that meeting, twenty-two world-renowned scientists joined His Holiness in a two-day inquiry on how best to institute collaborative re-search between Buddhism and modern science in the areas of attention and cogni-tive control, emotion, and mental imagery. For more information on this meeting, please visit its website: www.InvestigatingTheMind.org.

In June 2004, the Mind and Life Institute created the Mind and Life Summer Research Institute. This institute, which has become a very popular annual event, brings together graduate students, postdocs, and senior investigators in the fields of neuroscience, psychology, and medicine; contemplative scholars and practition-ers; and philosophers of mind for a weeklong residential science retreat consisting of presentations, dialogue, small groups, meditation practice, and faculty office hours—all focused on the scientific investigation of the effects of meditation and mental training on brain and behavior.

Mind and Life XII was held in Dharamsala in October 2004 on the topic of neuroplasticity. The scientific coordinator and moderator was Richard Davidson, and the participants were His Holiness, Fred H. Gage, Michael Meaney, Helen Neville, Phillip Shaver, Matthieu Ricard, and Evan Thompson.

Mind and Life XIII was another public meeting held at DAR Constitution Hall in Washington, D.C., in November 2005. This meeting was cosponsored by the Georgetown Medical Center and the Johns Hopkins University School of Medicine and was entitled The Science and Clinical Applications of Meditation. For two and a half days, the Dalai Lama and other contemplatives met with scientists and clini-cians before an audience of twenty-five hundred, exploring the neural mechanisms of meditation and how meditation has been used in the prevention and treatment of disease.

For more information about the Mind and Life Institute, please contact:

> Mind and Life Institute
> 589 West Street
> Louisville, CO 80027
>
> *www.mindandlife.org*
> *www.InvestigatingTheMind.org*
> *info@mindandlife.org*

NOTES

Most of the accounts of the science described in this book come from my interviews with the researchers who conducted it. Quotes not otherwise attributed are from those interviews or, if they are described in the text as something the scientist said to the Dalai Lama, from the Oct. 2004 Mind and Life meeting in Dharamsala.

CHAPTER 1 | Can We Change?: Challenging the Dogma of the Hardwired Brain

5 *No less a personage:* William James, *The Principles of Psychology* (Cambridge, Mass.: Harvard University Press, 1983), 110.

5 *Near the conclusion of his:* Quoted in Bruce Teter and J. Wesson Ashford, "Neuroplasticity in Alzheimer's Disease," *Journal of Neuroscience Research* 70 (Nov. 1, 2002): 402.

6 *As late as 1999:* D. H. Lowenstein and J. M. Parent, "Brain, Heal Thyself," *Science* 283 (1999): 1126–27.

12 *Consonances between Buddhism and science:* José Ignacio Cabezón, "Buddhism and Science: On the Nature of the Dialogue," in *Buddhism and Science: Breaking New Ground,* ed. Alan Wallace (New York: Columbia University Press, 2003), 11.

15 *Science was unknown in his:* His Holiness the Dalai Lama, *The Universe in a Single Atom* (New York: Morgan Road Books, 2005), 17.

15 *Between lessons in reading:* Ibid., 18. The rest of the Dalai Lama's description of his childhood discovery of science is based on his account in chapter 2 of *The Universe.*

16 *"There was a time:* His Holiness the Dalai Lama, *The Universe,* 19.

17 *"Looking back over my:* Ibid., 205.

18 *"Strictly speaking," the Dalai Lama:* Ibid., 24.

18 *"Therefore, when it comes to:* Ibid.

18 *Science's "inevitable dominance in:* Ibid., 10.

23 *She cautioned him that:* Ibid., 2.

23 *Recalling that first Mind:* Ibid., 36.

23 *"If as spiritual practitioners:* Ibid., 13.

23 *"Spirituality and science are:* Ibid., 4.

24 *"By gaining deeper insight:* Ibid.

24 *"The Buddhist terms in which:* Ibid., 150.

24 *And as he wrote:* The Dalai Lama and Howard C. Cutler, *The Art of Happiness: A Handbook for Living* (New York: Riverhead, 1998), 44–45.

25 *But in fact, Ramón y Cajal:* Quoted in Teter and Ashford, "Neuroplasticity in Alzheimer's," 402.

CHAPTER 2 / The Enchanted Loom: The Discovery of Neuroplasticity

An extended history of the discovery of neuroplasticity in the adult brain can be found in Jeffrey M. Schwartz and Sharon Begley, *The Mind and the Brain: Neuroplasticity and the Power of Mental Force* (New York: Regan Books, 2002), chapters 5–7.

28 *In 1912, two British neuroscientists:* T. Graham Brown and Charles Sherrington, "On the Instability of a Cortical Point," *Proceedings of the Royal Science Society of London B* 85 (1912): 250–77.

29 *In 1915, a neurologist:* S. Ivory Franz, "Variations in Distribution of the Motor Centers," *Psychological Review, Monograph Supplement* 19 (1915): 80–162.

29 *In 1917, Sherrington himself:* A.F.S. Leyton and C. S. Sherrington, "Observations on the Excitable Cortex of the Chimpanzee, Orang-utan and Gorilla," *Quarterly Journal of Experimental Physiology* 1 (1917): 135–222.

29 *In 1923, Karl Lashley:* K. S. Lashley, "Temporal Variation in the Function of the Gyrus Precentralis in Primates," *American Journal of Physiology* 65 (1923): 585–602.

30 *In 1949, Canadian psychologist Donald:* Donald O. Hebb, *The Organization of Behavior: A Neuropsychological Theory* (New York: Wiley, 1949).

32 *Kaas and Merzenich took:* M. M. Merzenich, J. H. Kaas, J. T. Wall, M. Sur, R. J. Nelson, and D. J. Felleman, "Progression of Change Following Median Nerve Section in the Cortical Representation of the Hand in Areas 3b and 1 in Adult Owl and Squirrel Monkeys," *Neuroscience* 10 (1983): 639–65.

33 *"These results," the scientists wrote:* Ibid., 662.

34 *"We propose that the differences:* M. M. Merzenich, R. J. Nelson, J. H. Kaas, M. P. Stryker, W. M. Jenkins, J. M. Zook, M. S. Cynader, and A. Schoppmann, "Variability in Hand Surface Representations in Areas 3b and 1 in Adult Owl and Squirrel Monkeys," *Journal of Comparative Neurology* 258 (1987): 281–96.

34 *Jenkins positioned a four-inch:* W. M. Jenkins, M. M. Merzenich, M. T. Ochs, T. Allard, and E. Guic-Roble, "Functional Reorganization of Primary Somatosensory Cortex in Adult Owl Monkeys after Behaviorally Controlled Tactile Stimulation," *Journal of Neurophysiology* 63 (1990): 82–104.

36 *And what had happened:* G. H. Recanzone, W. M. Jenkins, G. T. Hradek, and M. M. Merzenich, "Progressive Improvement in Discriminative Abilities in Adult Owl Monkeys Performing a Tactile Frequency Discrimination Task," *Journal of Neurophysiology* 67 (1992): 1015–30.

36 *In an experiment on four:* R. J. Nudo, G. W. Milliken, W. M. Jenkin, and M. M. Merzenich, "Use-Dependent Alterations of Movement Representations in Primary Motor Cortex of Adult Squirrel Monkeys," *Journal of Neuroscience* 16 (1996): 785–807.

37 *The motor cortex, they concluded:* Ibid., 785.

37 *"These idiosyncratic features:* M. M. Merzenich, G. H. Recanzone, W. M. Jenkins, and K. A. Grajski, "Adaptive Mechanisms in Cortical Networks Underlying Cortical Contributions to Learning and Non-declarative Memory," *Cold Spring Harbor Symposia on Quantitative Biology* 55 (1990): 873–87.

38 *The Silver Spring monkeys:* This account is condensed from Schwartz and Begley, *Mind and the Brain,* chapter 4. Another excellent narrative of this case is Caroline Fraser, "The Raid at Silver Spring," *New Yorker,* Apr. 19, 1993, 66.

40 *"Deafferented monkeys have a tendency:* E. Taub, "Movement in Nonhuman Primates Deprived of Somatosensory Feedback," in J. F. Keogh, ed., *Exercise and Sports Sciences Reviews* 4 (Santa Barbara: Journal Publishing Affiliates, 1977), 335–74.

42 *In a 1988 paper:* T. Pons, E. Garraghty, and M. Mishkin, "Lesion-Induced Plasticity in the Second Somatosensory Cortex of Adult Macaques," *Proceedings of the National Academy of Sciences* 85 (July 1988): 5279–81.

43 *The researchers reported their findings:* T. P. Pons, P. E. Garraghty, A. K. Ommaya, J. H. Kaas, E. Taub, and M. Mishkin, "Massive Cortical Reorganization after Sensory Deafferentation in Adult Macaques," *Science* 252 (1991): 1857–60.

44 *Pons explained what made:* Curt Suplee, "Brain's Ability to Re-wire after Injury Is Extensive; 'Silver Spring Monkeys' Used in Research," *Washington Post,* June 28, 1991, A3.

45 *For the experiments, Sur:* L. Von Melchner, S. L. Pallas, and M. Sur, "Visual Behaviour Mediated by Retinal Projections Directed to the Auditory Pathway," *Nature* 404 (2000): 871–75.

47 *On learning of his:* M. Merzenich, "Seeing in the Sound Zone," *Nature* 404 (2000): 820–21.

47 *In a series of experiments:* J. R. Newton, C. Ellsworth, T. Miyakawa, S. Tonegawa, and M. Sur, "Acceleration of Visually Cued Conditioned Fear through the Auditory Pathway," *Nature Neuroscience* 7 (2004): 968–73.

CHAPTER 3 | New Neurons for Old Brains: Neurogenesis

52 *As the Nobel Prize–winning:* Quoted in Bruce Teter and J. Wesson Ashford, "Neuroplasticity in Alzheimer's Disease," *Journal of Neuroscience Research* 70 (Nov. 1, 2002): 402.

53 *To his surprise, he found:* J. Altman, "Are New Neurons Formed in the Brains of Adult Mammals?" *Science* 135 (1962): 1127–28. An excellent account of the discovery of neurogenesis is Michael Specter, "Rethinking the Brain: How the Songs of Canaries Upset a Fundamental Principle of Science," *New Yorker,* July 23, 2001.

53 *In 1965, he reported:* J. Altman and G. D. Das, "Autoradiographic and Histological Evidence of Postnatal Hippocampal Neurogenesis in Rats," *Journal of Comparative Neurology* 124 (June 1965): 319–35.

53 *In 1967, he published:* J. Altman and G. D. Das, "Postnatal Neurogenesis in the Guinea-pig," *Nature* 214 (June 10, 1967): 1098–1101.

53 *In 1970, he described:* G. D. Das and J. Altman, "Postnatal Neurogenesis in the Caudate Nucleus and Nucleus Accumbens Septi in the Rat," *Brain Research* 21 (1970): 122–27.

53 *Michael Kaplan, a graduate assistant:* M. S. Kaplan and J. W. Hinds, "Neurogenesis in the Adult Rat: Electron Microscopic Analysis of Light Radioautographs," *Science* 197 (1977): 1092–94.

54 *In a paper that year:* F. Nottebohm, "A Brain for All Seasons: Cyclical Anatomical Changes in Song Control Nuclei of the Canary Brain," *Science* 214 (Dec. 18, 1981): 1368–70.

54 *In 1983, he reported:* S. A. Goldman and F. Nottebohm, "Neuronal Production, Migration, and Differentiation in a Vocal Control Nucleus of the Adult Female Canary Brain," *Proceedings of the National Academy of Sciences* 80 (Apr. 1983): 2390–94.

55 *The next year, he discovered:* J. A. Paton and F. Nottebohm, "Neurons Generated in the Adult Brain Are Recruited into Functional Circuits," *Science* 225 (Sept. 7, 1984): 1046–48.

55 *Rakic used the same:* P. Rakic, "Limits of Neurogenesis in Primates," *Science* 227 (Mar. 1, 1985): 1054–56.

55 *The field of neurogenesis:* E. Gould, B. S. McEwen, P. Tanapat, L. A. Galea, and E. Fuchs, "Neurogenesis in the Dentate Gyrus of the Adult Tree Shrew Is Regulated by Psychosocial Stress and NMDA Receptor Activation," *Journal of Neuroscience* (Apr. 1, 1997): 2492–98.

56 *As early as the 1940s:* D. O. Hebb, "The Effects of Early Experience on Problem-Solving at Maturity," *American Psychologist* 2 (1947): 306–7.

57 *At Harvard, David Hubel:* T. Wiesel and D. Hubel, "Comparison of the Effects of Unilateral and Bilateral Eye Closure on Cortical Unit Responses in Kittens," *Journal of Neurophysiology* 28 (1965): 1003–17.

57 *Using an inbred strain:* E. L. Bennett, M. C. Diamond, D. Krech, and M. R. Rosenzweig, "Chemical and Anatomical Plasticity of Brain," *Science* 146 (1964): 610–19; M. R. Rosenzweig and E. L. Bennett, "Effects of Differential Environments on Brain Weights and Enzyme Activities in Gerbils, Rats, and Mice," *Developmental Psychobiology* 2 (1969): 87–95.

57 *At the University of Illinois:* F. R. Volkmar and W. T. Greenough, "Rearing Complexity Affects Branching of Dendrites in the Visual Cortex of the Rat," *Science* 176 (1972): 1445–47

57–58 *But in 1997, Gage:* G. Kempermann, H. G. Kuhn, and F. H. Gage, "More Hippocampal Neurons in Adult Mice Living in an Enriched Environment," *Nature* 386 (1997): 493–95.

58 *A year after their discovery:* G. Kempermann, H. G. Kuhn, and F. H. Gage, "Experience-Induced Neurogenesis in the Senescent Dentate Gyrus," *Journal of Neuroscience* 18 (1998): 3206–12.

64 *And finally they did:* P. S. Eriksson, E. Perfilieva, T. Bjork-Eriksson, A. M. Alborn, C. Nordborg, D. A. Peterson, and F. H. Gage, "Neurogenesis in the Adult Human Hippocampus," *Nature Medicine* 4 (Nov. 1998): 1313–17.

66 *Gage and his team:* H. van Praag, G. Kempermann, and F. H. Gage, "Running Increases Cell Proliferation and Neurogenesis in the Adult Mouse Dentate Gyrus," *Nature Neuroscience* 2 (1999): 266–70.

66 *Indeed, within about a month:* H. van Praag, A. F. Schinder, B. R. Christie, N. Toni, T. D. Palmer, and F. H. Gage, "Functional Neurogenesis in the Adult Hippocampus," *Nature* 415 (2002): 1030–34.

67 *Gage and his colleagues:* H. van Praag, B. R. Christie, T. J. Sejnowski, and F. H. Gage, "Running Enhances Neurogenesis, Learning and Long-Term Potentiation in Mice," *Proceedings of the National Academy of Sciences* 96 (1999): 13427–31.

69 *In studies announced just weeks:* Brennan Eadie, Andrea Olson, and Brian Christie, "Voluntary Exercise Increases Neurogenic Activity in the Dentate Gyrus of the Adult Mammalian Brain: Fact or Fiction?" Poster presented at the annual meeting of the Society for Neuroscience, 2004.

70 *But in the first decade:* L. Santarelli, M. Saxe, C. Gross, A. Surget, F. Battaglia, S. Dulawa, N. Weisstaub, et al., "Requirement of Hippocampal Neurogenesis for the Behavioral Effects of Antidepressants," *Science* 301 (Aug. 8, 2003): 805–9.

CHAPTER 4 | A Child Shall Lead Them: The Neuroplasticity of Young Brains

74 *In 1688, an Irish philosopher:* A. Pascual-Leone and Roy Hamilton, "The Metamodal Organization of the Brain," *Progress in Brain Research* 134 (2001): 427–45.

76 *a one-year-old:* A. Gopnik, A. N. Meltzoff, and K. Kuhl, *The Scientist in the Crib: Minds, Brains and How Children Learn* (New York: Morrow, 1999), 186.

77 *By one estimate, some 20:* Lise Eliot, *What's Going On in There? How the Brain and Mind Develop in the First Five Years of Life* (New York: Bantam, 1999), 32.

77 *If we take 1,000:* Gopnik, Meltzoff, and Kuhl, *Scientist in the Crib,* 181.

77 *If a baby is born:* D. Maurer, T. L. Lewis, H. P. Brent, and A. V. Levin, "Rapid Improvement in the Acuity of Infants after Visual Input," *Science* 286 (1999): 108–10.

78 *In one now-classic experiment:* Gopnik, Meltzoff, and Kuhl, *Scientist in the Crib,* 103.

79 *Rats that are blinded:* D. Bavelier and H. J. Neville, "Cross-Modal Plasticity: Where and How?" *Nature Reviews | Neuroscience* 3 (2002): 443–52.

79 *Most studies had found:* Ibid., 444.

80 *It was 1983, and the:* H. J. Neville, A. Schmidt, and M. Kutas, "Altered Visual-Evoked Potentials in Congenitally Deaf Adults," *Brain Research* 266 (Apr. 1983): 127–32.

81 *In a series of studies:* H. J. Neville and D. Lawson, "Attention to Central and Peripheral Visual Space in a Movement Detection Task: An Event-Related Potential and Behavioral Study," *Brain Research* 405 (1987): 253–94; D. Bavelier, A. Tomann, C. Hutton, T. Mitchell, D. Corina, G. Liu, and H. Neville, "Visual Attention to the Periphery Is Enhanced in Congenitally Deaf Individuals," *Journal of Neuroscience* 20 (2000): 1–6.

82 *Neville therefore decided to investigate:* D. Bavelier, C. Brozinsky, A. Tomann, T. Mitchell, H. Neville, and G. Liu, "Impact of Early Deafness and Early Exposure to Sign Language on Cerebral Organization for Motion Processing," *Journal of Neuroscience* 21 (2001): 8931–42.

84 *To nail down the basis:* B. A. Armstrong, H. J. Neville, S. A. Hillyard, and T. V. Mitchell, "Auditory Deprivation Affects Processing of Motion, but Not Color," *Brain Research / Cognitive Brain Research* 14 (Nov. 2002): 422–34.

86 *Braille has its roots:* N. Sadato, "How the Blind 'See' Braille: Lessons from fMRI," *Neuroscientist* 11 (2005): 1–6.

87 *What he found was that:* A. Pascual-Leone and F. Torres, "Plasticity of the Sensorimotor Cortex Representation of the Reading Finger in Braille Readers," *Brain* 116 (1992): 39–52.

89 *This is what Pascual-Leone:* A. Pascual-Leone and F. Torres, "Plasticity of the Sensorimotor Cortex Representation of the Reading Finger in Braille Readers," *Brain* 116 (Feb. 1993): 39–52.

92 *The study was published:* N. Sadato, "Activation of the Primary Visual Cortex by Braille Reading in Blind Subjects," *Nature* 380 (1996): 526–28.

93 *Just as Hallett suspected:* H. Burton, "Visual Cortex Activity in Early and Late Blind People," *Journal of Neuroscience* 23 (2003): 4005–11.

94 *So Cohen and his colleagues:* L. G. Cohen, P. Celnik, A. Pascual-Leone, B. Corwell, L. Falz, J. Dambrosia, M. Honda, et al., "Functional Relevance of Cross-Modal Plasticity in Blind Humans," *Nature* 389 (Sept. 11, 1997): 180–83.

95 *In 2000, scientists described:* R. Hamilton, J. P. Keenan, M. Catala, and A. Pascual-Leone, "Alexia for Braille Following Bilateral Occipital Stroke in an Early Blind Woman," *Neuroreport* 11 (Feb. 7, 2000): 237–40.

95 *In a study with colleagues:* B. Röder, W. Teder-Salejarvi, A. Sterr, F. Rosler, S. A. Hillyard, and H. J. Neville, "Improved Auditory Spatial Tuning in Blind Humans," *Nature* 400 (1999): 162–66.

97 *After all, the visual regions:* S. J. Gilbert and V. Walsh, "Vision: The Versatile 'Visual' Cortex," *Current Biology* 14 (Dec. 29, 2004): R1056–57.

98 *The first thing Amedi found:* A. Amedi, N. Raz, P. Pianka, R. Malach, and E. Zohary, "Early 'Visual' Cortex Activation Correlates with Superior Verbal Memory Performance in the Blind," *Nature Neuroscience* 6 (July 2003): 758–66.

100 *Those who had been blind:* Amir Amedi, A. Floel, S. Knecht, E. Zohary, and L. G. Cohen, "Transcranial Magnetic Stimulation of the Occipital Pole Interferes with Verbal Processing in Blind Subjects," *Nature Neuroscience* 7 (2004): 1266–70.

100 *According to this idea:* Christian Büchel, "Cortical Hierarchy Turned on Its Head," *Nature Neuroscience* 6 (July 2003): 657–58.

102 *As Sadato puts it:* Sadato, "How the Blind 'See' Braille," 5.

103 *It was a relatively obscure:* G. H. Recanzone, C. E. Schreiner, and M. M. Merzenich, "Plasticity in the Frequency Representation of Primary Auditory Cortex Following Discrimination Training in Adult Owl Monkeys," *Journal of Neuroscience* 13 (1993): 87–103.

105 *The results were remarkable:* P. Tallal, S. L. Miller, G. Bedi, G. Byma, X. Wang, S. S. Nagarajan, C. Schreiner, W. M. Jenkins, and M. M. Merzenich, "Language Comprehension in Language-Learning Impaired Children Improved with Acoustically Modified Speech," *Science* 271 (1996): 81–84; and M. M. Merzenich, W. M. Jenkins, P. Johnston, C. Schreiner,

S. L. Miller, and P. Tallal, "Temporal Processing Deficits of Language-Learning Impaired Children Ameliorated by Training," *Science* 271 (1996): 77–81.

106 *Fast ForWord:* E. Temple, G. K. Deutsch, R. A. Poldrack, S. L. Miller, P. Tallal, M. M. Merzenich, and J. D. Gabrieli, "Neural Deficits in Children with Dyslexia Ameliorated by Behavioral Remediation: Evidence from Functional MRI," *Proceedings of the National Academy of Sciences* 100 (2003): 2860–65.

108 *In one of Neville's earliest:* Reviewed in H. J. Neville and J. T. Bruer, "Language Processing: How Experience Affects Brain Organization," in *Critical Thinking about Critical Periods,* ed. D. B. Bailey Jr., John T. Bruer, Frank J. Symons, and Jeff W. Lichtman (Baltimore: Paul H. Brookes Publishing, 2001), 151–72.

109 *In what Alvaro Pascual-Leone:* A. Pascual-Leone, A. Amedi, F. Fregni, and L. B. Merabet, "The Plastic Human Brain Cortex," *Annual Reviews of Neurosciences* 28 (2005): 377–401.

CHAPTER 5 | Footprints on the Brain: Sensory Experience Reshapes Adult Brains

110 *In one typical expirement:* L. G. Cohen, R. A. Weeks, N. Sadato, P. Celnik, K. Ishii, and M. Hallett, "Period of Susceptibility for Cross-Modal Plasticity in the Blind," *Annals of Neurology* 45 (Apr. 1999): 451–60.

112 *But two groups of scientists:* J. N. Giedd, J. Blumenthal, N. O. Jeffries, F. X. Castellanos, H. Liu, A. Zijdenbos, T. Paus, A. C. Evans, and J. L. Rapoport, "Brain Development during Childhood and Adolescence: A Longitudinal MRI Study," *Nature Neuroscience* 2 (1999): 861–63; E. R. Sowell, P. M. Thompson, C. J. Holmes, T. L. Jernigan, and A. W. Toga, "In Vivo Evidence for Post-adolescent Brain Maturation in Frontal and Striatal Regions," *Nature Neuroscience* 2 (1999): 859–61.

114 *They recruited people with normal:* A. Pascual-Leone and Roy Hamilton, "The Metamodal Organization of the Brain," *Progress in Brain Research* 134 (2001): 427–45.

118 *It has been around:* J. Herman, "Phantom Limb: From Medical Knowledge to Folk Wisdom and Back," *Annals of Internal Medicine* 128 (1998): 76–78.

118 *Ramachandran invited Victor Quintero:* V. S. Ramachandran and S. Blakeslee, *Phantoms in the Brain: Probing the Mysteries of the Human Mind* (New York: Morrow, 1998).

118 *"Where do you feel that?":* Sandra Blakeslee, "Missing Limbs, Still Atingle, Are Clues to Changes in the Brain," *New York Times,* Nov. 10, 1992, C1.

119 *Christina Saccuman of the San:* D. Perani et al., "Plasticity of Sensorimotor Maps in Hand Allograft Evaluated with fMRI," poster presented at the annual meeting of the Society for Neuroscience, 2004.

121 *After just those ten days:* E. Taub, N. E. Miller, T. A. Novack, E. W. Cook III, W. C. Fleming, C. S. Nepomuceno, J. S. Connell, and J. E. Crago, "Technique to Improve Chronic Motor Deficit after Stroke," *Archives of Physical Medicine and Rehabilitation* 74 (1993): 347–54.

122 *The crowning achievement for:* E. Taub, G. Uswatte, D. K. King, D. Morris, J. E. Crago, and A. Chatterjee, "A Placebo-Controlled Trial of Constraint-Induced Movement Therapy for Upper Extremity after Stroke," *Stroke* 37 (Apr. 2006): 1045–49.

124 *Treatment caused the area:* J. Liepert, H. Bauder, H. R. Wolfgang, W. H. Miltner, E. Taub, and C. Weiller, "Treatment-Induced Cortical Reorganization after Stroke in Humans," *Stroke* 6 (June 2000): 1210–16.

125 *In 2004, they reported:* S. Lum, E. Taub, D. Schwandt, M. Postman, P. Hardin, and G. Uswatte, "Automated Constraint-Induced Therapy Extension (AutoCITE) for Movement Deficits after Stroke," *Journal of Rehabilitation Research and Development* 41 (2004): 249–58.

126 *There was no difference:* T. Elbert, C. Pantev, C. Wienbruch, B. Rockstroh, and E. Taub, "Increased Cortical Representation of the Fingers of the Left Hand in String Players," *Science* 270 (1995): 305–7.

128 *In macular degeneration:* C. Baker et al., "Reorganization of Visual Processing in Macular Degeneration," slide presentation at the Society for Neuroscience, 2004.

129 *"Plasticity is an intrinsic property:* A. Pascual-Leone, A. Amedi, F. Fregni, and L. B. Merabet, "The Plastic Human Brain Cortex," *Annual Reviews of Neuroscience* 28 (2005): 377–401.

CHAPTER 6 | Mind over Matter: Mental Activity Changes the Brain

131 *During a visit to an:* His Holiness the Dalai Lama, *The Universe in a Single Atom* (New York: Morgan Road Books, 2005), 127.

132 *But "I thought then:* Ibid., 128.

133 *As he told scientists:* D. Goleman, *Destructive Emotions* (New York: Bantam Books, 2003), 207.

134 *As the English philosopher:* Carl Zimmer, *Soul Made Flesh* (New York: Free Press, 2004), 3.

134 *Considered the father:* Ibid.

135 *It is not simply:* C. McGinn, *The Mysterious Flame: Conscious Minds in a Material World* (New York: Basic Books, 1999), 18–19.

135 *Philosopher John Searle, who:* J. R. Searle, "A Philosopher Unriddles the Puzzle of Consciousness," *Cerebrum* 2 (2000): 44–54.

135 *That puzzle, of how:* R. W. Doty, "The Five Mysteries of the Mind, and Their Consequences," *Neuropsychologia* 36 (1998): 1069–76.

136 *As McGinn put it:* McGinn, *Mysterious Flame,* 28.

136 *Nobel Prize–winning neuroscientist:* R. W. Sperry, "Perception in the Absence of the Neocortical Commissures," *Research Publications Association for Research in Nervous and Mental Disease* 48 (1970): 123–38.

137 *Neuropsychiatrist Jeffrey Schwartz of the:* Schwartz's discovery of the power of mindfulness-based meditation to treat the dysfunctional circuits in OCD, as well as the history of attempts to treat OCD, are described at length in Jeffrey M. Schwartz and Sharon Begley, *The Mind and the Brain: Neuroplasticity and the Power of Mental Force* (New York: Regan Books, 2002), chapter 2.

139 *In* The Heart of Buddhist: Nyanaponika Thera, *The Heart of Buddhist Meditation* (York Beach, Maine: Samuel Weiser, 1973).

140 *They performed PET scans:* J. M. Schwartz, P. W. Stoessel, L. R. Baxter Jr., K. M. Martin, and

M. E. Phelps, "Systematic Changes in Cerebral Glucose Metabolic Rate after Successful Behavior Modification Treatment of Obsessive-Compulsive Disorder," *Archives of General Psychiatry* 53 (1996): 109–13.

142 *In 1989, scientists reported:* I. Elkin, M. T. Shea, J. T. Watkins, S. D. Imber, S. M. Sotsky, J. F. Collins, D. R. Glass, et al., "NIMH Treatment of Depression Collaborative Research Program: General Effectiveness of Treatments," *Archives of General Psychiatry* 46 (1989): 971–83.

143 *"The power of the cognitive:* G. Andrews, "Talk That Works: The Rise of Cognitive Behavior Therapy," *British Medical Journal* 313 (1996): 1501–2.

145 *So he made people sad:* Z. V. Segal, "Cognitive Assessment of Unipolar Depression: Measuring Products, Processes and Structures," *Behaviour Research and Therapy* 32 (Jan. 1994): 147–58.

147 *Treatment as usual left:* J. Scott, J. D. Teasdale, E. S. Paykel, A. L. Johnson, R. Abbott, H. Hayhurst, R. Moore, and A. Garland, "Effects of Cognitive Therapy on Psychological Symptoms and Social Functioning in Residual Depression," *British Journal of Psychiatry* 177 (2000): 440–46; J. D. Teasdale, Z. V. Segal, J. M. Williams, V. A. Ridgeway, J. M. Soulsby, and M. A. Lau, "Prevention of Relapse/Recurrence in Major Depression by Mindfulness-Based Cognitive Therapy," *Journal of Consulting and Clinical Psychiatry* 68 (2000): 615–23.

148 *In 2004, Teasdale and his:* S. H. Ma and J. D. Teasdale, "Mindfulness-Based Cognitive Therapy for Depression: Replication and Exploration of Differential Relapse Prevention Effects," *Journal of Consulting and Clinical Psychiatry* 72 (2004): 31–40.

148 *Neuroscientist Helen Mayberg:* H. S. Mayberg, J. A. Silva, S. K. Brannan, J. L. Tekell, R. K. Mahurin, S. McGinnis, and P. A. Jerabek, "The Functional Neuroanatomy of the Placebo Effect," *American Journal of Psychiatry* 159 (May 2002): 728–37.

149 *Depressed brains responded differently:* K. Goldapple, Z. Segal, C. Garson, M. Lau, P. Bieling, S. Kennedy, and H. Mayberg, "Modulation of Cortical-Limbic Pathways in Major Depression: Treatment-Specific Effects of Cognitive Behavior Therapy," *Archives of General Psychiatry* 61 (Jan. 2004): 34–41.

151 *In the mid-1990s, Pascual-Leone:* A. Pascual-Leone, D. Nguyet, L. G. Cohen, J. P. Brasil-Neto, A. Cammarota, and M. Hallett, "Modulation of Muscle Responses Evoked by Transcranial Magnetic Stimulation during the Acquisition of New Fine Motor Skills," *Journal of Neurophysiology* 74 (1995): 1037–45.

152 *"Mental practice resulted in:* A. Pascual-Leone, A. Amedi, F. Fregni, and L. B. Merabet, "The Plastic Human Brain Cortex," *Annual Reviews of Neuroscience* 28 (2005): 380.

152 *He tells the story:* His Holiness the Dalai Lama and Victor Chan, *The Wisdom of Forgiveness: Intimate Conversations and Journeys* (New York: Riverhead, 2004), 47.

158 *Nowhere was that shown:* G. H. Recanzone, C. E. Schreiner, and M. M. Merzenich, "Plasticity in the Frequency Representation of Primary Auditory Cortex Following Discrimination Training in Adult Owl Monkeys," *Journal of Neuroscience* 13 (1993): 87–103.

159 *Looking back on the discovery:* M. M. Merzenich and R. C. deCharms, "Neural Representations, Experience and Change," in *The Mind-Brain Continuum*, ed. R. Llinás and P. S. Churchland (Boston: MIT Press, 1996), 61–81.

CHAPTER 7 | Nature through Nurture: Turning On Genes in the Brain

162 *Psychologists and other experts:* The ERA (English and Romanian Adoptees) Study Team, led by Michael Rutter, has pioneered studies of these children. Among their recent reports are M. Rutter, T. G. O'Connor, and English and Romanian Adoptees (ERA) Study Team, "Are There Biological Programming Effects for Psychological Development? Findings from a Study of Romanian Adoptees," *Developmental Psychology* 40 (Jan. 2004): 81–94; C. Beckett, D. Bredenkamp, J. Castle, C. Groothues, T. G. O'Connor, M. Rutter, and English and Romanian Adoptees (ERA) Study Team, "Behavior Patterns Associated with Institutional Deprivation: A Study of Children Adopted from Romania," *Journal of Developmental and Behavioral Pediatrics* 23 (Oct. 2002): 297–303; T. G. O'Connor and M. Rutter, "Attachment Disorder Behavior Following Early Severe Deprivation: Extension and Longitudinal Follow-up," *Journal of the American Academy of Child and Adolescent Psychiatry* 39 (June 2000): 703–12; and T. G. O'Connor, M. Rutter, C. Beckett, L. Keaveney, and J. M. Kreppner, "The Effects of Global Severe Privation on Cognitive Competence: Extension and Longitudinal Follow-up," *Child Development* 71 (Mar.–Apr. 2000): 376–90.

162 *By the time:* Rutter, 2004.

164 *In the late 1950s:* M. X. Zarrow, G. C. Haltmeyer, V. H. Denenberg, and J. Thatcher, "Response of the Infantile Rat to Stress," *Endocrinology* 79 (Sept. 1966): 631–34; G. C. Haltmeyer, V. H. Denenberg, J. Thatcher, and M. X. Zarrow, "Response of the Adrenal Cortex of the Neonatal Rat after Subjection to Stress," *Nature* 212 (Dec. 1966): 1371–73; and V. H. Denenburg, J. T. Brumaghim, G. C. Haltmeyer, and M. X. Zarrow, "Increased Adrenocortical Activity in the Neonatal Rat Following Handling," *Endocrinology* 81 (Nov. 1967): 1047–52.

165 *In 1989, Meaney and:* M. J. Meaney, D. H. Aitken, V. Viau, S. Sharma, and A. Sarrieau, "Neonatal Handling Alters Adrenocortical Negative Feedback Sensitivity in Hippocampal Type II Glucocorticoid Receptor Binding in the Rat," *Neuroendocrinology* 50 (1989): 597–604.

167 *The mothers of handled pups:* D. Liu, J. Diorio, B. Tannenbaum, C. Caldji, D. Francis, A. Freedman, S. Sharma, D. Pearson, P. M. Plotsky, and M. J. Meaney, "Maternal Care, Hippocampal Glucocorticoid Receptors, and Hypothalamic-Pituitary-Adrenal Responses to Stress," *Science* 277 (Sept. 12, 1997): 1659–62.

169 *When Meaney did just this:* D. D. Francis, J. Diorio, D. Liu, and M. J. Meaney, "Nongenomic Transmission across Generations in Maternal Behavior and Stress Responses in the Rat," *Science* 286 (1999): 1155–58.

172 *Just a few months before:* I.C.G. Weaver, N. Cervoni, F. A. Champagne, A. C. D'Alessio, S. Sharma, J. R. Seckl, S. Dymov, M. Szyf, and M. J. Meaney, "Epigenetic Programming by Maternal Behavior," *Nature Neuroscience* 7 (Aug. 2004): 847–54.

178 *In the autumn of 2005:* A. B. Fries, T. E. Ziegler, J. R. Kurian, S. Jacoris, and S. D. Pollak, "Early Experience in Humans Is Associated with Changes in Neuropeptides Critical for Regulating Social Behavior," *Proceedings of the National Academy of Sciences* 102 (Nov. 22, 2005): 17237–40.

179 *The orphanage children had:* Ibid.

181 *In 2006, scientists at the:* Amie Ashley Hane and Nathan A. Fox, "Ordinary Variations in Maternal Caregiving Influence Human Infants' Stress Reactivity," *Psychological Science* 17, 550–56.

CHAPTER 8 | Blaming Mom?: Rewired for Compassion

186 *Attachment theory was created:* J. Bowlby, *Attachment and Loss,* vol. 1, *Attachment,* 2nd ed. (New York: Basic Books, 1969); vol. 2, *Separation: Anxiety and Anger* (New York: Basic Books, 1973); vol. 3, *Sadness and Depression* (New York: Basic Books, 1980).

186 *As advanced by American psychologist:* M.D.S. Ainsworth, M. Blehar, E. Waters, and S. Wall, *Patterns of Attachment: Assessed in the Strange Situation and at Home* (Hillsdale, N.J.: Erlbaum, 1978).

187 *A child who has:* K. A. Brennan, C. L. Clark, and P. R. Shaver, "Self-Report Measurement of Adult Attachment: An Integrative Overview," in *Attachment Theory and Close Relationships,* ed. J. A. Simpson and W. S. Rholes, 46–76 (New York: Guilford Press, 1998). Exhaustive descriptions of the different attachment styles and their connection to different upbringings can also be found in M. Mikulincer and R. Shaver, "Attachment Theory and Intergroup Bias: Evidence That Priming the Secure Base Schema Attenuates Negative Reactions to Out-groups," *Journal of Personality and Social Psychology* 81 (July 2001): 97–115.

192 *In the attachment questionnaire:* Brennan, Clark, and Shaver, "Self-Report Measurement."

197 *In two studies conducted:* Mikulincer and Shaver, "Attachment Theory and Intergroup Bias." Shaver and Mikulincer have described their work in numerous publications. (An excellent overview is M. Mikulincer, T. Dolev, and R. Shaver, "Attachment-Related Strategies during Thought Suppression: Ironic Rebounds and Vulnerable Self-Representations," *Journal of Personality and Social Psychology* 87 [Dec. 2004]: 940–56.)

201 *In a follow-up study:* Ibid.

203 *Mikulincer and some of his:* M. Mikulincer, O. Gillath, V. Halevy, N. Avihou, S. Avidan, and N. Eshkoli, "Attachment Theory and Reactions to Others' Needs: Evidence That Activation of the Sense of Attachment Security Promotes Empathic Responses," *Journal of Personality and Social Psychology* 81 (2001): 1205–24.

205 *In experiments carried out:* M. Mikulincer, P. R. Shaver, O. Gillath, and R. A. Nitzberg, "Attachment, Caregiving, and Altruism: Boosting Attachment Security Increases Compassion and Helping," *Journal of Personality and Social Psychology* 89 (Nov. 2005): 817–39.

CHAPTER 9 | Transforming the Emotional Mind: Challenging the Happiness "Set Point"

215 *Although there have been:* Clifford Saron, personal communication.

221 *In the research that sealed:* A. J. Tomarken, R. J. Davidson, R. E. Wheeler, and R. C. Doss, "Individual Differences in Anterior Brain Asymmetry and Fundamental Dimensions of Emotion," *Journal of Personality and Social Psychology* 62 (Apr. 1992): 676–87.

222 *In contrast, "no effort:* P. Ekman, R. J. Davidson, M. Ricard, and B. Alan Wallace, "Buddhist

and Psychological Perspectives on Emotions and Well-being," *Current Directions in Psychological Science* 14 (2005): 59–63.

223 *That 1977 paper:* R. J. Davidson and D. J. Goleman, "The Role of Attention in Meditation and Hypnosis: A Psychobiological Perspective on Transformations of Consciousness," *International Journal of Clinical and Experimental Hypnosis* 4 (Oct. 1977): 291–308.

223 *As he and senior colleagues:* R. J. Davidson, G. E. Schwartz, and L. P. Rothman, "Attentional Style and the Self-Regulation of Mode-Specific Attention: An Electroencephalographic Study," *Journal of Abnormal Psychology* 85 (Dec. 1976): 611–21.

223 *As part of that series:* R. J. Davidson, D. J. Goleman, and G. E. Schwartz, "Attentional and Affective Concomitants of Meditation: A Cross-Sectional Study," *Journal of Abnormal Psychology* 85 (Apr. 1976): 235–38.

225 *In 1992, he and colleagues:* Tomarken, Davidson, Wheeler, and Doss, "Individual Differences."

229 *The findings that, in highly experienced:* His Holiness the Dalai Lama, *The Universe,* 19.

234 *The month after the 2004:* A. Lutz, L. L. Greischar, N. B. Rawlings, M. Ricard, and R. J. Davidson, "Long-Term Meditators Self-Induce High-Amplitude Gamma Synchrony during Mental Practice," *Proceedings of the National Academy of Sciences* 101 (Nov. 16, 2004): 16369–73.

238 *One final spot of activity:* J. Brefczynski-Lewis, A. Lutz, and R. Davidson, "A Neural Correlate of Attentional Expertise in Long-time Buddhist Practitioners," slide presentation at the Society for Neuroscience, 2004; A. Lutz, J. Brefczynski-Lewis, and R. Davidson, "Loving-kindness and Compassion Meditation Results in Unique Patterns of fMRI Activation and Enhances the Reactivity of the Insula/Cingulate Neural Circuitry to Negative Stimuli in Meditators," slide presentation at the Society for Neuroscience, 2004.

CHAPTER 10 | Now What?

243 *In response to the signals:* A. Pascual-Leone, A. Amedi, F. Fregni, and L. B. Merabet, "The Plastic Human Brain Cortex," *Annual Reviews of Neuroscience* 28 (2005): 379.

244 *Or as his former mentor:* M. Hallett, "Guest Editorial: Neuroplasticity and Rehabilitation," *Journal of Rehabilitation Research and Development* 42 (July–Aug. 2005): xvii–xxii.

244 *Another condition that arises:* "Dystonia," American Association of Neuromuscular and Electrodiagnostic Medicine, http://www.aanem.org/education/patientinfo/dystonia.cfm; "Researcher Takes on Pianists' Injuries with Disklavier," May 16, 2003, http://www.giles.com/yamaha1/pr/mus/piano/2003/miller_0503.htm.

245 *Merzenich's team showed:* X. Wang, M. M. Merzenich, K. Sameshima, and W. M. Jenkins, "Remodeling of Hand Representation in Adult Cortex Determined by Timing of Tactile Stimulation," *Nature* 378 (1995): 71–75.

245 *Early findings suggest that:* N. N. Byl, S. Najaragan, and A. McKenzie, "Effect of Sensorimotor Training on Structure and Function in Three Patients with Focal Hand Dystonia," Society for Neuroscience abstracts (2000).

245 *Indeed, in a variation:* V. Candia, T. Elbert, E. Altenmuller, H. Rau, T. Schafer, and E. Taub,

"Constraint-Induced Movement Therapy for Focal Hand Dystonia in Musicians," *Lancet* 353 (1999): 42.

246 *Tinnitus, or ringing in:* A. R. Møller, "Symptoms and Signs Caused by Neural Plasticity," *Neurological Research* 23 (2001): 565–72.

248 *In a study Merzenich presented:* J. L. Hardy, B. Connor, J. Appelman, K. Schilling, D. Brenner, J. Dewey, D. Goldman, H. Mahncke, and M. Merzenich, "A Brain Plasticity–Based Training Program to Improve Memory in Older Adults: Pilot Results," slide presentation at the annual meeting of the Society for Neuroscience, 2005.

250 *the bible of mental illness: Diagnostic and Statistical Manual of Mental Disorders DSM-IV* (Washington, D.C.: American Psychiatric Association, 1994).

250 *In the last thirty years:* C. Brown, "The (Scientific) Pursuit of Happiness," *Smithsonian* (May 2004).

252 *Critics call this view:* Steven Rose, "The Rise of Neurogenetic Determinism," *Nature* 373 (Feb. 2, 1995): 380–382.

252 *"Neurogenetic determinism argues that:* Ibid., 380.

SHARON BEGLEY, science columnist and a senior editor at *Newsweek* magazine, was previously the science columnist for *The Wall Streeet Journal*,
where she inaugurated the paper's "Science Journal" in 2002. In addition to *Train Your Mind, Change Your Brain*, she co-authored *The Mind and the
Brain* and has won many awards for her articles. She is a frequent guest
on radio and television, including *The Charlie Rose Show, Today Weekend*,
and CBS's *The Early Show*. She lives in New York.